Highly Effective Marriage

NANCY L. VAN PELT

REVIEW AND HERALD® PUBLISHING ASSOCIATION
HAGERSTOWN, MD 21740

The author assumes full responsibility for the accuracy of all facts and quotations as cited in this book.

Texts credited to Amplified are from *The Amplified Bible.* Copyright © 1965 by Zondervan Publishing House. Used by permission.

Scripture quotations marked NASB are from the *New American Standard Bible,* © by The Lockman Foundation 1960, 1962, 1963, 1968, 1971, 1972, 1973, 1975, 1977.

Texts credited to NIV are from the *Holy Bible, New International Version.* Copyright © 1973, 1978, 1984, International Bible Society. Used by permission of Zondervan Bible Publishers.

Texts credited to NKJV are from the New King James Version. Copyright © 1979, 1980, 1982 by Thomas Nelson, Inc. Used by permission. All rights reserved.

Bible texts credited to RSV are from the Revised Standard Version of the Bible, copyright © 1946, 1952, 1971, by the Division of Christian Education of the National Council of the Churches of Christ in the U.S.A. Used by permission.

Verses marked TLB are taken from *The Living Bible,* copyright © 1971 by Tyndale House Publishers, Wheaton, Ill. Used by permission.

This book was
Edited by Cheryl Woolsey
Copyedited by Delma Miller and James Cavil
Designed by Emily Harding
Electronic makeup by Shirley M. Bolivar
Cover design by Genesis Design/Bryan Gray
Typeset: 10/13 Times

PRINTED IN U.S.A.

04 03 02 01 00   5 4 3 2 1

R&H Cataloging Service
Van Pelt, Nancy Lue
    Highly effective marriage

    1. Marriage.   I. Title.

    306.81

ISBN 0-8280-1420-5

Dedicated to my husband,
Harry Arthur Van Pelt

Wherever Harry is, there is . . .

Classical music playing (loudly)
A warning to "be careful"
A good morning hug
A goodnight kiss
A neatly made bed
A vacuumed carpet
A computer he's coaxing into action
A clean kitchen, with no mess or dishes in the sink
A lawn that needs mowing
A car with a tank full of gas
My greatest supporter.

Wherever Harry is, there are . . .

His slow (very slow) firm steps
Good clean jokes
Courtesies that come from the heart of a gentleman
Books and more books
Plans for going to our trailer at Fish Camp
Surprises galore.

Wherever Harry is, there is . . .

A pushover for a little sweet talk
A wink and a smile
Reading in bed
An electric blanket warmed to my liking
A spa heated to soothe my aching back
The greatest foot massager this side of heaven
The one who loves gadgets
One great lover and friend—
And someone I want to spend the rest of my life with.

Other books by Nancy L. Van Pelt

The Compleat Courtship
The Compleat Courtship Workbook
The Compleat Marriage
The Compleat Marriage Workbook
The Compleat Parent
The Compleat Parent Workbook
The Compleat Tween
Creative Hospitality
Get Organized!
How to Talk So Your Mate Will Listen and Listen So Your Mate
    Will Talk (Fleming H. Revel)
My Prayer Notebook
Smart Love: A Field Guide for Single Adults (Fleming H. Revell)

Seminar workshops based on *Highly Effective Marriage* are available. For further information, contact the author at www.heartnhome.com.

Visit our website at www.rhpa.org for information on other Review and Herald products.

Acknowledgments

No one ever writes a book "all by oneself," and this is certainly true in this case. *Highly Effective Marriage* has come to be not through my ideas alone, but because of many other people who gave of their time, talent, and ideas. It has resulted from teaching hundreds of family life classes over the past 25 years of my career, as well as from counseling couples from all walks of life. It has come as a result of attending seminars and talking with pastors and marriage counselors. It is the product of research in a multitude of books written by professionals.

Specifically, I am indebted to:

Alberta Mazat, a specialist in the field of sexuality, who provided technical advice for the chapter dealing with sexual fulfillment.

Ronald M. Moore, a physician in private practice for more than 30 years in Fresno, California, who reviewed the sexual material to assure medical accuracy.

Doreen Clark, my faithful secretary, who skillfully prepared the manuscript for publication.

All the seminar participants, whose experiences have testified that these principles work.

My husband. No one can calculate the gratitude that a spouse deserves when an author is absorbed in producing a book of this magnitude. My debt goes deep for his patience and ever-loving ways with me. He's absolutely the greatest!

And to God be the glory!

—Nancy L. Van Pelt

Contents

Part 4: Why Can't a Woman Be More Like a Man?

Part 5: Who's In Charge Here, Anyway? (Solutions to Power Struggles)

Part 6: Good Sex Doesn't Just Happen

Part 7: Preventing Marriage Burnout

Before You Begin

A fulfilling and highly satisfying marriage can be the most critical factor in achieving happiness throughout life. Ninety-six percent of all Americans marry at some point in their life. A good marriage, what I call a "highly effective marriage," can be one of life's greatest joys and the single most important factor in making life worthwhile.

Although people like to *get* married, it is more difficult to *stay* married. Current divorce statistics run at about 50 percent. When both partners are under the age of 21 or have dropped out of high school to get married, the divorce rate soars to 80 percent. In spite of such dismal statistics, we continue to marry rapidly. And divorced people remarry even more quickly. Four-fifths of all people who divorce remarry within five years, and most of those within three years of their divorce. Unfortunately, more than half of those remarriages will end in divorce again! Obviously we have a strong desire to be married but lack understanding about what it takes to make marriage work.[1]

The past 25 years of my life have been dedicated to family life education, with an emphasis on marriage. As a family life educator, certified through the National Council on Family Relations, I have taught literally thousands of couples who have attended my marriage seminars. I have talked with hundreds of couples whose marriages ranged from disastrous to fabulous.

About 10 percent of all marriages are what might be termed highly effective marriages. Since 50 percent end in divorce, the remaining 40 percent fall between poor and fairly good.

So why do we keep marrying when marriage is so often fraught with difficulties? People marry for love, companionship, for a family. They marry for friendship and intimacy. The promise of love and happiness appears so desirable that we think we can beat the odds! Even when it is a widely published fact that half of all marriages end in divorce, people still marry.

A word about remarriage. Following divorce, people jump right back into another relationship, and these new relationships stand an even greater chance of encountering serious conflicts than do first marriages. If you are already divorced and contemplating remarriage, I beg you to read my book *Smart Love* to gain perspective.[2] Marrying hastily may seem like a quick way to relieve some of your pain. But marriages on the rebound have a very high failure rate. I recommend that people not remarry for a minimum of two years after divorce. People who have just gone through the divorce process need time to recover from the psychological shock of divorce before jumping "heart first" into another relationship without using their heads. Second-time-around marriages based on "heart first" leaps usually don't last a year.

You don't want to make the same mistakes the second time around. Since we are creatures of habit, frequently blind impulse lures us into like situations, in which we replay painful events over and over. Regardless of the quality of your first marriage, you are partly responsible for its demise. You must realize this so you will not repeat the same mistakes. One way to prevent this is to acquire as much knowledge as possible about yourself and how you respond in a relationship. Self-knowledge will greatly assist your transition into a new marriage.

This brings me to the purpose for this book—to increase your opportunity to achieve a successful, highly effective marriage. You can be among the 50 percent who make it, and even among the 10 percent who enjoy superior marital happiness.

This book teaches, step by step, how to achieve success. Other books often discuss creative divorce and why relationships fail, rather than how to succeed. They teach couples how to "fight fair" instead of how not to fight. They point to human strategies for success, when this book suggests divine guidance blended with practical biblical instruction.

Marriage cannot make anyone happier who does not bring the ingredients for happiness into it. —**Sydney J. Harris.**

Within the pages of this book are two essential resources: detailed descriptions of important relationship skills and how to build them, as well as step-by-step plans for effecting change where it is needed. Neither one is sufficient by itself.

If your car or washing machine broke down, I doubt you'd attempt to fix it without fully understanding its complex mechanism. Even a set of the most expensive and sophisticated tools won't help if you don't know how to use them. Likewise in marriage. Not only do you need tools such as relationship skills, but you also should have an in-depth understanding of how and why changes in your behavior will improve your marriage, and knowledge of how to implement the changes. With these resources, you will be able to achieve your goal of a highly effective marriage. Here's what you'll discover in this book:

Part 1: Her Needs/His Needs—Decoding the Mystery. The first chapter, "Marriage—Playing the Game for Keeps," introduces you to Nolan Ryan, the miracle man with an amazing baseball career. But the most amazing aspect of Nolan's life is that he is just as successful in his role as a husband. You will examine how commitment and expectations shape your vision of what marriage can and should be.

The next two chapters describe "her needs and his needs." You will learn about men's and women's greatest emotional needs. When men and women are asked in surveys how well they are doing in meeting the emotional needs of their partners, the vast majority believe they are doing well. However, when their partners are asked if their needs are being met, they reveal much room for improvement! Either we don't know what we are doing or our partners are misinterpreting what is being done. Take your pick. Meeting these simple needs provides the foundation for a caring relationship. When these needs are met, we want to stay married. When they go unfulfilled, we feel hurt, alienated, and distant from our partners.

Confidential to "Second Time Arounder": Marriage is like the Army. Everybody complains about it, but a surprising number reenlist.

Part 2: How to Live With an Imperfect Mate. You'll learn about the "emotional bank account" model of relationships. You'll begin to understand that you are making either deposits or withdrawals in the account on a daily basis. When we are loving and kind, hundreds of credits flow into our mate's EBA, creating the feeling that we are loved and accepted the way we are. When we are criticized, the account can be seriously overdrawn.

Many people think they aren't compatible because one is a night person and the other prefers going to bed early. But it's not the differences between partners that cause problems. It's how the differences are handled when they arise. Every couple must learn how to live with and manage these differences. Practical steps are outlined for becoming a more accepting person, as well as the limits of acceptance.

Part 3: Why Can't My Partner Understand What I Say? What are the reasons couples can't communicate? Much of the problem revolves around the fact that people enter into relationships with no training in communication and no agreed-upon rules or skills for handling the strong negative feelings that are an inevitable part of marriage. Without skills, partners in the face of conflict often resort to destructive guerrilla tactics that can seriously wound each other.

Partners in happy relationships develop good listening skills. These skills have nothing to do with forcing agreement or giving advice. Listening involves understanding and accepting differences in personality as well as likes and dislikes. In a happy marriage a person can count on his or her mate's being a good friend and listening without judging. Chapter 9, "Listening—A Way to Show

You Care," describes good listening skills. Chapter 10, "How to Talk to the One You Love," covers how to talk when you are irritated or angry over something and offers a share-care plan for solving conflicts. As a couple master the skills of effective listening and talking they build the foundation for closeness and intimacy in their relationship.

Part 4: Why Can't a Woman Be More Like a Man? In this section, we not only look at the physical differences between males and females but also discuss differences in their brains. These differences offer some explanation of how the different sexes can process the same information but come up with totally different conclusions, and how these differences can affect health. Armed with this information, you'll be able to figure out why males and females respond and behave so differently.

Part 5: Who's in Charge Here, Anyway? There are peaceful solutions to dominance, submission, and power struggles. Since power struggles tear at the very fabric of relationships and leave people feeling isolated, hurt, and hopeless, we'll search for a model of support that provides each partner with a balanced sense of control, enabling both partners to think of themselves as competent.

Another facet of relationship-building explored in this chapter is how a couple can achieve spiritual oneness. The longer I continue in my ministry to families, the more convinced I become that the answer to marital distress is not to be found in more romance, fun, and excitement, or in better problem-solving skills—important as those are—but in the type of depth that comes when a couple worships and prays together.

A marriage may be made in heaven, but the maintenance must be done on earth.

Part 6: Good Sex Doesn't Just Happen. This section tackles reports of an epidemic of widespread sexual dissatisfaction among married couples. For those who live complicated, busy lives, there may never be enough time or energy to feel sexual desire. Problems arise when there is a marked difference between the needs and desires of husband and wife.

Explored in these chapters are the complex and intricate sexual response systems designed by our Creator purely to provide sexual pleasure and to bond husband and wife to each other. Maintaining a fulfilling sexual experience that will last for decades of loving requires deliberate action and energy, along with patience, understanding, and creativity.

Part 7: Preventing Marriage Burnout. The final chapters explore how to keep a marriage on track romantically. After couples have been married awhile, the tendency is to give work and children their freshest energy. Marriage gets what's left over. How can a couple make love and romance last a lifetime? The pressures on husband and wife sharing a lifetime together are enormous. At times problems will become intense and seemingly unbearable. What can be done to protect a marriage from marital burnout—from fizzling over the long haul? Explored here are creative ways to keep relationships romantic. The challenge of being married is learning to keep a relationship romantic, interesting, and alive through all the changing years of marriage.

It's possible that after reading this book with your partner, you'll realize you need more help than you can possibly get from a book. You may recognize, perhaps for the first time, that there are problems bigger than you can handle alone. Rather than giving up, accept the fact that your marriage may be stalled in a phase of distress and that you need outside help to survive the crisis. Even the strongest of couples occasionally need direction to see a clear path through a difficult problem. If this is your situation, by all means seek couple counseling.

Finally, I want to compliment the truly outstanding marriages, the highly effective marriages, in which devoted and loving couples are weathering the joys and sorrows of married life together. If you are one of those couples, I congratulate you. You make my work with families rewarding. You are living examples of my vision for what marriage can be—couples who pledge themselves to each other "for better or for worse," and then work to make it better.

—Nancy L. Van Pelt

[1] Harvey L. Ruben, *Supermarriage* (New York: Bantam Books, 1986), pp. 11, 12.
[2] Nancy L. Van Pelt, *Smart Love—A Field Guide for Single Adults* (Grand Rapids: Fleming H. Revell, 1997).

Chapter 1

MARRIAGE

Playing for Keeps

Nolan Ryan, legendary pitcher for the Texas Rangers, has had an amazing baseball career. Some of his record-breaking feats include striking out his 5,000th batter, pitching seven no-hit games, and winning 324 games. But the most amazing aspect of Nolan Ryan's life is not only that he was successful on the field but that he is just as successful in life—as a husband, father, and businessman. What are his secrets for living wisely?

In his autobiography, *Miracle Man,* Nolan says that the most important number in his life is "one." There has been only one woman in his life—Ruth—the only girl he has ever wanted to be with since he was a teenager. Throughout his life this has never changed. He considers Ruth his number one best friend. Nolan says that like most guys (especially athletes), he had to learn the hard way how to treat Ruth right. Before they had children, Ruth was stuck in New York while Nolan was on the road with the Mets. When he got home he wanted to stay home, but Ruth wanted to go out. They both had to learn to compromise and be sensitive to the needs of the other.

The biggest adjustment they had to make came when they had children. Nolan, like most other men, had no idea how drastically children would impact his marriage. He comments that most men just keep on doing what's important to them, and their wives end up with all the work. He started out that way. Ballplayers are especially guilty of pushing all parenting obligations off on their wives because they are on the road and gone from home much of the time.

According to Nolan, all men have to learn sooner or later that it takes a tremendous amount of time and effort to raise responsible children. When dumped on the wife to shoulder alone, this responsibility greatly restricts her life. Nolan had to understand that he was not the only one in the marriage who had dreams and goals—that Ruth had some dreams of her own. This was a difficult lesson for someone who became the immediate center of attention everywhere he went just because he could throw a baseball.

Nolan is the first to admit his marriage isn't perfect. Like any other couple, Nolan and Ruth have had their ups and downs. But the two of them have worked through their downs and celebrated their ups. Many professional athletes think they are above any laws of the land or any rules. They think they are entitled to do whatever they please without answering to anyone. To Nolan's way of thinking, it really says something about values when a superstar athlete with the AIDS virus is made into a hero. If a female athlete announced that she had slept with a couple hundred men and had AIDS, she would hardly be considered a superstar. She would be called a tramp.

Nolan is committed to his marriage. In spite of all his efforts to stay in shape, continue with the game, and win, Nolan says that his family is his main priority. When Nolan was playing in the majors, he commuted on off days to be with his family during baseball season. In the winter he stayed close to home.

Nolan and Ruth often work out together. When they find time to vacation—between baseball and overseeing their four ranches and two banks—they share activities like skiing and diving with their three children. They both believe a healthy lifestyle benefits their three children. They have worked hard to instill in them the proper values in life and let them know the rewards received from living in accordance with them, even though the rewards are not always immediate.

Marriage is not something one tries on for size, and then decides whether to keep; it is rather something one decides with a promise, and then bends every effort to keep.—Leon R. Kass.

Since Nolan and Ruth have achieved celebrity status, they could be at a charity ball or a dinner every night of the week. But they recognize that within a few years their children will be out of the nest. Their week is planned around everyone's hectic schedules. Many forces battle to pull the family apart, but "we've worked to stay together," Nolan states.

If you press him, you can get Nolan to tell stories about the greatest game he ever pitched or other great moments in his career. He needs no prompting, however, to tell stories about his family. One of his favorites is about the time he and Ruth were on a road trip and Reese—who was left in charge of the house—accidentally locked one of their three hunting dogs inside. The dog panicked, destroyed a curtain, and caused $1,000 in damage trying to find a way out. Reese called a decorator and used his own savings to pay for the damage; he never asked his parents for help. Ruth was flabbergasted, but Nolan recognized that the time, effort, and values they had poured into their children were paying off.

There's something for all of us in examining how Nolan Ryan has ordered his life priorities, how he feels about his wife, his children, his values, and his pursuit of a healthy lifestyle.[1]

The Benefits of Staying Committed

The Ryans freely admit their marriage isn't perfect and they've had to work through ups and downs. Talk to any couple who have been married 30 or 40 years. If they are truthful, you'll hear about the bad times as well as the good. But when a couple make it over the long haul, you'll find two strong people who have worked hard to honor the commitment made on their wedding day.

You might ask a couple married this length of time if they ever thought of abandoning ship. Ask about the crisis periods—the big stuff such as career changes, business failures, bankruptcy, the death of a child or another close family member, loss of mental or physical health, financial stress, lawsuits, an out-of-wedlock teen pregnancy, a time when decisions must be made regarding care of aging parents, or their struggles during retirement when they started getting in each other's way. What held the couple together?

Surviving all the crises of marriage over the span of 30, 40, and 50+ years takes commitment. Romantic feelings fail during the tough times. Sex doesn't seem very important, either. Material possessions may not mean much. Now it's the two of them against the world, toughing it out, testing all their resources. Will they make it?

During the early years the couple may not make it unless they have a strong commitment. Some studies show that half of all divorces take place during the first two years of marriage.[2] During the early years there is a tendency to dramatize the importance of every problem, and the D word rears its ugly head. After 30 years of the good times along with the bad, a couple learns that not every bad time signals divorce. They will survive this crisis, as they have survived many prior crises. Their commitment to survival carries them through.

There are two things you shouldn't enter into prematurely: divorce and embalming.

—Charles Swindoll *(Strike the Original Match).*

Every relationship seems to have its droughts, its dry spells when growth stops and boredom sets in. This can be a dangerous time for couples, especially if a member of the opposite sex comes on the scene during the drought and awakens romantic and/or sexual desire. This is another time that commitment plays a strong role. Can a couple survive the droughts?

It's the kind of commitment we make in marriage that allows us to experience trust, respect, and intimacy. It's hardly possible in a temporary relationship, when you are aware that you could easily be replaced, to develop the openness and trust that comes with commitment. But when you know in the deepest part of your soul that your partner is absolutely committed to you forever and ever, what a powerful difference it makes in your relationship! You know you can reveal things about yourself to this person that no one else is aware of. All of the carefully guarded feelings, memories, and experiences you've kept hidden inside can now be shared with someone who will understand you, love you, and never reject you. A type of trust takes over that forever bonds you together in love.

The wedding vows include promises of love and devotion. The knowledge that you have a partner in life who is devoted to you and loves you is one of the most fulfilling feelings in life. This knowledge of an everlasting kind of love gives a deep inner security that allows you to overcome the struggles of life.

All marriages are happy. It's the living together afterward that causes all the trouble.

When both members of a couple are 100 percent committed to each other, and their commitment has been tested and has endured, uneasy fears of abandonment are significantly eased. Whether ever verbalized or not, this fear haunts many, both male and female. We tremble at the thought of facing the future alone without someone at our side to help us over the rough times.

This is why the wedding vows are so important. These vows mean that your partner has promised to stick with you through thick and thin. Your partner will be loyal to you, even when you are away from each other. It is a promise that says you will always have someone there for better or worse, in sickness and in health, till death parts you. Always and forever.

Commitment Isn't Enough

Researchers can now predict with more than 90 percent accuracy who will enjoy a successful relationship and who will suffer distress and divorce. To a large degree the findings in these studies do not line up with popular opinion of what makes marriage work or fail. I've generalized the discrepancies below.

POPULAR OPINION: Whom you marry determines your chances for a happy marriage.

STUDIES SHOW: Marital happiness has little to do with whom you marry and everything to do with how you cope with conflict.

POPULAR OPINION: Personality flaws and irritating faults are the underlying cause of marital distress.

STUDIES SHOW: Personality flaws and irritating faults do not predict marital happiness or marital stability.

POPULAR OPINION: Compatibility and similar likes and dislikes determine relationship success.

STUDIES SHOW: It's not how similar or different you are; it's how you handle differences when they arise that counts.

POPULAR OPINION: Problems experienced during early years will heal themselves and get better in time.

STUDIES SHOW: Problems worsen over time, and it's much wiser to deal with them early, when they are easier to handle.

POPULAR OPINION: Men and women have different needs in marriage and have different approaches to intimacy.

STUDIES SHOW: The major difference between men and women in marriage lies in the way they handle conflict rather than in their approach to intimacy.

POPULAR OPINION: When a couple loves each other enough and are really committed, they can solve any problem.

STUDIES SHOW: Love is needed to begin a relationship, but it doesn't provide enough fuel over time to keep the relationship successful. Nor does commitment. Again, it's how couples manage conflict that makes the difference.[3]

Highly effective marriages are the result of more than just compatibility and commitment. Effective communication and conflict management skills are vital. There will always be differences of opinion over likes, desires, and how to get things done. Setting up a home together provides fertile ground for disagreements over how to earn and spend money, keep house, raise children, and spend free time, as well as how to meet each other's needs.

High Expectations

In previous decades roles were clearly defined by society, and a couple could fit into these roles, which limited potential conflict. Today roles have changed, and every couple must work out their own unique compromises. Couples today want more than just security. They are looking for an emotionally rewarding relationship that provides contentment and happiness. When these expectations are not met, disillusion and disenchantment often set in. The high divorce rate may be partly a result of the excessively high expectations we have for marriage, rather than an indication that people are turned off to marriage. The desire to marry has changed little, but the expectations of what marriage can provide have changed greatly. The only way to achieve these high expectations is through the use of communication and conflict management skills.

There is no place we can go to earn a degree in how to be married. We can't purchase a guarantee that ensures us a successful, happy marriage. That's not how marriage works. But several years ago a fascinating study was launched by the Department of Human Development and the Family at the University of Nebraska. The purpose of the study was to discover what specific qualities go into making strong families.

Strong families from a variety of racial and ethnic backgrounds were selected and asked such questions as "How do you deal with conflict?" "Do you experience power struggles?" and "How do you communicate?"

Nick Stinnett writes of his findings: "Altogether we studied 3,000 families and collected a lot of information. But when we analyzed it all, we found six main qualities in strong families. Strong families (1) are committed to the family; (2) spend time together; (3) have good family communication; (4) express appreciation to each other; (5) have a spiritual commitment; and (6) are able to solve problems in a crisis." [4]

How to put these six factors to work in marriage is the task of this book. Each reader needs to ponder how to apply them to his or her own marriage. Success comes with a price tag: time. Time spent, undivided attention given, energy expended.

Commitment isn't just something that is spoken of in front of a minister during the wedding ceremony. It may begin there, but commitment is a process that continues daily. It has to do with setting priorities and eliminating things that compete with your number one priority—your partner. It is observed and measured in units of time, attention, energy, and willingness to make changes, compromise, and say "I'm sorry."

"By wisdom a house is built, and by understanding it is established; by knowledge the rooms are filled with all precious and pleasant riches," King Solomon observed in Proverbs 24:3, 4 (RSV). Building such a marriage, establishing it with knowledge and filling the rooms with "precious and pleasant riches," doesn't just happen. It is the result of commitment to each other and God, as well as following some well-defined principles for happiness. Are you game? Stick with me! We'll be examining these principles in the coming chapters.

---

[1] Nolan Ryan and Jerry Jenkins, *Miracle Man* (Waco, Tex.: Word Publishing, 1992).

[2] Jeanette C. Lauer and Robert H. Lauer, *Till Death Do Us Part: A Study and Guide to Long-term Marriage* (Binghamton, N.Y.: Haworth Press, 1986), p. 50.

[3] Clifford Notarius and Howard Markman, *We Can Work It Out* (New York: Putnam, 1992), pp. 20, 21.

[4] Nick Stinnett, *Secrets of Strong Families* (Boston: Little, Brown and Co., 1985), quoted in a church newsletter.

Chapter 2

Her Need For . . .

*O*nce upon a time a husband and wife were getting all snugly in bed. The passion began to build. Suddenly the wife stopped and said to her husband, "Honey, I don't feel like it. I just need you to hold me." Confused, the husband said, "What?" His wife launched into an explanation that he just was not in tune with her emotional needs as a woman. The husband realized that nothing was going to happen that night and he might as well accept it.

The next day the man decided to take his wife shopping at her favorite department store. He walked through women's dresses and selected three very expensive outfits for her to try on. She was flabbergasted at his efforts to please her, tried on all three, but couldn't decide which one she wanted. Magnanimously he told her to take all three.

Next he suggested she might need shoes to match. She selected three pairs worth $200 each. Then they went to the jewelry department, where she selected a necklace and earrings. The wife began to think her husband had flipped out, but she was so excited she didn't care. She saw a tennis bracelet displayed on a shelf and begged for it. "Honey, you don't play tennis," the husband cautioned, "but if you like it, then let's get it."

The wife was delirious with excitement by now and could not imagine what must be going on in her husband's head. "OK," she finally said, "let's go to the cash register."

"Oh, darling, you misunderstood," her husband told her. "We're not going to *buy* all this stuff."

The wife's face went blank.

"No, honey, I just wanted you to *hold* all this stuff for a while."

Her eyes narrowed angrily. She was about to explode when her husband said, "You just aren't in tune with the sexual or financial needs I have as a man!"

Men and women have different emotional needs, yet most are only vaguely aware of the differences. When questioned in surveys about meeting each other's needs, both sexes feel that while they are giving adequately to their mate, their partners neither acknowledge nor appreciate what they give them. Actually both partners give to the relationship, but they usually give what they themselves want, not what their partners desire! As a result, both end up feeling frustrated and resentful.

For example, a woman thinks she is acting loving when she asks caring questions or expresses concerns. This can be very annoying to a man. He may feel that she is trying to control or manipulate him in some way. This is confusing to her because if he offered her the same type of concern, she would appreciate it and feel loved. Her efforts at showing she loves him irritate him.

Being cared about is something so desperately needed in this depersonalized world that people will crawl across a thousand miles of desert to get it.— **Wilber Sutherland.**

When a woman gets upset, a man often tries to ease the situation by telling her not to worry and get so upset over things. He responds to her the same way he relates to the situation. He doesn't recognize that his efforts to minimize the problem invalidate her feelings and make her long for understanding and support. When she grows even more upset by his attempts to show her that she doesn't need to be so upset, he gets confused. He can't understand why his attempts to help have failed.

Most men fall short of being able to define what *their* most important needs are, let alone define what their wife's needs are. And most women, though they tend to see themselves as experts on relationships, fail to understand their husbands' needs.

Look, for example, at the busy executive bent on climbing the corporate ladder. He has the pressures of competition, expectations of his own and those of his boss, and all the crises of the professional workplace to battle. His wife has her own battles. She may be struggling with toy-strewn rooms, pinching and tattling, and toddlers screaming "No! No!" while her husband is taking a client to lunch. Or she may be pushing commands on a computer or meeting the demands of patients under her care. Often she must face the same crises of the workplace her husband has to deal with.

After the stress of the day, he needs a little peace and quiet in order to refocus. She needs a little attention and intimate conversation in order to refocus. She tries to connect with him, ask about his day, tell him about hers—but all she gets out of him are meaningless grunts as he heads for the family room to relax with Monday night football.

Can this couple help each other be happy and still have their own needs met? Yes! But they first need to understand the nature of their differences. I've narrowed the emotional needs of the sexes down to four each.

Her Needs	His Needs
1. A woman needs frequent demonstrations of love and affection.	1. A man needs admiration for appearance, abilities, and character traits.
2. A woman needs emotional security.	2. A man needs approval and support.
3. A woman needs appreciation for her domestic efforts and attractiveness.	3. A man needs respect.
4. A woman needs romantic attention.	4. A man needs sexual fulfillment.

Now let's explore these needs in more detail:

1. Her Need for Love and Affection. Love is essential for the survival of all humans, from babyhood on. But the way each sex needs love to be expressed is different.

Often before marriage, when a young man attempts to win the heart of the woman he adores, he persists night and day with loving words and romantic gestures. But once she becomes his bride, he often fails to recognize her intense need to feel loved on a day-to-day basis for the rest of her life.

Because of her capacity for affection, daily expressions of romantic love are vital to a woman's existence. These are the key to her self-worth, her satisfaction with married life, and her sexual responsiveness. If a man feels trapped in a bored, tired marriage marked by a dull sex life, he might look to himself for part of the answer. By consistently and thoughtfully expressing affectionate attention, many men could melt the heart of even the most frigid wife.

One bewildered husband complained of not being able to understand his wife. "I have given her everything she wants and needs. We have a custom-built home in the best section of town, with our own satellite dish and a big-screen TV. She has more jewels and furs than she can wear. We belong to the best country club around and recently cruised the Caribbean. I'm a faithful husband who doesn't drink or beat the kids. But she says she's miserable, and I can't figure out why!"

This man doesn't realize that his wife would trade the custom-built house and its conveniences, as well as the country club and cruises, for a few words of affection and his undivided attention. Satellite dishes, big-screen TVs, and membership in country clubs do not make a woman feel cherished, but being somebody's sweetheart does.

Many men are unaware of a woman's continuing need for romantic love and affection. When a couple seeks my counseling services, I frequently ask them to grade their marriage on a scale of 1 to 10, with 10 being high and 1 low. I ask for the male evaluation first. The average male (regardless of the state of his marital affairs) usually grades the relationship at eight, with seven being low.

Before marriage the three little words are "I love you." After marriage, they are "Let's eat out."

Where does his wife grade the relationship? Three, or maybe four. One woman graded her marriage at minus two. Where did her husband grade it? Ten! He said they were perfect for each other, and didn't understand the problem.

Why do males view their marriages so differently from females? When it comes to marriage, many men are willing to settle for a business arrangement of sorts. As long as they get meals served on time, have clean clothes to put on in the morning when they need them, and sex when they ask for it, the tendency is to shrug their shoulders and say, "Everything is fine around here." Their basic needs are being met.

This is not so with women. Affectionate attention may be an added benefit to a man, but to a woman it is an absolute necessity. Women in a "business arrangement" marriage are crawling their emotional walls—and their husbands aren't even aware of it.

When women reach out for reassurance. A young bride of a few weeks was lying on the bed with her head resting on her husband's shoulder. After a long silence she asked, "What are you thinking about?"

(Men, if you and your wife are lying on the bed with her head resting on your shoulder and she asks what you are thinking about, *PLEASE BE THINKING ABOUT HER!)*

"Oh," her husband replied, "I was just wondering what I should tell the boss tomorrow when he asks about the job I've been working on."

"Oh," she said. Then she waited.

Any man with a grain of knowledge about a woman's needs would have known that she was waiting for him to ask her what *she* was thinking about. But this husband didn't. Instead he asked, "Are you going to fix supper pretty soon?"

She clenched her teeth and flatly announced that she would fix it in a little while.

"Well," he offered cheerily, "I'll be glad to teach you how to make sloppy joes the way my mother makes them."

That did it! She blew sky-high. He was puzzled and hurt. He didn't understand why she was so angry, and he felt she was being unreasonable.[1]

Of course, if she was expecting him to read her mind and know what she wanted him to ask her, she *was* being unreasonable! But a sensitive husband will learn to recognize the signs of his wife reaching out to him for affection. And he should offer plenty of loving attention without being asked.

A woman yearns to be someone special to her husband—to feel loved and cherished. This explains why anniversaries are more important to her than they are to him and why she feels so frustrated when her husband forgets such courtesies. It also explains why a woman constantly "reaches" for her husband, not so much in a physical sense, but in an emotional way. She needs to connect with him, feel close to and intimate with him in ways that he may not fully understand.

If you want your wife to listen to you, talk to another woman.

One famous minister and family counselor has observed that a woman's need for love and affection from her husband is so great that if she cannot achieve it one way, she will instinctively try another. If her efforts at communication are sabotaged by her husband's silence, she has many alternatives at her disposal. She may become angry over an insignificant matter, or accusatory, or depressed.

In an almost frantic attempt to force any kind of communication, she will push any button on his control panel. When a man reaches overload and finally erupts with anger, a wife feels she has gotten some type of response. At a totally unconscious level this wife is saying, "I'd like first-class love from you. If I cannot have that, I'll settle for attention. If I can't get your attention, I'll go for your sympathy. If that fails, I'll get you where it hurts. I'll have an accident or a symptom."[2]

Many more women than men go to doctors for imaginary symptoms. It may cost a lot, but at least they have a male's attention, if only for a few minutes. There are a lot of husbands out there who could save themselves a bundle of money by paying some notice to their attention-starved wives.

A woman's need for romantic attention and affection might be compared to an empty 55-gallon barrel. A smart man begins filling her barrel first thing in the morning. Before getting out of bed he'll wrap his arms around her and whisper sweet nothings (five gallons). During breakfast he compliments her on something (another five). Before hustling out the door he gives her a hug and kiss (five more). During a coffee break he phones to let her know he is thinking of her (another five).

At night when he comes in the door, before greeting the kids or petting the dog he gives her a warm hug, a genuine smile, and a kiss with some meaning (10 gallons). He compliments her on the evening meal (another five). Even though he chauffeurs the kids to and from a meeting, pays bills, and works on the computer, he gives her 10 minutes of his undivided attention to talk about something important (15 gallons); and he caresses her lovingly as they pass in the hallway (five). When he crawls into bed that night he can rest assured that he has filled her emotional love barrel to the 55-gallon mark (without spending a dime!)

How long should 55 gallons of love and attention last? When she goes to sleep that night, her barrel springs a leak and drains empty. A smart man understands that her love barrel needs daily input in order for her to remain happy.

Expressing affection. Men need to make a conscious decision to express love. Even if you've said it all before, say it again. Even if you think she already knows how much you love her, say it again. Tell her how much you love her. Tell her you think she's a great cook. Tell her that you think she has gorgeous legs.

Thinking nice things doesn't count. Say them out loud. When you say nothing, she assumes you don't care. That is translated as *he doesn't love me anymore.* And remember, a woman doesn't want to have to ask you if she's loved. She wants it verbalized spontaneously. Try some of the statements listed below.

Every day is a better day for me because of you.

The happiest day of my life is the day I married you.

I love you more today than on our wedding day. You make my life complete.

You mean more to me than I can ever tell you.

Former President Harry Truman was an incurable romantic. He pursued his wife, Bess, for years before she finally agreed to marry him. He first asked her in 1911, but they were not married until 1919. Marriage did not end their romance, however. Whenever he was away from Bess, Harry wrote her love letters. After Bess Truman's death in 1982, more than 1,200 letters from Harry were found in her home. He never stopped courting his wife or letting her know she was loved, even after many years of marriage.[3]

Affection can be shown overtly through hugging and kissing, but it can also be shown in low-key, subtle ways through quiet acts of tenderness. Hold hands while you watch TV. Give her an affectionate pat. Run your fingers through her hair. Displays of this kind of affection have a contented, dreamy quality, like sitting in front of a cozy fire and enjoying the flames as they leap and dance. Nothing needs to be said.

2. Her Need for Emotional Security. Emotional security is the ultimate goal in a woman's life. She looks for reassurance regarding her place in her husband's affections by asking him to do something for her she could easily do for herself. His willingness serves as a measure of his love and adoration. A woman doesn't want to have to compete with anyone else or anything else for her husband's time and attention.

Sometimes a woman expects her husband to do what she wants done without being asked. Why? Because she sees this as an evidence of an even greater degree of love for her. She may not always tell him what she really wants done. And if his mind-reading abilities fail him and he does not do what she desires, she becomes indignant.

For example, I like Harry to fill the gas tank in the car. This has nothing to do with whether I believe putting gas in the car is a male thing to do. I am very capable and self-sufficient and could easily do the job myself. But when Harry assumes this responsibility, I feel that he's taking care of me and am reassured of my place in his affections.

At times this need for emotional security can go one step further. A wife may deny that she wants something she actually wants. If her husband takes her at her word, she feels troubled. She believes that she should be so important to her husband that he will understand and meet her desires, regardless of what she says or does.

Often misunderstandings happen in the bedroom because of this kind of thinking. The man makes sexual advances, and the woman withdraws. In an effort to be considerate of her wishes, he turns over and tries to sleep. At this point, she might cry or nurse hurt and angry feelings. Why? She assumes she should be so irresistibly attractive that her husband will persist in his efforts despite all obstacles she puts in his way. If he doesn't, she concludes that he doesn't care the way he used to. Her emotional security, her place in his affections, is threatened.

Granted, a woman should recognize how unrealistic it is for her husband to recognize her wants despite what she says and how she acts. If she doesn't always know what she wants, how can she expect her husband to? But she doesn't always realize this. Sometimes a woman can behave in uncomprehensible ways, but if she admits as much, and asks for patience, her husband will have an easier time feeling his way toward understanding her.

A man can satisfy his wife's need for emotional security by letting her know that she's the one for him—that given another opportunity he would choose her all over again. If he has a roving eye and she notices how he checks out the physical equipment of other women, she feels threatened. No one expects a man to put blinders on, but he should take care to keep his wife reassured of her number one place in his heart. Any time he feels she might feel insecure in his affection, he might slip his arm around her and say, "There's no doubt about it, honey. No one can compare to you!"

Among the large collection of cards I have received from Harry over the years is one that reads: *"Before I met you I was troubled with evil thoughts . . ."* Inside it reads: *"Now I enjoy them!"* And in his own handwriting, he added: *"With you!"* to make certain I felt secure in his affections.

Often a husband who would never think of having an affair with another woman gets involved with his profession, business, sports, TV, videos, a hobby, or even his church, to the exclusion of his wife. One woman told me her husband was having a torrid affair, and she was sick of it. Every night after dinner he disappeared into the other room and became involved with his computer! "I could fight another woman," she said, "but how do you fight a computer?" A wife needs her husband to so value her well-being that he takes the effort to let her know of her priority in his life.

The late Dennis Guernsey tells in his book *Thoroughly Married* of a family dinner hour that changed his life. His wife had prepared pepper steak, his personal favorite. She placed the serving plate directly in front of him. He served himself the largest steak and then passed the serving dish on to his children. His eldest daughter asked, "Daddy, why do you always take the biggest piece?" He mumbled some type of response. After dinner, however, he went for a walk to sort through his jerk-prone habits and to ask himself why he served himself first and most.

The next evening he deliberately served his wife first with the best of everything. His children immediately noticed and wanted to be served also. He simply told them that Mom was his wife and deserved to be cared for first. He went on to explain that he hadn't been doing a very good job but was planning to do better, beginning right away.

His wife, who had been in the kitchen during this exchange, rounded the corner and caught on to what was happening. The smile that lit her face could have illuminated the entire house. Someone was going to look after her.[4]

It is easy for a woman to get to feeling more like an object than a person. Any husband can prevent this by making her feel special, cherished, and valued. Every day he needs to do something that says "You are important to me." A woman needs this to be expressed in both words and actions.

Bill Havens was an Olympic-class champion who never made it to the Olympics. He had to make the decision whether to leave his pregnant wife and head for the Olympic Games or stay by his wife's side and be present for the birth of his child. Bill was favored for a gold medal in canoeing, but he gave up the gold in favor of being with his wife for their baby's birth. Although he never regretted the decision, he always wondered if he had made the right decision.

Thirty years later the nagging question was answered beyond the shadow of a doubt. His son sent a telegram from Helsinki, Finland, to say, "Dad: Thanks for waiting around for me to get born in 1924. I'm coming home with the gold medal you should have won." Bill Havens never won the Olympic gold, but he's always been a winner in the eyes of his wife. He placed his marriage and his wife's needs above his own personal goals.[5]

3. Her Need for Appreciation for Domestic Efforts. A woman needs to feel that her domestic efforts are appreciated. One woman told me she felt her husband loved her only when she kept the house spotless. She longed for him to know, however, that without his love and affection she didn't have the energy to clean the house. Any woman who feels loved only for what she does feels used, not loved. Love must be given as a gift with nothing asked in return. Genuine love says, "I love you for who and what you are, even if you don't keep the house spotless 24 hours a day."

A woman wants to know a man cares about her world. A man can show her he cares by becoming involved with her life. He can help her or actually take over some task. Prepare a meal. Clear the table. Load the dishwasher. Give a child a bath. Put a child to bed. Vacuum the house. These things spell **LOVE** in capital letters.

Whether a woman works full-time in the home or outside the home, her husband can appreciate what she does to keep the home running smoothly. A large number of women today manage their homes as well as their careers outside the home in a laudable manner. A few words of appreciation for this dual role would soothe the stress of their day.

A Woman Needs Appreciation for Her Efforts to Look Attractive. A woman needs to feel attractive. A frustrated woman's feelings were expressed in an open letter to her husband through a popular newspaper column. She complained how different things are now than they were in their early years together and how he criticized her for the way she looks. When they were dating, he couldn't see enough of her. This attitude continued through their honeymoon and early months of marriage. She was number one in his life.

As the newness of their relationship began to wear off, she got shoved farther and farther into the background. Next, he began going places with his buddies, as he had done before he was married. His ego and job took first place over his home and family. She confessed that after several pregnancies her figure wasn't what it used to be but asked what *his* excuse was for gaining weight. She spent four or five days and nights every week alone with the kids, being both mother and father to them. Her husband felt he deserved an award if he was home for supper two nights a week.

She admitted that he supported the family faithfully, but a paycheck wasn't enough to nurture a marriage or raise responsible kids—she and the kids needed his presence too. She asked point blank how long he intended to ignore the warning signals the older children were already giving because of the distress they felt from being separated from their father so much.

"So if I eat more than I should," she concluded, "it's only because I am so unhappy over our life and your refusal to take an active part in it."

The columnist responded that she was betting she'd get at least 100 letters from men, wanting to know if their wives had written that letter!

A woman needs to hear again and again from her husband just how attractive she is. Compliments on her hair, figure, or dress are always in order. She especially needs these assurances as she passes 40. Women cannot ignore the fact that a younger woman can appear very attractive to older men. And they are painfully aware of what the passing years are doing to their face, hair, and figure. They need plenty of reassurance that they are still attractive, interesting, and sexy to their husbands, in spite of the passing years.

A man who was nearing 40 himself told his wife that when she reached 40 he would trade her in on two 20s. "Forget it, honey," she quipped. "You aren't wired for 220!"

Many women complain that their husbands show attention or give compliments only when they want sex. A wife who never receives attention except during intercourse will grow to reject her husband and their sexual relationship, so the man who wants his wife to welcome his advances will compliment her often. When out socially, he can make it a point to single her out several times during the evening. If he compliments her on her appearance in front of others, he makes double deposits in her emotional bank account.

Try praising your wife, even if at first it frightens her.

Not only do men need to understand how important a compliment is to their wives, they should understand how to give a compliment. Compliments should be specific. Look her over. What specific article of clothing do you like on her? Is there anything about her hair or makeup that makes her look attractive? What do you like about her figure? Does she move in a way that is sexy or appealing?

Ask yourself, what can I say to my wife to make her feel loved and special in five seconds or less? "You're a real looker!" That comment has punch and is a hundred times better than saying, "You look nice." On a scale of 1 to 10, "you look nice" rates a one. It may be better than saying nothing, but only barely.

Lisa and Randy planned a wonderful evening out to celebrate their anniversary. Lisa bought a new dress for the occasion, then had her hair styled and her nails done. She spent a long time dressing, making sure everything was perfect. She did this partly to reassure herself that she could still be attractive to her husband, but also to show him she loved and cared about him.

Randy was waiting in the family room watching TV when Lisa finally waltzed into the room. "Well, here I am!" she said, taking a spin around the room to give him a look at the finished product.

Randy didn't even flip off the TV.

"How do I look?" Lisa asked, getting a definite edge in her voice.

"You look nice," he said absently, getting up to look for his car keys.

"Nice!" she repeated to herself as she did a slow boil.

"Well, what do you want me to say?" he countered.

As you can imagine, the evening went downhill from there!

Since some men need all the help they can get on verbalizing compliments, here are some suggestions:

Honey, you look great in that dress. It shows off your waistline.

Your hair looks pretty when you wear it that way.

You look like a million bucks in that outfit. It's a beautiful color on you.

Looking at you is one of my favorite pastimes.

Complimenting your wife will not only help you meet one of her basic emotional needs but will arouse her feelings for you. Whenever a man does this for his wife, it will pay rich dividends in the bedroom as well as in other areas of your relationship.

4. Her Need for Romantic Attention. Some men know exactly what their wives want in the romance department. Others are a little slow in learning. Shirley had been married to Larry for two years. For a Valentine's Day gift the first year, he gave her a calculator. She was hurt but forgave him. He was so wonderful in other ways she overlooked the offense. She thought he'd learn what women want for Valentine's Day and change.

Shirley was dead wrong. Seven years later she was still receiving practical items such as a new set of pots and pans, a sewing machine, electric can opener, and microwave oven. The eighth year he forgot altogether. After 24 hours of silent treatment he knew she was mad, but he still didn't catch on. In desperation he went out and bought a dozen rather wilted red roses—*on special*—and was even more puzzled by her exasperation.

Steve, another distraught husband, called to say his wife, Deanna, had just asked for a divorce. He hadn't seen this coming and was absolutely dumbfounded. When he had asked her why she wanted to divorce him, she asked, "What color are the walls in the kitchen?" He responded with the how-am-I-supposed-to-know routine, and she stormed out, saying, "That's why I'm divorcing you!"

At work Steve paid attention to every detail. At home he paid little attention to anything—his wife, his children, or the home itself. He was oblivious to everything that was not specifically job-oriented. He had lived in that house for 11 years, yet had no idea what color the kitchen walls were. Now he didn't understand why his wife wanted out. I do. His wife felt invisible, unimportant, unloved. She felt that she was nothing more to Steve than a cook, house cleaner, servant, sex partner, and someone to raise his children. She no longer felt important to him.

When this happens in a relationship, when a husband no longer demonstrates to his wife that he cares, a woman may become angry, resentful, or outright bitter and will begin to distance herself. Deanna had tried to look pretty for this man, but he never noticed. She had cooked his favorite foods, but he never noticed. She went out of her way to please him, but he never noticed. In desperation she muttered under her breath, "I could have my head shaved and Steve wouldn't notice the difference. He lives on another planet."

During our courtship I couldn't have asked for more from Harry in the romance department—flowers, dinners, phone calls, and letters every day. And he continues these attentions. I could paper China's entire Great Wall with all the cards Harry has given me over the years. My favorite card says "I miss you so much that when I think of you tears well up in my eyes . . . And they roll down onto my hot little body and turn to steam!" Harry, Harry, Harry!

However, the card I treasure most is the one he gave me on our twentieth wedding anniversary. I read it quickly and was ready to toss it aside when words he had penned himself caught my eye and left me breathless: "And may the next 20 be even happier!" Wow! Do some guys know how to melt a woman's heart! Harry understood that I didn't want to hear from the card company (even though it urges one to "care enough to send the very best"). It was Harry's sentiments that melted my heart, not those written by the card company.

Men, the little bit of time you spend finding something appropriately romantic to give your wife will pay off huge dividends. Pay attention to her comments when you are shopping together. What does she pick up and admire? What does she give her friends and family? Many women don't mind being asked what they'd like (if you ask in general terms, long before any event), but most women want you to pay enough attention to their wants and whims that you know what to give them. Knowing is half the gift.

And women, don't crush your husband's efforts at gift-giving by showing ingratitude through disappointment or criticism. It took me a while to learn how to accept gifts from Harry. I am practical and thrifty by nature, and I worry about finances when Harry gives me extravagant presents. One anniversary he presented me with expensive perfume. I questioned his wisdom in this. My mother, who was visiting, overheard my reaction and took me aside to teach me a lesson.

Returning a gift, exchanging it for something else, or putting it away without using it are discourtesies nearly unforgivable. A garment that doesn't fit may be exchanged for another size. If you don't like something, use it for a time and then put it away. You show appreciation for the giver when you appreciate the gift. Choose your words carefully in order to thank him for his thoughtfulness.

Men, you won't go wrong if you send your wife flowers, write her a note, or send a card. Romance her when you are tired (after a hard day at work). Romance her when you are really tired (after a week at work with no breaks). Romance her when you are really, really tired (after *The Late Show*).

Meeting these legitimate female needs with a little imagination and planning make a woman feel cherished. This is what wooing is all about. And it costs so little. Once she thinks you don't romance her enough, she'll think you don't love her enough—and when she believes that, you *will* pay.

. . .

21 Ways to Love Your Wife

1. Give her a hug and a kiss before getting out of bed.
2. Smile when you look at her.
3. Call her during the day to say you miss her.
4. Turn out the lights and eat dinner by candlelight.
5. Play her favorite music and invite her to cuddle with you on the sofa while you listen.
6. Ask about her day and how things went.
7. Wash her back while she's in the tub or shower.
8. Dry her back while she is in the tub or shower.
9. Put a love note in her lunch or purse.
10. As a surprise, pick her up after work.
11. Tell her how much you enjoy talking with her.
12. Tell her, in front of your children, what a good mother she is.
13. Slip your arm around her as you sit together in church.
14. Ask her for a date to be enjoyed without the children.
15. Get up 10 minutes early and ask her to join you for a chat while you sip a hot drink.
16. Before you fall asleep at night, wrap your arms around her and whisper words of love.
17. Ask her opinion about a recent news report or sermon at church.
18. Give her a hug for no reason at all.
19. Compliment her in front of a friend.
20. Use endearing words with her often.
21. When you are out socially, wink or blow a kiss to her.

[1] Adapted from Jack and Carole Mayhall, *Marriage Takes More Than Love* (Colorado Springs, Colo.: Navpress, 1978), pp. 37, 38.

[2] Cecil Osborne, *The Art of Understanding Your Mate* (Grand Rapids: Zondervan Pub. House, 1970), p. 53.

[3] H. Norman Wright, *Holding On to Romance* (Ventura, Calif.: Regal Books, 1992), p. 137.

[4] Dennis Guernsey, *Thoroughly Married* (Waco, Tex.: Word Books, 1975), p. 57.

[5] Ken R. Canfield, *Seven Secrets of Effective Fathers* (Wheaton, Ill.: Tyndale House, 1992), p. 43.

Chapter 3

HIS NEED FOR . . .

*I*f you want a man to keep loving you," a prominent pastor's wife tells women, "you only have to do one thing—appreciate him and let him know you do." This bit of old-fashioned, homespun advice would save many marriages if women would only practice it.

One disillusioned man said he was recently elected president of a large organization in his town. Diligently, he prepared his acceptance speech that he delivered at a banquet attended by all the members, their wives, and other dignitaries. When he finished speaking, many friends crowded around to congratulate him on how well he'd done. Although he appreciated their response, the one person whose appreciation he wanted most of all—his wife—said nothing. The hurt went deep as he recognized that he must search elsewhere for appreciation.

1. A Man Needs Admiration for Appearance, Abilities, and Character Traits. Yes, a man appreciates honor and acclaim from others—but most of all, he needs his wife to think he is great. Every man needs a fan club, and his wife should be president. He needs her to cheer him on—not just when he's winning, but during the inevitable low times as well. That's when he really needs her to say, "You can do this. You've done well before. You can do it again. I believe in you." He needs to feel there is someone on his team that he can always count on. That someone should be his wife.

The saying "Behind every great man is a great woman" should be amended to read, "Behind every great man is an admiring wife." Biographies of great men prove this, and the lives of great men demonstrate it. A man thrives on a woman's admiration. Although not much is written about it, many men owe deep gratitude to their wives for this type of emotional support. Without it their confidence—the major factor in their success—might have crumbled.

Some unknown genius put together a 24-hour recording that turns out tender messages for admiration-starved men. Men can dial this number and hear a woman's sultry voice croon, "You're the most exciting man I ever met." After a pause for effect, the voice continues breathlessly, "I wonder if the real woman in your life recognizes how lucky she is." Softly she adds, "I do." After the laughter died down in one seminar where this recording was described, three men raised their hands and asked, "What did you say that number was?"

What does a man want admiration for? Let's explore three categories:

Appearance. To many men, physical appearance ranks high. These men want specific masculine qualities admired—their physique and strength. One woman told me, giggling, "You know what my husband does sometimes? Every once in a while he comes home from work, sheds all his clothes right down to his undershorts, and then parades through the house beating on his chest, making Tarzan calls." This husband was begging for attention.

I can live for two months on a good compliment.—**Mark Twain**

During a seminar I asked the women, "What is the last thing your husbands heard before they left for work this morning?"

One woman blurted out, "How much my back hurt!"

"What's he going to hear at work today?" I asked. The woman gulped as she recognized that he worked in an office with many well-groomed, attractive women who often complimented him on his appearance, his work, and his good manners.

"Never," I told these women, "let your husband leave the house without putting your arms around him and whispering something in his ear about how much you admire him." This is what he will remember about you throughout the day. You are filling his need and not leaving him wide open for some cute little trick to flaunt her stuff, thinking your husband a great candidate for her next conquest. By complimenting your husband first thing in the morning, you bond him to you throughout the day.

Someone tells the story of a young wife who had a terrible morning. Her hubby couldn't find a shirt to wear; he complained about breakfast and spilled milk all over the table and floor. After she finally hustled the children out the door, the two had a real free-for-all fight. As her beaten husband left for work, he shouted back at her, "Why did you ever marry me in the first place?" Without thinking she shouted back, "Because you look just like Tom Cruise!"

She was horrified by her answer. She'd married him because she loved him, of course, and his resemblance to Cruise was part of a fantasy she had about him. She put in a miserable half hour before the phone rang.

"You know what I like about you?" her husband asked, a new jauntiness pervading his voice.

"I can't imagine," she answered.

"Your unerring judgment and superb taste," he said. "Not to mention your eye for great looks."

Watch your husband the next time you see him studying his appearance in the mirror. His hairline may be receding a little, and he may be sprouting a slight paunch around his belt line. But this is of little consequence. He squares his shoulders, sucks in his abs a little, and says to his mirror reflection, "You tiger, you!" Any time your husband feels like a tiger, he thinks he can conquer the world. And when he feels like this, *you* will be richly rewarded.

Skills, talents, and abilities. What skills, talents, and abilities does your husband have? Harry is a talented artist. Sometimes I pause before one of his favorite paintings and compliment him, as I have many times before, on his exquisite work. He revels in this praise.

Compliment your husband on the skills and abilities he demonstrates in connection with his work. You may never have been to his place of employment, but you can still be a good listener and admire what he tells you. If you want him to tell you about his work and his accomplishments, you'd better learn how to encourage and motivate him at work. When he has a great idea, tell him so. When he gets a promotion or a raise, be his greatest supporter.

Friends of ours own property at Fish Camp, three miles from the south entrance to Yosemite National Park. Harry and I have been invited to park our trailer there. Some of our most memorable summer fun is spent at Fish Camp cookouts. Leroy, another frequent guest, is a gourmet cook. Often Leroy takes on planning and preparing a meal for the entire crowd, which might number 20. Everything he cooks, even under camp conditions, is specially seasoned, cooked to perfection, and tastes superb.

Talent like this deserves recognition. Whether a man is mechanical, proficient at the computer, a mathematics whiz, an avid reader, or a great joketeller, a wife should see to it that she satisfies his need for appreciation.

Just yesterday Harry fixed a problem with the car engine. He promptly told me about it and then took me to the garage to show me what he had done. Since my knowledge of cars is limited, it did little good to show me. Why did he bother? He needed the pat on the back and the affirmation, and I was glad to lay it on him!

Character traits. Whether your man is honest, responsible, always on time, has scrupulous morals, is deeply religious, or has integrity that can't be beat—speak up. Is he devoted to his occupation? Did he show courage during some harrowing experience? Does he faithfully bring home a paycheck to support you and the children?

Many women accept financial support for years without offering a word of appreciation. Don't assume your man knows how much you admire his character traits. He needs to hear you say it. It will encourage him to even greater heights of integrity and spur him on during low periods.

Does your man encourage you to develop your own talents and interests? Does he prepare a meal? mow the lawn? paint the house? share in the care of the home? do his part in caring for the children? remember anniversaries and birthdays without being prompted? Such courtesies require appreciation. Does he devote time and energy toward making your marriage superior? Is he a responsible, caring, and dedicated father? Appreciation will reinforce his desire to continue.

A husband who prefers to remain anonymous parodied a well-known poem this way:

> If with pleasure you are viewing
> Any work a man is doing,
> If you like him or you love him,
> Tell him now.
> Don't withhold your approbation
> 'Til the parson makes oration
> As he lies with snowy lilies o'er his brow.
> For no matter how you shout it,
> He won't really care about it;
> He won't know how many teardrops you have shed.
> If you think some praise is due him,
> Now's the time to slip it to him,
> For he cannot read his tombstone when he's dead.

Remember, a man falls in love with the woman who makes him feel stronger, more capable, more intelligent, and sexier than he's ever felt before. A man falls in love because of the way a woman makes him feel about himself.

When a man no longer feels good about himself when he is with his wife, he becomes vulnerable to another woman. This is what affairs are all about. He probably is not really "in love" with the other woman. He craves the feeling he gets about himself when he is with the other woman.

Ladies, you can relight those fires you once had burning with your husband. Help your husband feel good about himself when he is with you. Nourish his needs on a daily basis in order to make him want to stay home and not go elsewhere.

Some women are in dire need of reprogramming their thinking and behavior. They respond automatically to their children's needs but neglect their husband's. But remember, marriage, because it lasts for a lifetime, is primary.

The five-second compliment. One woman admitted that she had made a serious mistake. She had not been telling her husband how much she admired his work and how proud she was of his abilities. She began giving him five-second compliments several times a day. It was as good as an ego vitamin, she announced with joy. Her husband's self-confidence increased, his libido was energized, and he became much more affectionate with her. All this accomplished in five seconds!

If you need some help in expressing admiration, here are some suggestions on how to say it:

Honey, you're really smart. The way you handled that business deal was brilliant!

Your bod really makes that shirt look good on you.

Thanks for cleaning up that mess.

I appreciate your willingness to drive me there.

Build him up every chance you get. When he feels good about himself he will naturally love you more and be more responsive to your needs. Initially it may take a little effort. But make it a habit, and you'll have a husband who adores you and wants to satisfy your needs in return.

If a man could verbalize what he wants from his wife, it might sound something like this:

I want to know why I'm important to you. And I need to hear it every day, not just once.

Tell me daily what you admire. Compliment every admirable quality.

I want to be your leading man, your hero, and protector.

Tell me why I matter to you.

Honest admiration is a tremendous need for a man. When a wife tells her husband she admires something he has done, this inspires him to achieve even more. He sees himself as capable of handling new responsibilities and improving skills beyond what he is presently accomplishing. This inspiration encourages him to respond more positively to the responsibilities and challenges of life.

Admiration not only motivates a man to push ahead, but it also provides a present-moment reward for his achievements. When a man's wife expresses appreciation for his supporting her, it makes long, intensive hours worthwhile. A man needs to be appreciated for what he already is, not for what he could become with her help.

Admiration also helps a man believe in himself. This is especially necessary for a man with low self-esteem. Admiration will help him during low periods. Unless a wife assists her husband gently in building a more positive self-image, he will only become more and more defensive about his shortcomings. Some men refuse to attend marriage seminars, see a counselor, read a book on marriage, or accept help of any kind. Such men have such fragile self-esteem that even the slightest criticism is devastating to them.

Admiration is the opposite of criticism. Criticism causes a man to be angry and defensive, but admiration energizes him and motivates him to carry on and excel. A man wants and needs his wife's approval. A steady diet of criticism is dangerous to anyone's mental health. But self-esteem can be improved within an environment created by someone who values and admires their accomplishments. When a man is appreciated by a woman who supports and encourages him, it sparks genius and potential.

2. A Man Needs Approval and Support. Learning to approve of and support a man is a real art. Few things make a man feel more loved and valued than being reassured that you grasp his point of view, even if you don't share it. Even a minimum attempt at such understanding of feelings can make an enormous difference, especially when things are not going well with a couple.

You can also demonstrate support by apologizing when it's called for. An outright apology lets him know you consider his gripe valid and worth respecting. When you apologize, you don't always have to say "I'm sorry." You could say, "You're right. I was wrong." Admitting that you were wrong can have a powerful, positive effect on the conversation that follows. Even if you can't see his point of view, let him know you are trying.

Husbands need someone with whom they can share their ideas of how things ought to be. They need to test and sample responses from their wives. They need someone to confirm their ideas. This confirmation, when it comes from someone who cares, reinforces their self-image and makes them feel more confident and secure.

Young husbands just beginning their careers particularly need approval. Filled with ideas, proposals, and zeal, they itch to prove there is a better way. But often their colleagues are busy with their own plans, or may throw a wet blanket on new ideas. Young husbands need someone to reinforce their mental picture of themselves when they get their turn at the helm.

*There is no greater love than the love that holds on where there seems nothing left to hold on to.—***G.W.C. Thomas**

A man needs understanding of the heavy responsibilities he carries for supporting the family. One woman told me her husband came home from an unusually trying day at work and was in a terrible mood, ready to pick a fight over the least little thing. Instead of arguing or defending herself against his attacks, as she ordinarily would, she left him alone while she fixed dinner.

Over dinner she held her tongue and told him how much she appreciated how hard he worked to support the family. She went on to tell him that she knew it wasn't always easy for him to work at his less-than-perfect job. After dinner, for the first time since they were married, her husband didn't leave the table immediately but sat and talked to her for a good hour. He appreciated the support she offered during that difficult period.

It isn't easy to support and encourage a man when he changes careers or suggests a move to another location or state in order to better himself in his career, especially if it appears he is making a poor choice. But if a man isn't happy in what he's doing, his wife can't be happy either. The odds against a man's winning in another field may be slim. His friends may be telling him he won't make it. But if a man wants a change, he needs a wife who will support him.

Moodiness, depression, and discouragement are common among men. And the more intelligent, talented, and aggressive the man, the deeper his fall into depression. These men have high goals and aspirations for the future, and when things don't go well for them it hits them hard.

A woman has the power to restore the broken pieces of a man's soul. Instinctively a man knows this and will turn to his wife in his hour of need if she has proved supportive in the past. What he wants and needs is your understanding and support during a difficult time. He comes to you to have his doubts removed, his self-esteem reestablished, and his soul restored. When he talks about his troubles, let him. Let him tell you without trying to remove the problem or give him advice.

Accept his discouragement for what it is—a temporary emotion or mood. Let him know you believe in him. Offer him hope for the future and your belief that he can survive.

A top government official told his wife, "If you ever lost faith in me, I'd be finished. But as long as you believe in me, I can lick the world." A wife needs to demonstrate to her husband, without a moment's doubt, that she has faith he can do whatever he wants to do and be successful—even if they have only a sandwich to split between them.

Offer reassurance during the low periods. If your husband fails to get a hoped-for promotion or raise, you can still express confidence in his ability to try again or to carry on. As one woman put it, "It is vital to preserve your husband's respect for himself."

In an interview Nancy Reagan once said that although she married her husband for what he was, not for what he accomplished, she felt it essential to encourage him to do what was interesting and challenging for him. "If it's what he wants," she said, "you will benefit in the long run."

Agreeing with your husband's ideas, suggestions, or solutions is another form of approval. Remember, every time you give a compliment or express pride in your partner, you strengthen the bond between you. Try out some of the supportive phrases below.

I believe in you.
You can do it!

You can count on me to be there for you.
I think you can handle this successfully.
You can do it!

3. His Need for Respect. Scripture is clear on this point: "You wives must submit to your husbands' leadership in the same way you submit to the Lord" (Ephesians 5:22, TLB). Wives are to reverence or respect their husbands. The dictionary definition for *respect* refers the reader to the word *admire* and then gives this denotation: "regard for and appreciation of worth, honor, and esteem." The definition of *reverence* is: "a feeling of profound respect, often mingled with awe and affection."

The secret of happy marriage is simple: just keep on being as polite to each other as you are to your best friends.— Robert Quillen.

How is respect measured? Words can convey respect or disdain. Do you speak in a respectful tone of voice? Do you talk down to your husband or order him around as you might one of the children? Respect—or lack of it—can also be communicated through nonverbal behavior. A roll of the eyes or deep sigh can convey "How can you be so incredibly stupid?" without a word said.

A woman sets the attitude of respect in the home. When a mother respects her husband, the children learn attitudes of respect for their father. A wife should always respect her husband's ideas and opinions, but this becomes doubly true in the presence of other family members and friends. Showing disrespect in private is bad enough; but when a wife demonstrates a lack of respect in front of others, she breeds contempt—in his attitude toward her as well as in the minds of the observers.

When a wife builds her husband up in the presence of others, not only does she demonstrate respect, but others respect her loyalty. When children observe their mother always treating their father respectfully, they too will develop attitudes of respect for Daddy. It is the woman in the home who sets the atmosphere of respect for the entire family.

Respect means treating a man like an equal, not a child. When a woman says "Remember to pick the children up after school" or "How many times do I have to ask you to come to the table on time?" or "Don't you think you need to wear a sweater?" she gives the impression that her husband is totally incompetent and needs her to run his life and tell him what to do.

When a woman acts like a mother and treats her man like a little boy, he will live up to her expectations of incompetence. When she scolds him, reminds him of things to remember, does things for him that he should be doing for himself, or corrects him and gives him directions on how to do something he should know how to do—she is not respecting his abilities as an adult.

Acting like your husband's mother will destroy your relationship. He will eventually resent you and rebel against you when he wants his independence. The more incompetent he feels, the lower his self-esteem and the more incompetent he will act.

The wife is the loser in all this. When a man does not feel good about himself he is incapable of loving her the way she wants to be loved. It is difficult for him to be happy with himself or his wife. This eventually affects her feelings about him because she can only respect, admire, and appreciate him when he is confident and competent.

A newly married male whose marriage was already in trouble because of serious mothering on the part of his new bride bitterly complained to me, "Who can have sex with his mother?" His young wife was shocked into the realization that mothering quickly kills passion. It affects female desire as well. How romantic and responsive can a woman be to a man she's treated like a child all day?

Show confidence in your husband's abilities. Relax, and trust him to figure out the way to solve his problems, whether he's lost on the freeway or stuck in the middle of negotiations with his boss. Trust and confidence translate into respect and increased self-esteem, and you as a woman will find the emotional security *you* need as you give your man the opportunity to prove himself competent.

4. His Need for Sexual Fulfillment. In the same way many men do not understand a woman's need for romance, most women do not understand how important sexual fulfillment is to a man. Before a man can fulfill his wife's emotional needs, he must know that his wife finds him sexually attractive.

Many a man who misses an anniversary catches it later.

Call it a double bind or the ultimate impasse, but we're back to the old idiom "A man gives love in order to get sex, and a woman gives sex in order to get love." A woman needs to feel emotionally satisfied before she can fulfill her husband's sexual needs; and a man requires sexual fulfillment before responding to his wife's need for affection, caring, and romantic attention.

Sex does something for the male besides satisfying his urgent sexual needs. Sex is a confirmation of a woman's desire and love for him, as well as a reaffirmation of his self-worth and masculinity. Only when his self-worth has been affirmed does he feel virile. Indeed, so great is a man's need for sexual fulfillment that Willard F. Harley, author of *His Needs, Her Needs,* places it first in a list of things that a man can't do without.[1]

A man must feel wanted and needed, not simply endured. Some women perform the sex act as if they were paying compulsory dues to a professional organization. In one large survey on male sexuality, hundreds of men were asked why they liked intercourse. The reason men gave most often for liking or wanting intercourse was the feeling of being loved and accepted by their wives. Their answers were summed up by one man who said, "Intercourse continually reaffirms my close attachment with my mate. It tells me she loves me. It gives me confidence. It makes me feel wanted."

There's a vital connection between a man's masculinity and his sexuality. Women tend to judge their husband's sexual needs by their own. When a man's sexual needs are ignored, initiation of sex resisted, or when a woman merely tolerates their sexual relationship, he feels rejection of his very maleness. It destroys his sense of self. But when he functions as a man should function, it reaffirms his maleness. By so doing he also proves to his wife (from his viewpoint) that he loves her.

The media portrays men as sexually assertive and confident. But truthfully, the average male worries a great deal about his ability to "perform." Males fear inability to maintain an erection, impotence, and premature ejaculation. Being able to perform has a certain competitive quality that makes him question his ability to be a sufficiently skillful lover to satisfy his wife. Men question whether they can perform as well as or better than other men and whether their desires are normal or perverted. They wonder if they are expecting too much, or too little. Some men also fear they are too sex-driven.

All of these fears make a man extremely vulnerable to acceptance and rejection. When approaching his wife for sex he has in effect laid his maleness on the line. If she rejects him she has in effect rejected a vital part of him, his maleness. Deep down he is asking, How am I doing as a lover? When a wife anticipates and enjoys sex, this increases his confidence regarding his masculinity as well as his ability as a lover.

This confidence will carry over into other areas of his life—his marriage, parenting, and his work. He'll be ready to tackle the world with confidence. His battery is fully charged. A good sexual encounter boosts a man's self-esteem, pats him on the back, and affirms his OK-ness. Don't fail to meet this need.

A good sexual relationship also affair-proofs your marriage. When a man marries, he promises to remain sexually faithful for a lifetime. He willingly makes this commitment because he trusts his wife to be as interested in him sexually as he is in her and trusts she will be sexually available when he needs her. Unfortunately some men discover this to be one of the biggest mistakes of their lives. If a man's spiritual or moral convictions are strong, he may live with the commitment he made and make the best of it. Many cannot or will not, and so look for sex elsewhere.

Some men seem to lose their reasoning abilities in their attempts to fill their sexual needs. Even men in leadership positions—politicians, pastors, and leaders of large churches—have thrown away their reputations, position, wealth, achievements, children, and families in order to fill this need that they themselves do not fully understand. I have listened to stories from such bewildered leaders, shocked at their own indiscretions. In most cases such men are so motivated by their need for sex and what it does to reinforce their maleness that their intellect becomes clouded and their integrity is sacrificed.

Emotions often build up inside a man. He may be worried about some project at work that isn't going well. Or he may be concerned over the health of his parents. Since men have been trained to hold their emotions in check, he likely feels helpless, confused, and fearful. When these feelings build up inside him, he doesn't know what to do about them; but he knows he needs a release of some kind. Suddenly he's in the mood for sex. In sex he finds an outlet for his repressed emotions.

When a man makes sexual advances, he is asking for more than sex. He is asking that you accept him. He's looking for emotional closeness. Sex may be the only way he's ever learned to get close. And he may be totally unaware of what he is really asking for. Sometimes a man will reach out for sex when he needs reassurance and comfort. Sex has made him feel better before, and he looks to it once again to soothe and comfort him.

To a man, sex is another language to communicate love to his wife. A man's unspoken emotions can be released acceptably through sex when he doesn't know how to say what he's feeling. This creates no problems when a wife understands the process. But both must recognize that sex provides only temporary relief for pent-up emotions. It doesn't really solve the problem he is experiencing or help him verbalize under stress.

A man feels rejected when his sexual advances are rebuffed. Indifference or mere tolerance hurt him more than anything else. He may still make love to you and enjoy it; but when you become eager for his lovemaking it does something for his sense of maleness that nothing else can do. Loving you in return becomes sheer pleasure to him.

A story is told of a bird lover who bought a parrot to keep her company. She returned it to the pet store the next day, complaining that the bird didn't talk. The pet store owner asked if the parrot had a mirror in its cage. "Parrots love mirrors and often begin talking when they see their reflection in the mirror," the store owner explained. The new bird owner bought a mirror and went home with her parrot.

The next day the bird lover was back at the pet store firmly stating that the parrot still wasn't talking. She demanded a talking parrot. The pet store owner didn't want to lose the sale. He encouraged her to purchase a ladder. "Parrots love ladders," he said. "A happy parrot soon becomes a talkative parrot." The woman listened to this new advice, bought a ladder for the cage, and went home.

The following day the owner of the parrot appeared again at the store, complaining that the parrot still did not talk. This time the store owner suggested a swing for the parrot. "Once he starts swinging," the store owner chirped, "he'll talk up a storm." The woman reluctantly bought a swing, went home, and put it in the parrot's cage.

When she showed up the next day, she was even more upset. "The parrot died," she told the pet store owner.

Shocked, the man asked, "Before the parrot died, did he ever say anything?"

"Yes," the woman replied. "Just before he died he asked in a weak squawk, 'Don't they sell any *food* at that pet store?'" [2]

In the same way, all the "bells and whistles" that go with marriage—fancy homes, exotic vacations, cabins in the mountains, powerful positions, and big salaries—guarantee us nothing in the happiness department without "food." And the food that nourishes a marriage is meeting emotional needs.

---

[1] Willard F. Harley, Jr., *His Needs, Her Needs* (Grand Rapids: Fleming H. Revell, 1994), p. 42.

[2] Adapted from Randy Fishell, "Simple Pictures Are Best," *Adventist Review*, Dec. 18, 1997, p. 25.

Chapter 4

#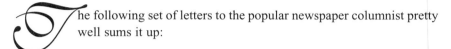

The following set of letters to the popular newspaper columnist pretty well sums it up:

Dear Ann Landers:

My husband and I just celebrated our twentieth wedding anniversary. He's a good provider, no bad habits, a wonderful father to our children, and everyone who knows him thinks he's great. So what am I complaining about?

The man does not stop talking. The first thing I hear in the morning is his voice. At night when I turn out the lights, he's still talking. He asks me a question and answers it himself. He tells me he wants an opinion, and then he gives me one. He repeats a conversation, and before I can comment he tells me what he thinks. When we're out socially, I never get a chance to open my mouth. People must think I'm a blooming idiot. Some of our friends don't know I have vocal cords. Any advice?

Signed: Wed to a Talking Machine

Dear Wed:

After 20 years, accept the fact that this man is not going to change. It will save wear and tear on your blood vessels. And please read the next letter.

Dear Ann Landers:

I've been married for 22 years to a man who will not talk to me. He refuses to discuss family problems and makes no comment whatsoever when I present family problems with which I need help.

I've tried every approach imaginable—from the nonchalant, casual, "What do you think about this, dear?" to the impassioned request, "I need your help desperately," and finally the screaming anguished pleas: "Will you answer me!" His response is a blank look and stony silence. Once in a while he mumbles, "I hadn't thought about it."

My husband is an intelligent professional man who has a lot on his mind—but who doesn't these days? I ask very little of him. I am tired of making all the decisions alone. I'm on the verge of blowing my mind. Any suggestions?

Signed: Wife of the Great Stone Man

Dear Wife:

After 22 years, accept the fact that this man is not going to change. It will save wear and tear on your blood vessels.[1]

Acceptance. No other quality is so vital or so fundamental to marriage. And it is certainly the foundation of a highly effective marriage. Love comes first, but acceptance of a partner must be practiced on a day-to-day basis or love will not last. When we are accepted by our mates, we feel appreciated, approved of, and ultimately encouraged to be all that we can be. But when our mate tries to improve or change some habit or behavior of ours, we feel hurt.

My own marriage is a prime example here. When I discovered Harry, I thought he was wonderful. He was adaptable and easygoing, as compared to my more structured and organized life. He was mannerly, thoughtful, caring, handsome, and treated me like a queen. We enjoyed many of the same activities, never argued or disagreed on anything. I thought I had succeeded where all other women had failed—I had located The Perfect Man.

During a portion of our courtship we were separated. I pursued higher education while he served his country in the Army. So our courtship was carried on via letters and phone calls. He remained PERFECT. (I still have some of those letters to prove that this is the way I thought of Harry during those years.)

But the minute the "I Do's" were completed (probably on our way to the honeymoon site) I was already into my husband improvement mode. I knew what I was doing, but I tried to state it so sweetly that he wouldn't notice that I was making suggestions or trying to change him. My requests always began with a "Honey" or "Darling," and I timed my appeals carefully.

I couldn't believe that Harry actually resisted my well-thought-out, well-timed suggestions. I persisted. He either bristled or ignored me. Sometimes I thought he repeated the detested behavior deliberately just to spite me. But I wouldn't give up. I knew we could have a great marriage if Harry would just improve in a few areas.

I redoubled my efforts. Things got worse. I would back off and try again. This man simply did not understand how I wanted to help him become the best man possible. I thought if only he would listen to me, there would be no end to what he could accomplish and how blissful the two of us could be. But all my efforts to help him failed, and things between us got worse.

One night, 15 years into our marriage, we had a major disagreement. This was The Big One. We both hurled vicious accusations. Exhausted from our unresolvable problems, we threatened divorce. One hurtful remark in particular stuck in my mind: "Since the day we married," Harry told me, "you've done nothing but try to change me. You don't love me or care about me. I am not going to change for you or anyone."

I thought about what he had said. "You don't love me." Harry just couldn't understand that I was trying to change him because I loved him. "I am not going to change for you or anyone." There it was. After 15 years of marriage I realized that if our marriage was going to survive, *I* was going to have to change. This was a new thought. I had been so busy blaming him for our problems that I was blind to my own faults.

As I stomped off to bed alone, I recalled a book a friend had given me that tells how to understand and treat a man. While reading it earlier, I had become so furious over some of the advice that I had thrown the book under the bed. I didn't even want to see it, let alone evaluate what it might mean to my marriage. As I mulled my present situation over in my mind, I thought of the discarded book. I retrieved it and began reading.

I won't say I *liked* what I read. But I was convinced the book was right: I had never given Harry the acceptance he needed. My constant suggestions that he change this or do that made him feel "less than." Fifteen years of my nagging and complaining, though my intentions were good, had almost destroyed our relationship. We had come within a hairbreadth of calling it quits.

A good husband should be deaf and a good wife should be blind.

I read that book over and over, contemplating and evaluating each new concept. The very point that I had objected to the most became the salvation of our marriage. A few days later Harry and I had a state-of-the-marriage meeting. I told Harry that I had learned he didn't need my suggestions for improvement—he needed my acceptance and encouragement. I assured him I was going to become a new wife. And I've been in the new wife mode ever since.

Is it easy for me? Definitely not! Some of us are more compelled to change our mates than others. My very temperament continues to push me in that direction. Sometimes I fail. I catch myself, or Harry lets me know I've stepped over the line again.

We all have blind spots in relationships in which we fail to see situations clearly. This is my blind or weak area. I will always struggle with acceptance. Perhaps you can understand why I consider this chapter so important. This is where I nearly lost my marriage, but where it was made new again. Constantly teaching the subject, as well as writing about it, has helped me grow.

What Is Acceptance?

The dictionary definition uses the following terms: to receive with favor, approval, willingness; favorable reception; welcome; regarded as normal or right. When dating Harry I did everything within my power to give him approval, and I did it willingly. No one coerced me into it. I was falling in love with this man, and I wanted to show him that I welcomed him, that I received him favorably, that I regarded everything he said or did as normal and right. Harry was The Perfect Man, remember?

What happened that nearly destroyed our marriage? After our marriage I showed disapproval of him. I no longer welcomed him or received him favorably. Everything (or nearly everything) he said or did I regarded as unacceptable and wrong. I thought he needed to change, remember?

If you had your choice of the type of person you wanted to live with in a life-long commitment, would you choose an accepting person, or a critical person? It's a pretty obvious choice.

In order to maintain a friendship with someone, we must practice a good measure of acceptance. When a friend does something we don't like, we excuse it, forgive it, or forget it. "That's just the way she does things," we say with a smile. Within marriage, we aren't quite so forgiving.

What does it mean to accept your mate at face value? What is involved in acceptance? It means that you view your partner as a worthy person. That you like them just the way they are. That you respect their right to be different or dissimilar from you. That you allow them to possess their own feelings about matters regardless of how they may differ from yours.

Though it can be a highly rewarding experience to accept another person just as they are without thought of change, it is not always easy to do. In the process we will need to ask ourselves some frightening questions. Can I accept the fact that my partner responds to life's problems differently than I do?

In our home, for example, when we encounter a problem I want to discuss it NOW, achieve a quick solution, implement the plan, move on, and forget it. Harry solves problems much differently. He wants all the details laid out on the table. He explores all the options, moving through an analytical process of slow-moving negotiations with a lot of talk. If his emotions have been running high, he has difficulty laying them aside, moving on, and forgetting the problem as I prefer to do. I have to ask myself, can I accept this difference in problem solving? Can I permit my partner to have different likes and dislikes than I have? Harry loves buttermilk and cottage cheese. I think of these foods as spoiled. Harry likes classical music and has a library of classical compact disks, including Beethoven's Fifth Symphony and Tchaikovsky's !812 Overture. The heavier, louder, and less melodic (to my ears) the music, the better he likes it. I have little appreciation for classical music, though I have to admit that during our dating days I professed to be a great admirer of Beethoven and his type!

Can I respect my partner's right to choose his own beliefs and develop his own values? We're talking politics and religion here. Some women are convinced that it is their obligation to convert their unbelieving husbands. Through nagging, moralizing, lecturing, reminding, or begging they attempt to coerce or trick their husbands into attending church. They resort to any measure or tactic, often to the detriment of the husband's well-being.

This demanding, self-righteous attitude is probably as offensive a sin as is the husbands' alienation from religion. These women often take on the role of the Holy Spirit, feeling compelled by an unseen power to bring—or drag, if necessary—their men to church.

Acceptance of others doesn't come easily. We tend to cluster around us those who think, feel, and act as we do. When our loved ones fail to live up to our preconceived ideas of what is "right" or "wrong," we attempt to change their ideas and prove ourselves right. We persecute them with unacceptance. We gather our self-righteous robes around us and look down on the very ones we have pledged to love, honor, and cherish until death parts us—because they don't believe the way we do. Yet this separateness of the individual, this right each person has to use their experience in their own way and to discover their own meaning, is one of the most priceless privileges in life.

Does this mean that we should pretend that our mates are perfect? Of course not! It means that we recognize the imperfections but make a conscious choice to concentrate on all the good qualities, all the possibilities that lie within our partners. We accept the total person—faults and all. There is a biblical base for this concept rooted in Philippians 4:8: "Whatever is true, whatever is noble, whatever is right, whatever is pure, whatever is lovely, whatever is admirable—if anything is excellent or praiseworthy—think about such things" (NIV).

Some feel they have been practicing acceptance because they have mustered the strength to restrain criticism. They may say nothing, but grimaces, soulful looks, long sighs, a roll of the eyes, and painful silences get the message across louder than words.

Acceptance is not tolerance—putting up with or enduring faults. It does not mean dishonesty—forcing ourselves to believe that we are married to the perfect person. It doesn't mean resignation—giving up because our spouse refuses to change. When I accept my partner I see the total person—faults and good qualities. I am content with what I see. And I prove my contentment by not trying to make my partner over.

Acceptance—An Irrepressible Need to Be Loved and Approved

We are all created with a need to be loved and accepted, an almost insatiable longing for someone to cherish and like us for who and what we are regardless of how we look or act. This need to be loved and accepted is evident even in the animal kingdom, especially among elephants.

In India, elephants who are to be trained for service are put in isolation for three days. These animals react to loneliness much the same as humans would— they grieve and fret and long for their peers. When they are most vulnerable, they are brought to a nighttime ceremony of fire. For many hours in the flickering light, they are screamed at, intimidated, stroked, and ordered back and forth. By morning, half-crazed, the elephants yield to man as their master.[2]

A parallel exists between these elephants and us fragile human beings. We too are social creatures, born with irrepressible needs to be loved and accepted by our parents and peers. We long for acceptance even more from our mates.

A loving spouse can see the good in you even when you can't.

A man visited a ranch in Zimbabwe where cattle were being bred and raised. There among several hundred steers was a full-grown female elephant who had been "adopted" when she was young. She spent her days associating with cattle, trying hard to be accepted. Because the elephant was smarter than the cattle, she sought ways to win their respect. She used her trunk to unlock the gate for them, even though she had no interest in escaping. And, believe it or not, she even tried to learn how to moo so she could sound more like the "in" group. If this is the length that an animal will go to for acceptance, to what lengths will humans go?

To a large degree we marry someone who fills this craving within us. This craving operates 24 hours a day. When our needs for acceptance are not met, we feel rejected, alienated, and deeply hurt. We begin to dislike the very ones we love the most, and do not care to be near them or talk to them. When our mate fills our need for love and acceptance, however, our closeness is reaffirmed. We have good feelings about ourselves, our mate, and our relationship.

The Key to Acceptance

An important prerequisite to accepting a mate at face value is the ability to accept yourself just as you are. To the same degree you are able to accept yourself you will be able to accept your partner.

Self-worth is an honest appraisal of one's self. You make no false claims. Rather, you accept your weak areas as well as your strengths and feel you deserve the respect of others. You have learned to build on strengths and compensate for weaknesses. You have learned to live with the limitations you have been unable to change. From time to time you fail, but you are able to pick up the pieces and move ahead. You try to be sincere and open, and consider yourself a worthy person.

These healthy attitudes free you to pay attention to others. You are as tolerant of the weaknesses of others as you are of your own. You appreciate the differences of others instead of resenting, fearing, or ridiculing them. You realize that our differences make each human being unique. Healthy self-respect also frees you spiritually, for you more fully appreciate God's acceptance of you and your potential for good.

Low self-esteem causes defensive and inappropriate communication patterns to dominate in order to protect a weak sense of being. When you have low self-esteem, desperation overwhelms you as problems resurface. Since you possess neither the coping mechanism to resolve problems nor the ability to put new skills to work, you sink deeper into self-defeating patterns.

Obviously this affects your marriage. Someone with a poor self-image is often unhappy and will likely suffer from depression or lash out at others with blame for the hurt and pain. Your weak self-image forces you to try to prove something to your partner just to make a point.

There is no greater barrier to a highly effective marriage than deep-seated feelings that you are unlovable. The first love affair you must negotiate successfully is a love affair with yourself. Only then will you be fully able to love another person and allow that person to love you. Without the knowledge that you are lovable, your partner's love will never be quite real or convincing. In many insidious ways you will unknowingly attempt to undermine it.

Dr. Stanley S. Heller, who was selected by *New York Magazine* as one of the top New York psychiatrists, has said, "The most important quality in any marriage is the emotional health of each person." [3] It is more difficult than ever to find an emotionally healthy partner because a record number of people are growing up in dysfunctional homes—families that have been ravaged by divorce, alcoholism, drug abuse, and emotional, sexual, or physical abuse.

People from these backgrounds carry devastating wounds, though they may be hidden. Their personal pain drives them to search for someone who can heal their pain, soothe their wounds, and put together all the broken pieces of their lives.

We all carry wounds of one kind or another, for we all come from imperfect homes. We all were born flawed! But we can learn to accept ourselves and learn to deal with our flaws, rather than run from them or blame others. We can learn to like ourselves just the way we are.

Before we can achieve a successful marriage with someone else, we need to have a healthy, loving relationship with ourselves. As Oscar Wilde once said: "To love oneself is the beginning of a lifelong romance."

---

[1] Ann Landers, in Chicago *Tribune.* Permission granted by Ann Landers/Creators Syndicate.

[2] James C. Dobson, in *Focus on the Family Newsletter,* February 1993.

[3] Van Pelt, *Smart Love—A Field Guide for Single Adults,* pp. 31, 32.

Chapter 5

Habits That Destroy Relationships

*A*ny habit that makes your spouse unhappy threatens the love and security of your relationship. A single act may be tolerated; but when even thoughtless acts are repeated and become predictable, the damage to the relationship is multiplied.

Willard F. Harley in his book *Love Busters*[1] created the term "Love Bank" to describe how love feelings are created and destroyed. Every experience we have with our spouses affects the balance held in our Love Bank. We are either making deposits or withdrawals in the account throughout each day. When things go well and we are loving, kind, supportive, and understanding of our partners, hundreds of credits flow into our Emotional Bank Account (EBA) and create the feeling that our partners are loved and accepted the way they are. When things go badly, huge withdrawals are made from the EBA. At times the account can be seriously overdrawn, and the relationship goes into a serious deficit. Should negative feelings continue to dominate, a couple can even begin to hate each other—every action, even an innocent or unknowing act, is interpreted as uncaring and insensitive.

Let's look at some of the most destructive habits that make withdrawals from our EBA. When engaged in repeatedly, they can threaten the very solemnity of the marriage vows.

Destructive Habit Number 1: Nagging

One of the most common Love Busters used by women, although men are certainly not exempt, is nagging. The dictionary defines nagging as "to torment by persistent faultfinding or complaining." Wise King Solomon said, "A constant dripping on a rainy day and a cranky woman are much alike! You can no more stop her complaints than you can stop the wind or hold onto anything with oil-slick hands" (Proverbs 27:15, 16 TLB*)*.

A noted psychologist made a detailed study of thousands of marriages and found nagging the worst fault of wives. The Gallup Poll confirmed this: nagging tops the list of feminine faults.

A typical nag list from the feminine gender might read as follows: He never fixes anything around the house, never takes me anyplace, won't get up in the morning, watches television too late, gets up too early, won't go to church, spends money foolishly, lives beyond our means, won't talk with me, doesn't understand my feelings, pays no attention to the kids, forgets birthdays and anniversaries, isn't home enough, never says a decent word unless he wants sex, is stingy with me, is too quiet, leaves the toilet seat up, never picks up his clothes, uses bad grammar, has terrible table manners, drives like a maniac, tells the same jokes over and over, brags too much, swears in front of the children, refuses to exercise, eats too much, spends too much time golfing, doesn't pay bills on time, constantly flips TV channels, is too domineering or passive or indecisive. Where, oh where is the perfect man?

Women often consider it a gesture of love to nag or offer advice. Men do not. Women must learn that there is an unwritten code by which men operate: *a man offers another man advice only when it is specifically asked for.* Out of respect for one another, a man will allow his buddy to solve his own problems unless called upon.

Take your life in your own hands, and what happens? A terrible thing: no one to blame.—Erica Jong.

One woman found herself angry with her husband for some of the very reasons mentioned previously. Inadvertently her husband conveyed insults to her through his manner and personality. For example, just before retiring each evening, he would ask, "Did you lock the back door?" She always answered affirmatively, "Yes, dear. I just locked the back door." At this point her husband walked to the door to verify that it was indeed locked. There were only two ways for this wife to interpret his behavior. Either he thought she was lying about whether she had locked the door, or else he didn't think she had the brains to remember whether she had locked it or not. Both alternatives made her furious. This scenario symbolized a dozen other sources of conflict between them.

Then one night as the husband proceeded to check the lock on the door immediately after she had just told him she'd locked it, the Lord spoke to her. "Take a good look at your husband," the Lord said.

"What do You mean, Lord?" she questioned.

"Well," the Lord replied, "I have made your husband a door checker. He's a detail man. That's why he's such a good accountant. He can examine a list of figures and instantly locate an error that others have overlooked. I gave him that ability to handle accounting procedures. Yes, I made your husband a *door checker*, and I want you to accept him that way."

The Lord didn't exactly speak to me in this manner—although I frequently wish He had done so to wake me up a little sooner—but it was almost as dramatic. In my case, He spoke to me through a book. Is the Lord sending you a message? Will you listen? Are you willing to make the necessary changes to become a more accepting person?

Destructive Habit Number 2: Angry Outbursts

Bursts of anger are little more than attempts to punish our partners because they have done something that displeases us. In an angry flash we try to "teach" the other person a lesson by saying something hurtful. Each of us has a private arsenal of weapons we draw upon at these times when we need them. These may take the form of shouting, put-downs, criticism, or sarcastic name-calling. Some couples resort to profanity, striking each other, throwing things, kicking, and pulling hair. Whatever the form, these actions cause huge deductions from the EBA. Each of us has the capacity of hurting our spouse more deeply than can anyone else. Our spouses are extremely vulnerable to our anger.

You may think anger appropriate because of what your spouse did that incurred your wrath. Although anger is sometimes justified, in the vast majority of cases it is ugly and usually creates more problems than it solves. Even if anger solves the immediate problem, it will likely create more problems than it solves. The angrier you are the more ugly the things spat out during the outburst, the more devastating the results on the relationship. Not only do displays of anger hurt the spouse at which they are directed, but they usually make a complete fool of the angry spouse.

Males can usually take more angry outbursts than females. Females can tolerate less, as they are more emotional and sensitive. Not only are females generally more easily hurt by angry words, but it takes them longer to recover. Remember: *Any time anger succeeds in marriage it does so at the expense of romantic love.*

There are ways to control such angry outbursts. In the next chapter on communication, I explain how to vent feelings without hurting, threatening, or destroying your partner. A simple communication skill, dubbed "I messages," can transform a marriage riddled with angry outbursts. If angry outbursts play even a small part in your marriage, they must be eliminated if you hope to have a healthy romantic relationship.

Destructive Habit Number 3: Criticism

If you want your marriage to end, criticize your partner. This is the advice of marriage counselors and experts of all kinds, based on recent research. These studies suggest that the marriages most likely to end are those in which some or all of four behaviors are chronic—and criticism heads the list. The others that follow in quick succession are contempt, defensiveness, and withdrawal. Psychologist John Gottman and other respected researchers in the field have found they are the strongest predictors of separation and divorce.[2]

It is not the amount of empathy, understanding, love, support, or respect that predicts who is going to make it or who is going to divorce, but the "zingers," or negative behaviors that are far more predictive over time. According to another researcher, Howard Markman, Professor of Psychology at the University of Denver,[3] one "zinger" erases 20 positive acts of kindness. Anger alone is not so harmful to a marriage unless that anger is blended with criticism, contempt, and defensiveness.

Constant criticism or contempt on the part of either partner is predictive of marital distress and divorce, and it leads to a vicious cycle. The wife criticizes or blames her husband; the husband becomes defensive and either withdraws from the discussion or defends himself by also going on the attack. The result is a highly destructive fight that can end in a verbal battle and physical abuse. This leads to what is termed by professionals "flooding," when spouses are so overwhelmed by negative emotions that their EBA is so vastly overdrawn that even reserve funds are depleted. Once this occurs, further discussion is fruitless and spouses must call time-out until they have calmed down. Third-party intervention will likely be necessary to help the couple control this negative cycle.

Destructive Habit Number 4: Irritating Habits and Annoying Behaviors

For some unknown reason, women seem to find their husbands more annoying than husbands find wives irritating. On a late-night talk show a comedian quipped, "Women always marry a man and hope he'll change. Men always marry a woman and hope she'll never change." And there's some truth to this. Women seem to go into a relationship saying, "There are a few things I don't like about him. But when I get through with him, you'll hardly recognize him."

Men usually go into a relationship saying, "I feel like a king when I'm with her. She's wonderful. I hope she never changes. I always want to feel like this when I'm with her." It is this feeling that pushes him toward marriage. He wants to be her hero for the rest of his life. But once a wife focuses on weaknesses and tries to change her husband, love begins to die.

Whether this tendency comes from male or female, it has a negative effect on a marriage. A withdrawal occurs from the couple's EBA. Should all the reserves be used up, there will be nothing left to draw on.

One woman was irritated over several of her husband's behaviors—his poor posture, eating habits, tone of voice, and choice of clothes. None of these behaviors was intentionally done to irritate her, and none was inherently "evil." All were an innocent part of his personality. Another woman with a different personality might not be the least irritated by these behaviors and be delighted to have this man as her husband.

I encouraged this woman to become more accepting; and I also suggested to the husband that he curb these behaviors so annoying to his wife. Instead of cooperating, he tried to convince me that he should be able to do whatever he pleased. If his wife didn't like it, she could "lump it." She needed to become more accepting, he objected. When we are annoyed over someone else's behavior, we consider them annoying, selfish, and inconsiderate. But when our behavior annoys someone else, we insist that we have a right to act the way we want to and the other person should have to accept us. A double standard indeed.

George and Jean had a different problem. What annoyed Jean so much about George was not his personality but rather his activities. When they were dating, he always chose their activities. Either she'd engage in the activity of choice or he'd go without her. During the early years of their marriage he played racquetball with his friends, attended sporting events, or watched sports on television. Although Jean tried to enjoy sporting events with him, she tired of the constancy. During Monday night football she began to watch something else on another TV in the house. During baseball games to amuse herself she would score all hits, runs, and errors on a score sheet. George knew Jean resented his activities, but he continued them anyway. Although he was not deliberately trying to hurt Jean in the pursuit of his own interests, he did so at the expense of their relationship.

Stack every bit of criticism between two layers of praise.

An interest in sporting events is not wrong; but when it annoys a partner, one must consider the cost. George argued that if Jean didn't like sports it was her problem. In actuality it was *their* problem. George needed to accept responsibility for the way his behavior affected his wife. It took him some time to understand how love works. Originally he had put enough deposits in their EBA to keep Jean feeling loved and satisfied. But his continual withdrawal against her protests depleted the reserve. Their account had a zero balance. Once he understood the connection between his behavior and her feelings and how it affected her love for him, he agreed to pursue at least one activity they both could enjoy and limit his involvement in other sports.

Some marriage counselors advise that a couple should never plan an activity that does not have the enthusiastic support of a mate. And this goes for both parties. Enthusiastic support does not mean begging, pleading, or badgering a partner about a fishing trip or cruise until the partner can take no more and caves in. This is not "enthusiastic support."

Irritating habits and annoying behaviors affect a marriage in much the same manner as do other negative behaviors—huge withdrawals from the EBA. This is true for both sexes. We all crave acceptance in humongous doses. But it is particularly hurtful for a wife to try to change her husband because it erodes his primary needs for appreciation, admiration, and approval. It is impossible for him to have these basic needs fulfilled while his wife is trying to change him.

This is an extremely difficult concept for some women to grasp. In some cases it is almost as if a woman is compelled by an unseen power to point out her husband's mistakes or change some behavior. It is a natural reaction for women to desire change in their relationships and want improvement. Even if a relationship is already good, often a woman will see ways in which she thinks it can be better— if only her partner would do so and so. In spite of the fact that she loves him devotedly and thinks of him as "wonderful," she is still inclined to improve him.

When she sets about her Husband Improvement Plan, a woman is motivated by love. But her mate perceives it not as love but as rejection and manipulation. And resistance appears to be the major male reaction to this lack of acceptance.

---

[1] William F. Harley, Jr., *Love Busters* (New York: Simon & Schuster, 1994), p. 67.

[2] John Gottman, *Why Marriages Succeed or Fail* (New York: Simon & Schuster, 1994), pp. 20, 21.

[3] Alison Bass, "Experts Hone In on Why Marriages Fail," Boston *Globe* (quoted in The Fresno *Bee,* Dec. 5, 1993).

Chapter 6

The Effects of Destructive Habits on Relationships

 et's look at how destructive habits of nagging, angry outbursts, criticism, or irritating habits and annoying behaviors affect a marriage.

Destructive Habits Create Tension

Let's say your partner repeats a behavior that irritates you so much you are almost at the breaking point. You mention it to your partner a time or two. No response. You mention it again. He tells you to "cut the nagging." But it's driving you crazy. You try to overlook this behavior, but it is so objectionable that you can't stop mentioning it. What is likely to happen?

Even though you may feel your intentions are good, destructive habits create tension in the home. At first your mate may become defensive or lash back: "I do not. . . . You're not so hot yourself, you know," or some similar response. A wife may pout, become depressed, or punish you through the silent treatment. A husband may become openly hostile and angry. A wife may become withdrawn, depressed, and distant. There may be little sharing. The couple lives under one roof yet seldom speaks about anything meaningful. Since acceptance is a basic human need, each may seek to have the need for acceptance filled outside the marriage relationship. He may throw more of himself into his career, his golf game, or accessing the Internet. She may spend more time with her friends, donating time at the church, or shopping. All of these activities may be legitimate but used primarily to escape an unpleasant atmosphere. The stage has also been set for a third party to begin meeting unfilled needs. Either partner could easily slip into an adulterous affair where needs of acceptance and approval are often met.

Children also suffer from the tension in the home. Even though they may not hear or understand the words spoken, the angry, critical atmosphere, painful silences, and deep hurt exhibited provide painful evidence to children that all is not well. With the security of their home being disrupted, they become anxious.

Destructive Habits Kill Love

It is next to impossible to feel tender love for someone who criticizes you or evidences disapproval about something they dislike. Once such things have been verbalized, feelings of love vanish. You may not even want to be in the same room with the person who has criticized you, let alone touch the person. And the thought of a sexual encounter at this point is out of the question. A man once told me that his wife had berated him for so many years, criticized everything he said or did, demasculating him in hundreds of insidious ways, that he had no sexual desire for her whatsoever. He had plenty of sexual desire for other women, whom he vigorously sought, but feelings for his wife were dead and without hope of resurrection.

If a man had enough horse sense to treat his wife like a thorough-bred, she wouldn't turn into a nag.

It is difficult for a man to love a nagging woman. Her nagging triggers thoughts of his childhood when his mother reminded him to "put on his galoshes, button his coat, wipe his nose, and not to talk with his mouth full." A psychiatrist once asked a critical wife, "When you tear your husband down all the time, how can you expect him to love you? If he wants to find out what's wrong with him, let him go to a counselor and dislike the counselor for pointing out the truth. A wife can't afford to provoke her husband to hate."

Criticism also crushes a woman's tender feelings for her husband. Under a barrage of criticism and faultfinding she will become depressed, angry, and bitter. She may not have the energy to keep up with her employment, the household chores, care of the children, or meal preparation when all she gets for her efforts is criticism. She will either distance herself from her husband, seek relief through an affair, or become an angry, bitter nag in return.

Whenever you criticize your partner, you endanger your love relationship. Sometimes one partner will even request that the other evaluate his performance (as with a pastor and his wife). When he delivers a sermon he asks his wife to give him an evaluation. A wife who attempts to give even "helpful suggestions" will find her relationship with her husband endangered. Every negative comment takes something away from the relationship. Lovers should not become each other's critics.

Destructive Habits Arouse Defenses

Being accepted as we are is a basic human need and is ideally fulfilled when we marry. But when we receive censure and unacceptance from the one we love it hurts self-esteem and arouses resentment. One's first line of defense under attack may be to stage a counterattack. Or it may evidence itself through being stingy, stubborn, lazy, uncooperative, unloving, silent, withdrawn, or through other acts of hostility. The more the other partner nags, complains, or criticizes, the more one's resentment may increase. Indeed, an unaccepted person may even spend time away from home in the arms of someone who does accept him and loves him just as he is. A resentful person often secretly vows to get even someday, somehow.

Destructive Habits Don't Produce Change

After teaching a lesson on acceptance, I spoke with a woman who confessed that she had been trying to change her husband for 35 years. She admitted devoting two days of every week to her project. Her Husband Improvement Plan had failed miserably and now she felt lonely, tired, and bitter. Through her tears she lamented the 35 years spent in a useless pursuit.

Another woman attending a seminar told how she had listed her husband's faults on the back of a calendar. Yes, she actually filled 12 blank pages with his numerous shortcomings. What did she get in return? Not only did her husband leave her, but her teenage son got so sick of her constant faultfinding and critical attacks that he also left home to get away from her. Neither of them changed their ways. Soon after his departure, her husband was hospitalized with a life-threatening medical condition. This brush with death shocked the woman into a new appreciation of her husband's worth. After a period of soul-searching and a true conversion, she changed her ways. Both husband and son returned home, and the home was reunited in a new way.

Considering the problems created through attempts to reform a mate's behavior—the tension created in the home, the effect on a couple's communication, as well as the effect on the children—one might well ask one's self, "Is it worth it?" Is changing your mate to suit your ideas of how he or she should act more important than achieving a supportive relationship and emotionally secure children?

Words of advice from Paul in Galatians 5:15 warn us: "If you keep on biting and devouring each other, watch out or you will be destroyed by each other" (NIV).

Another Part of the Problem—You!

Why have you attempted to change your partner? Why did I attempt to change Harry? Because he needed to change to become a better person. Secondly (although I hate to admit it), if my husband changed I would benefit through his improved behavior, more acceptable personality, and more positive attitudes. Maybe you too, through feminine insight or masculine logic, have detected areas in your mate's life that need improvement so you could be happier. Maybe you have convinced yourself that you are trying to help your spouse overcome weak areas as well as destructive habits and achieve a more acceptable personality for his own good.

On the surface this sounds justifiable and perhaps even noble; yet a basic Christian principle is being violated. The heart of the Christian message is rooted in changing ourselves, not in our ability to change another person. Jesus instructs those who feel such a compulsion to remove "the plank out of your own eye, and then you will see clearly to remove the speck from your brother's eye" (Matthew 7:5, NIV).

An insidious motive lies behind criticism as well as all attempts to reform another person. We put others down in order to cover up our own feeling of inferiority. By belittling the worth of others we attempt to build our own shaky self-esteem.

Putting others down and criticizing them fails to prove that we have personal worth. Anyone who really understands the roots of self-esteem knows that critical people have major self-esteem problems. Whenever we criticize someone, we place him in an inferior position. This automatically puts him on the defensive, and drives him away.

Something should happen to our attitudes when we choose the Christian lifestyle. We should become *more accepting* of our partners. Since we fully recognize the accepting and forgiving attitude God extends toward our personal idiosyncrasies and imperfect behavior, we should be more willing to extend this same attitude toward others. God totally accepts us, with all our imperfections, faults, failures, and messed-up lives. He accepts us the way we are—as sinners. We don't have to prove our worth to Him. Why do we demand more of our partners? Since Christ is our example in all things, the knowledge that we are freely accepted by Him with all our imperfections should liberate us to be more accepting of others, not less accepting. Once this truth sinks in, we are able to develop a greater appreciation for ourselves as well as for our mates.

How to Point Out Mistakes (if You Must)

No husband or wife is required to sit idly by while a mate tactlessly offends them or others through destructive habits or annoying behaviors. There are times when offensive behaviors as well as mistakes should be pointed out, and you may be the only person who cares enough to do this. How do you do it? The same way porcupines make love: very carefully.

Learn how far you can go. Let's say your spouse refuses to wear a seat belt. In a nice, helpful manner without irritation in your voice, you remind him to put on his seatbelt. You notice that he resents even a gentle reminder. Then let it be. Your husband needs to be able to decide on his own whether to wear a seat belt, even at the risk of his life! Each time you make the suggestion to wear a seat belt, he thinks it an imposition of your values on him.

Whenever you think your spouse is making a mistake, subtle suggestions, disrespectful judgments, and helpful hints will not straighten him out. A far more effective approach is to understand why your partner does not wish to wear a seat belt and respectfully negotiate a resolution that also takes your emotional reactions into account. An I-message would be an effective method of stating your feelings: "I get really frightened when you don't wear a seat belt because if we ever had an accident you could be seriously hurt." There's no blaming, judging, or put-down. You simply express your feelings regarding the possible outcome after an accident.*

Before criticizing your wife's faults, you must remember it may have been these very defects which prevented her from getting a better husband than the one she married.

Should you shout, "You're stupid not to wear a seat belt!" not only is this an ineffective way of persuading your mate to wear a seat belt, but it will also make a huge withdrawal from your EBA.

When some wives criticize their husbands even in the slightest way, it signals all-out war. Others can make a helpful suggestion and it will be taken in the manner intended. Each of us has to understand the boundaries of how far we can go with our own partner. Learn about sensitive areas that might set off World War III as well as the difference between inciting anger and talking things out. Even then some of us might benefit by trying to feed our partners constructive suggestions in smaller doses.

Watch your timing. Comedians, politicians, and great lovers are well aware of the importance of timing. You may have a legitimate complaint, but your timing may be off. Bedtime and mealtime are two occasions to avoid conflict. Factors such as fatigue, hunger, and emotional stress decrease mental efficiency and increase irritability. You may wish to wait until the incident has passed because often both partners may be too close to a situation to view it with clarity. It is senseless and unproductive to attempt to solve a problem when both partners are upset. "Take time to cool down and gain perspective first," is good advice. By allowing the emotions of the moment to cool, you will gain perspective and wisdom. Ask a person to mend his ways when he or she can do something about it.

Guard your manner and tone of voice. When speaking to a spouse we can assume one of three roles: parent, adult, or child. Many people have shared with me that they can't stand the insulting manner in which their spouses speak to them. On one occasion I counseled a young couple attending my marriage seminar. Although they had been married only six weeks, their marriage was already in deep trouble because of the wife's tendency to assume the mother role. Not only did she get her husband up on time in the morning, but she laid out his clothes, combed his hair, put his lunch in his hand, and saw him off to work on time. When he returned home she took over again, managing his time as well as telling him what was and was not acceptable for him to be doing until he went to bed. After hearing her side of the story, I asked for his input. He would begin a sentence and she would cut him off. I'd ask again and she would jump in and correct him. In spite of my pleas that she allow him to speak, she constantly interrupted, saying he was not telling the truth or he didn't understand. I had to ask the wife to leave the room in order to hear the husband's side.

When alone, I asked if he understood the role patterns each had assumed. Without hesitation he responded, "She's the mother, and I'm the son." Then he added bitterly, "And it is very difficult to have sex with your mother." At 26 he was in his sexual prime, and yet the roles each had assumed and the manner in which they were speaking to each other were destroying their sex life.

Avoid speaking to your spouse as a parent punishing a child for misbehavior. Partners should always speak to each other as equals, adult to adult. Even if your partner should speak to you as a parent, you do not need to assume the child role. You can still respond as an adult. Your relationship with one another is more important than the relationship you hold with anyone else on earth, including your children. Guard it carefully.

One thing should bring comfort to those who find the habits, behaviors, and faults of their partners nearly unbearable, especially when exhibited in public: *others are usually much more accepting of our mate's idiosyncrasies than we are.* After all, they do not have to live with the fault. This knowledge alone should free us from a portion of our drive to reform our mates.

Husbands and wives in a highly effective marriage should feel free to discuss whatever disturbs them, but it should never be in the form of a direct attack. The surest way to weaken affection is to tell someone what is wrong with him. Nothing destroys the EBA more quickly than a running account of faults. In order to feel loved, we must feel understood, not criticized or condemned.

Furthermore, you can attempt to point out the mistakes of a partner only when you have earned the right. You must first have demonstrated your unfailing respect for your partner as a person. Since even constructive criticism plays havoc with self-esteem, "advice" can be delivered only in an atmosphere of love, kindness, and respect. Only then will you have the right to discuss a hot topic with your mate, all the while remembering your partner may have a few gripes about you too.

---

*See my book *How to Talk So Your Mate Will Listen and Listen So Your Mate Will Talk* (Grand Rapids.: Fleming H. Revell, 1989), chapter 4, for a complete explanation of how to use I-messages effectively.

Chapter 7

How to Become a More Accepting Person (if You Really Want To)

*B*efore you jump into the change myself/change my partner mode, do an attitude check. The following suggestions can help bring balance to your perception of what needs acceptance and what needs to be changed in your relationships.

What to Accept, What to Change

1. Separate the Deed From the Doer. Acceptance does not always mean "liking." But even an objectionable behavior or situation can be viewed without open hostility. During the course of marriage, there are dozens of human differences with which we must learn to live, even if we don't *like* them. Whether a matter of promptness, church attendance, speech mannerisms, or personal preference of any kind, through prayer and practice we can learn to raise our tolerance levels and accept basic differences by separating the deed from the doer.

It's just not humanly possible to feel accepting toward our mates all the time. Some behaviors such as drinking, smoking, gambling, swearing, laziness, dishonesty, or vulgarity will always be unacceptable. But the ability to separate the deed from the doer is crucial. When your child writes on the wall, it's the deed, the writing on the wall that is bad, not the child. In the same manner, marriage partners should be able to know that while not everything they do may be applauded, they are nonetheless loved and accepted.

It is difficult to act in a Christlike manner when we are being treated unfairly but God would have us be loving even when we are not loved in return. We must attempt to view unacceptable behaviors and idiosyncrasies much as God does. He hates the sin in us but loves us, the sinner, with an undying, forever love. We can strive to attain this Godlike attribute.

2. View Your Mate's Personality Differences as Complementary to Your

Own. One of the things that I find most difficult to accept in my husband is his total unawareness of the passing of time. He can make a "quick trip" to the grocery store and take so long in finding his way home again that I could file for divorce on grounds of desertion! He can run to a neighbor's house to borrow a tool and not return for hours. He can be late for supper even after just phoning me to say he'll be right home.

I have come to realize that time means something different to him than it does to me. In my family of "efficiency experts" we were barely allowed bathroom privileges while traveling, and since birth I have been trained to make use of every minute.

Harry and I are a classic example of an "imperfect fit" in a marriage. Given our radical differences, we could easily drive each other crazy, and we sometimes do. But there is a much better alternative. We choose to recognize and value the manner in which each of our strengths balances out the deficiencies of the other. Although it took me a while, I've learned to appreciate Harry's easygoing, relaxed nature, which creates opportunities for me to enjoy frequent present-moment experiences I often miss in my rush toward productivity.

My "productive" temperament is not superior to his easygoing one. Why should I force Harry into my mold when his entire system is geared to operate at another speed? Through acceptance, I finally learned that *different* does not mean *wrong.* This freed me to accept his slower, more relaxed manner as an attribute that complements my more high-pressured drive to produce. Some accomplishments in life cannot be measured in terms of production.

Harry and I actually complement each other in a beautiful way: Harry needs me to speed him up a little, and I need him to slow me down a little. We are more complete as a couple because of the differences we bring to the relationship.

One of the worst mistakes you can make is to try to re-create your spouse in your own image. You will never succeed, and you will embitter your mate. But if you view the differences between you as complementary, it softens the sharp edges of the differences. You will begin to appreciate, rather than resent, your mate's personality.

If you look at your partner as an unacceptable person who possesses a host of unacceptable, negative traits, you'll probably never see the abundance of positive qualities your partner possesses, because you aren't looking for them. If you decide to change your perspective and see only the best in your spouse, you can do that also. We recognize that our friends have idiosyncrasies and weaknesses, yet we still respect and appreciate them. The same should hold true in marriage.

3. Express Acceptance Out Loud. Most of us tend to think of acceptance as an attitude that can't be verbalized. Since you love your mate, the tendency is to think that your mate automatically knows and understands that he or she is accepted. Although acceptance originates from our thinking processes and how we view our mate, it must also be demonstrated through actions as well as the spoken word. Acceptance is something that needs to be verbalized. Tell your mate that you accept and like them just the way they are.

One of the most welcome expressions is "I like you just the way you are." Other good acceptance expressions include: "You are a nice person [and then name a quality you like about your mate]" or "I like the way you do things," "You are everything I had hoped and dreamed you would be." Mention specific areas in which your mate has fulfilled your hopes and dreams.

Such verbal demonstrations of acceptance are a needed part of everyday life when things run smoothly, but are needed more desperately when your partner hurts. During such times they need to hear meaningful words of acceptance—not just for the things they have done but for what they are as a person. Perhaps the greatest thing you can ever say to your partner (outside of "I love you") is "I like you—just the way you are."

The difficulty with marriage is that we fall in love with a personality but must live with a character.—

Peter Devries.

At first you may find it difficult to express acceptance in words, as your words may sound insincere. But stating it out loud while you are still in the process of becoming a more accepting person is an important segment of practicing acceptance. Rather than rejecting this step because it makes you feel uncomfortable, act from principle, recognizing that it fills a human need. Your mate desperately needs to hear this from you, especially if your relationship has been riddled with destructive habits. In the end you will find that the more you express acceptance out loud, the more it will help you grow toward complete acceptance.

4. Add Humor to Irritating Situations. This may sound like a ridiculous tactic to use when addressing a serious subject such as acceptance. But the importance of using humor when you are trying to deal with irritating faults cannot be overemphasized. The ability to laugh at yourself and with your partner will do more to take the edge off marital discord than anything else you can do. Laughter is a wonderful tonic when you are handling problems.

Charlie Shedd has commented that when a couple learns how to laugh and make light of faults and mistakes, a wonderful transformation takes place in the home. "High heaven has special clean-up squads," he writes, "which respond to these signals. They come to sweep away the broken pieces and give that marriage a fresh beginning." [1]

The next time your mate repeats an annoying habit that drives you up the wall, make a ridiculous crack about it and laugh till the tears come. It is possible to put a comic side to irritating faults. Laughter lessens the sting and soothes the irritation of the moment.

5. *Recall the Original Romantic Feelings You Had for Each Other.* Daily irritations and annoyances sometimes allow us to lose sight of how we looked at each other before we were married. That's why it is important to recall the original feelings you had for each other when you were dating, to rehearse mentally the way you saw each other then. There's not a doubt that those feelings were heightened and exaggerated by infatuation and passion; nevertheless, they contained a central core of emotional truth and caring.

To recapture that feeling, plan an evening in front of the fireplace to look at old pictures, listen to the music that meant so much to you then, or revisit a place you went while courting. Recalling such things will help you recapture the intrigue, emotion, and joy you experienced when you first discovered each other.

The story is told of a French writer who sat down at a table and dipped a roll in his tea. The familiar aroma unleashed a flood of memories from his mother's kitchen. As a result, he wrote a 1,000-page memoir of his childhood experience that became a literary classic. In the same way, you can recall how you once viewed your spouse through the eyes of romantic love. This is not dishonesty or denial. It's a matter of adjusting your perception.

Getting Rid of Your Own Bad Habits

Now let's put the shoe on the other foot. Has it ever occurred to you that your habits might be just as annoying to your partner as theirs are to you?

The tendency is to focus on the irritating faults and annoying habits of our partners rather than recognizing that we may have some faults that are just as annoying or irritating. If you wish to test this theory, ask your mate to list behaviors they'd like you to change. (Better limit it to three behaviors, so they don't run out of paper!)

Any behavior that causes your partner unhappiness puts your marriage at risk. Annoying habits, irritating faults, and disgusting mannerisms all destroy romantic love. One occurrence is bad enough, but an annoying behavior that is repeated over and over multiplies the damage to your relationship as it is repeated. A bad habit is like a leaky roof. If it isn't repaired, it will cause more and more damage until the plaster caves in and the ceiling is destroyed.

Research indicates that men seem to be less motivated to change their annoying behaviors for a woman's sake. Apparently many of them feel that this kind of change threatens their manliness.[2] However, women also often view requests for change as a threat to their sense of identity. Rather than viewing change as a threat, consider dealing with your personal habits as a simple matter of consideration and caring. If you want to live peaceably with a spouse, one you care for and want to make happy, it only makes sense to make some accommodations for their feelings.

To show a willingness to change, I usually ask one or both partners to sign a commitment to act more considerately in the future. The agreement might read as follows:

Even when one partner is not willing to work on the relationship or effect

---

I recognize that my behavior is causing my partner unhappiness and hurt. I agree to follow a course of action to stop my annoying behaviors and irritating faults in order to preserve our love and protect the future of our marriage.

Husband's Signature

Wife's Signature

Date

---

change, the other partner can alter their own habits. Frequently the change becomes so significant that the "silent partner" will join the willing partner in working on the relationship.

Changing Yourself

Sandy was very unhappy because her husband constantly made belittling cracks at her expense. The man was a good-natured person, but his sarcasm was hurtful. Sandy asked him not to do it. He would apologize but do it again. Nothing she said made any difference.

Her counselor suggested the next time her husband made a sarcastic remark that she reach for a notebook, glance at her watch, noting the time, and write down what was said. The first time she did this, he asked what she was doing. The counselor had warned her that her response must contain no put-downs or judgments. She responded without a trace of rancor in her voice. "Sometimes you say the most memorable things. Our relationship is so important to me that I want to make a record of them."

At first he would apologize or laugh and say, "Your shrink put you up to this, didn't she?" But Sandy refused to be drawn into a discussion of what she was doing. She did not become angry, explain herself, or debate him. (This took some effort on her part!)

During the second week of this experiment there were no incidents. But during week three he slipped back into a sarcastic mode. When he slipped, she simply reached for her notebook without comment. During the fourth and fifth week there were no incidents. Then he slipped once, stopped himself, and apologized.

Sandy's husband had developed a bad habit of which he was barely conscious. All Sandy was doing was raising her husband's consciousness level to a specific situation. She was changing her situation by changing her own reactions.

Eileen encountered another typical problem. She complained that her husband wouldn't talk with her enough to meet her needs. She prodded, nagged, and complained. She read all the books about How to Get a Man to Open Up to You, went to communication seminars, and scheduled time to talk. It was all futile. When her time, energy, and patience were exhausted, he talked no more than he ever had.

Finally Eileen began to realize that she was not responsible for her husband's behavior nor could she change it. The only person over whom she had control was *herself.* With effort she stopped prodding him to talk. She stopped complaining and nagging. She made herself less available for conversation and actually began to cut conversations with him short. When she wished to converse, she talked, regardless of his two-syllable replies, but otherwise she filled her time by joining a women's bowling team and taking a night school course.

For the first three or four weeks her husband appeared to enjoy being left alone and relieved to have Eileen go her own way. Then he became curious about his wife's new behavior. Where was she going? What was she doing? Whom was she with? When he questioned her, she responded briefly and went about her business. He started to get a little jealous of all the time she was spending elsewhere. One day he confronted her with an amazing request: "Honey, I think we need to start spending more time together, don't you?"

This woman put to practice a classic principle she had learned about intimacy. She had learned that pushing for intimacy often pushes a spouse away. Eileen drew her husband back to her by changing her own behavior, not pushing for change in him.

Whenever you change the manner in which you have been reacting to a situation, you change the situation. The significance of this point slips by many people's attention. *Any situation can be changed by changing your reaction to it.*

When making any behavioral change, however, you must anticipate certain normal reactions. When one partner initiates change, the other partner's behavior may become even more annoying. They will often consciously or unconsciously push your buttons even harder, trying to reestablish the old familiar patterns of interaction. You must remain firm. If you are consistent with your new behavior, your partner will have to learn new patterns of reaction.

Your new behavior must be repeated consistently for 21 to 45 days in order to become an established habit. If you've had a habit of reacting a certain way for 20 years, you can't expect change in yourself or your partner just because you react differently twice.[3]

The very act of doing something you don't usually do seems to have a constructive impact. Constructive change in one person usually opens the way for constructive change in the other. With some people the change will come quickly, easily, and openly. Barriers built up over the years may come tumbling down quickly.

The most impressive example of tolerance is a golden wedding anniversary.

With others, reactive change comes much more slowly. But change will come. The type of change you will get cannot always be predicted in advance. It may not always be positive. If not, go back to the drawing board and draft a new plan. But change in your behavior will always produce change.

Rather than expecting a specific result when you attempt to initiate change, use the examples from the stories I've related to inspire creative behavioral changes of your own. Your partner's responses are not under your control. Remember Einstein's definition of insanity: doing the same thing again and again, but expecting different results.

In summary, keep the following principles in mind.

1. We can change no one by direct action.
2. We can change only ourselves.
3. When we change ourselves, others tend to change in response to us.

Create a Strategy for Change

Habits tend to hang on tenaciously. This shouldn't surprise us, because that is exactly what a habit is—a pattern of behavior that we have programmed into our own personal computer, our brain. Does this mean we can't do anything to change a bad habit? Are we doomed for the rest of our lives to nagging, criticizing, angry outbursts, and other negative behaviors? No. Here are some practical pointers.

- *Ask for God's help.* Scripture tells us, "Apart from me you can do nothing" (John 15:5, NIV). You simply cannot expect to make any permanent positive change in your life without His help. Base change on the realization that your ability to break a bad habit comes from God.

- *Choose the best time to make a change.* "There is a time for everything, and a season for every activity under heaven" (Ecclesiastes 3:1, NIV). Tackle the breaking of your negative habit when you are not under extreme stress. Avoid such times as major holidays. A good time to make a change is when you are under strong conviction that a change needs to be made.

- *Focus on one negative habit at a time.* Don't try to overcome several bad habits at one time. Select one habit and set small goals for yourself. This makes change in habit patterns more manageable and less intimidating. Small successes along the way will encourage you to continue. Mark Twain once said, "Habit is habit, and not to be flung out of the window by any man, but coaxed downstairs a step at a time."

- *Replace the bad habit with a good one.* Replace a nagging comment with a compliment for something done well. Reprogram constant criticism by making a list of 10 of your mate's best qualities and reading these qualities out loud three times a day. Negative thinking can be reprogrammed by replacing it with something positive. Repeating a memorized portion of Scripture might serve you well here.

- *Don't give up when you fail.* One wise person quipped, "Quitting a habit is easy, but starting again is just as easy." So don't give up when you find yourself falling back into old habit patterns. Consider it a learning experience and begin repeating these steps. Studies show that the more times a person has tried to give up smoking, for example, the greater are their chances of success the next time. Keep on keeping on!

The effort you put into changing your own annoying behaviors and irritating faults will not go unnoticed. Check your EBA. You'll likely find an accumulating amount of rewarding dividends.

Must I Accept Everything?

Should you become a doormat? Do you have to accept every mean, degrading, ugly, vicious thing your mate does? Should you permit a mate to stomp all over your rights and dignity, saying nothing at all, to preserve the concept of acceptance? No! No! No! You are an individual, a person to be respected, a human being with a will of your own.

For example, you need not accept infidelity. Marital partners have the right to expect strict fidelity, even in these times of changing moral values. The Word of God, as well as the laws of the land, supports this view. Husbands and wives are within their Christian right in obtaining a divorce when adultery is involved.

But it would be wise to take a complete self-inventory before pursuing a divorce. Is there any behavior you have that might drive a mate away or provide the excuse your mate needed to commit adultery? If so, with some serious changes on your part you might be able to rescue your marriage. It is often possible for a partner with biblical grounds for divorce to rescue a marriage. Remember that Scripture permits but does not command divorce on grounds of adultery.

Other cases may involve such serious offenses as incest, homosexuality, lesbianism, desertion, nonsupport, mental incapacity, physical abuse, gambling, alcoholism, drug abuse, and other addictions. None of these situations can or should be handled by blaming yourself or simply completing a self-inventory. Embarrassment and shame often keep individuals from sharing their personal pain with someone. But each of these situations needs individual attention and immediate intervention by professionals.

Other regrettable situations arise in which acceptance is a challenge. But there is nothing as beautiful as a loving relationship in which each adapts to and accepts the other as they are. The following story was written by a surgeon who witnessed a divinely inspired act of accommodation and acceptance.

I stand by the bed where a young woman lies, her face postoperative, her mouth twisted in palsy, clownish. A tiny twig of the facial nerve, the one to the muscles of her mouth, has been severed. She will be thus from now on. The surgeon has followed with religious fervor the curve of her flesh; I promise you that. Nevertheless, to remove the tumor in her cheek, I had to cut the little nerve.

Her young husband is in the room. He stands on the opposite side of the bed, and together they seem to dwell in the evening lamplight, isolated from me, private. Who are they, *I ask myself,* he and this wry-mouth I have made, who gaze at and touch each other so generously, greedily? *The young woman speaks.*

"Will my mouth always be like this?" she asks.

"Yes," I say, "it will. It is because the nerve was cut."

She nods, and is silent. But the young man smiles.

"I like it," he says. "It is kind of cute."

All at once I know who he is. I understand, and I lower my gaze. One is not bold in an encounter with a god. Unmindful, he bends to kiss her crooked mouth, and I so close I can see how he twists his own lips to accommodate to hers, to show her that their kiss still works. I remember that the gods appeared in ancient Greece as mortals, and I hold my breath and let the wonder in.[4]

This is the heart cry that rises from each of us. How we long for one person on this earth to accept and love us just the way we are—crooked mouth and all. This should be our objective in marriage—to be that person for our mate.

---

[1] Nancy L. Van Pelt, *Compleat Marriage* (Hagerstown, Md.: Review and Herald Pub. Assn., 1979), p. 153.

[2] Willard F. Harley, *Love Busters* (Grand Rapids: Fleming H. Revell, 1992), pp. 220-223.

[3] Maxwell Maltz, *Psycho-Cybernetics* (Hollywood, Calif.: Wilshire Book Co., 1960), p. xv.

[4] Richard Selzer, M.D., *Mortal Lessons: Notes on the Art of Surgery* (New York: Simon & Schuster, 1976), pp. 45, 46.

Chapter 8

WHY WE COMMUNICATE THE WAY WE DO

Patricia pulled nervously at a tissue as she spoke. "Our first date was very romantic and unforgettable. We went to dinner but never tasted the food. We were so enraptured with each other, we talked for hours and lost all track of time. I felt I had known him all my life. I had had numerous relationships with men, but this one was different.

"When John finally asked me to marry him it was inevitable. In the beginning, our marriage was much like our courtship. We shared everything and considered ourselves best friends; we shared things we would never tell anyone else. Sometimes we'd lie in bed holding each other, talking until the wee hours of the morning.

"Gradually, over the years, each of us has pulled back and closed down. There is little to say to each another. Sometimes I have little feeling for this man I once adored. I think he feels much the same way.

"What happened? Nothing dramatic. We got so busy with our separate worlds we hardly noticed that we weren't friends anymore. The signals were all there, but we refused to recognize them. He'd bury himself in the antique car he was rebuilding. I became very resentful and shut him out just for spite. The couple who didn't have enough hours in the day to discuss life didn't exist anymore.

"Our friends used to tease us because we would get so wrapped up in talking with each other, they didn't want to interrupt us. That seems like a long time ago. Now we stay together because of the children. We have lived this way for so long now, it would be very difficult to open up to each another again.

"I doubt if we could talk in a way that wouldn't threaten or interrupt the comfort zone we have each established. Our relationship may not be great, but it is predictable and there is a sense of security in our misery. Now we are strangers. We have lost the ability to care or see things from the other's viewpoint."

People marry dreaming of a lifelong intimate friendship with their mate. Instead, most marriages end up purely "functional," where partners perform the duties of provider, nurturer, parent, sex partner, cook. The functional marriage is incomplete and unsatisfying.

The great news is, a functional marriage can be transformed into a highly effective marriage by establishing an intimate communication system. Communication is what sparks the caring, giving, sharing, and affirming that are present in intimate friendship.

Why Couples Can't Communicate

Many reasons exist for the inability to communicate. Perhaps the most obvious is that most of us have never been taught effective communication skills. When we have never learned proper skills we continue to function in the ineffective ruts we create for ourselves.

Another reason couples fail to communicate adequately is they are afraid to share real thoughts and feelings with their mates. There is justification for such fear. Who hasn't opened up to a partner and been rebuffed? Some get hurt so badly they crawl permanently inside a shell and refuse to come out.

Every conversation is influenced by the misunderstandings and unresolved problems from the past. The greater the hurt and anger from the past, the less likely the couple can continue to communicate without third-party intervention.

Learned Patterns From the Past. The manner in which you speak and listen today is affected by what you learned as a child when growing up. You carefully observed how family members talked, listened, and responded. You may have observed positive patterns such as respect, directness in asking for things, and cheerfulness—and you may have observed destructive patterns, such as hostility, mind reading, silent treatment, and yelling.

You began to experiment with what would work for you, and you most likely carried these same patterns with you into your marriage. You may have learned to have what you consider to be quiet, respectful discussions. But this pattern of communication may not work well with a mate who learned to settle matters through loud negotiation and arguing.

Social Conditioning. Boys and girls also learn to communicate with their peers, especially between the ages of 5 and 15. Little girls play most frequently in pairs, with a series of "best friends." The relationship between the girls is solidified by private talk and the sharing of secrets. The information isn't important, but the experience of sharing it with a best friend is. Little boys, on the other hand, play more frequently in groups, often outdoors. There is less talking and more activity when boys get together. A new boy is easily admitted to the group, but once in he must jockey for position and status within the group. Such attitudes are reinforced through the growing-up years.

When a woman gets married she thinks she has found an improved version of her best friend and confides in him through private talks and shares "secrets." Many of her secrets involve how to improve the marriage.

The husband has never heard so many secrets in his life and concludes there must be something terribly wrong with the relationship. This puts him on the defensive! He doesn't need the heart-to-heart talks as much as he may miss doing things with male friends, where activities played a major role.

The woman feels tremendous inner satisfaction while she is talking. The husband senses real trouble, since they have to keep discussing things! Their relationship can weaken as she pushes for more intimate talks about what she feels is wrong and he tries to prevent them. One thing is for sure, males and females have very different ideas on how to communicate and become best friends.

An argument is the longest distance between two points.—**Dan Bennett.**

Temperaments

Nothing may have a more profound influence on your style of communication than your temperament. Temperament is a combination of inherited traits that affect your behavior. These traits are passed on through the genes and are largely responsible for your actions, reactions, and emotional responses as well as how you communicate.

The following brief description of the four temperaments introduces you to the communication patterns most likely used by each.*

Sanguine. Sanguines are outgoing, exuberant conversationalists who love to talk and can easily dominate conversations. A compulsiveness compels them to tell long, dramatic, detailed stories, which make them favorites at social gatherings. This compulsion to talk makes them very poor listeners. A short attention span and the fact that they are easily distracted further complicate their ability to listen. They tend to be loud persons who explode easily.

Choleric. Cholerics speak freely but more deliberately than sanguines. They dislike the long, detailed stories of the sanguine. They would tell the same story, but skip insignificant details, press their point home, and move to the next point of interest. Cholerics find it easy to make decisions for themselves and others but can often be opinionated, domineering, and bossy. Cholerics usually think they are right—and because of their keen and practical minds, usually are! Cholerics make good debaters but argumentative and sarcastic marriage partners.

Melancholy. Melancholies are introverts and are exceptional analytical thinkers. They speak only after careful analysis. They thrive on detail and are dominated by a variety of moods swings. Sometimes melancholies are outgoing, friendly, and extroverted, but they vacillate to being withdrawn, depressed, and irritable. They are extremely sensitive and tend to take everything personally. Of all the temperaments, they have the most difficulty expressing their true feelings.

Phlegmatic. Phlegmatics are quiet, slow, more deliberate, and noncombative speakers. They rarely get angry and will go to almost any length to avoid unpleasant confrontations. They never laugh very loud or cry very hard and most often appear "expressionless," which makes them difficult to read. They are always the same: steady and dependable. Their natural dry sense of humor can be a joy—except to a spouse. They are usually easy to live with unless their slow and methodical manner becomes a source of irritation to a more aggressive partner.

For effective communication: present your message so that it matches the way your spouse responds to life and processes information.—H. Norman Wright.

No temperament type is superior to another. Each communicates in a different and distinct manner. Usually we are blends of all four, with one or two dominating. I am chol-san, and nothing can change that. Understanding the temperaments helps me understand my mel-san husband's style and why he goes on and on about things. Our inherent temperaments play a big part in determining how we communicate as a couple.

Is There Hope for Achieving Better Communication?

The happiness of a couple, to a large degree, can be measured by the effectiveness of their communication. Effective patterns of communication allow the couple to negotiate problem areas, fulfill needs, avoid misunderstandings, and develop intimacy over the years.

When a relationship is riddled with ineffective patterns, the couple will misinterpret motives, needs will go unmet, problems will go unsolved, and hostility will increase. As the years roll on, the chance for solving these problems lessens because of ingrained habit patterns and deep-seated resentment.

Many people get so caught in a web of inadequate communication habits that they give up. Others *say* they want to improve communication, but they lack know-how and commitment to break negative habits and establish new ones.

You may or may not be aware of what you should or should not be doing. But by becoming more aware of the patterns you and your partner are using, you can avoid typical pitfalls that trap thousands, greatly improve your chances for learning to communicate at new and deeper levels, and understand your mate better.

---

*For a complete analysis on temperament types see Tim LaHaye's *Your Temperament: Discover Its Potential* (Wheaton, Ill.: Tyndale House Publishers, 1984).

Chapter 9

LISTENING—
A WAY TO SHOW YOU CARE

esearchers estimate that we spend more than 70 percent of our waking hours communicating with others—speaking, listening, reading, or writing. More than 33 percent of that time is devoted to talking and more than 42 percent to listening. Since a commanding amount of time is spent in listening, it assumes primary importance in our lives.[1]

In a communication survey I conducted on hundreds of people attending my family life seminars, 55 percent admitted their partners accused them of not listening. Women complained their husbands wouldn't listen to them, and men said their wives never heard what they were told. Yes, listening is a problem within marriage.[2]

Listening Bloopers

Poor listening stems from bad habits. Two of the most irritating of these habits are interrupting and lack of eye contact.

Interrupters spend their time forming a reply while waiting for a split second when they can break in. It may be a human tendency to jump in when something triggers a thought. But you must let your partner finish a thought regardless of how boring it seems. Sanguines in particular have trouble with interrupting, since everything said reminds them of a story that demands being told immediately— even in the middle of yours.

A lack of eye contact conveys disinterest, distrust, and a lack of caring. In deteriorating relationships, couples rarely look directly into each other's faces. The magic of looking into each other's eyes is gone.

Some couples avoid eye contact for weeks or months at a time. Lack of eye contact is used as punishment and to show displeasure. Consciously refusing to maintain eye contact with a partner is cruel. Those in deteriorating relationships and those wishing to become better listeners can begin reestablishing intimacy through eye contact.

Other annoying listeners include the following:

- people who make you feel you are wasting their time
- people who pace back and forth as if in a hurry to get away
- people who finish your sentences
- people who restate what you say, putting words in your mouth
- people who contradict what you say before you even state your case
- people who use speaker phones
- people who stand too close or too far away—depending on your cultural preference!

Listening Know-how

Listening sounds simple, but it is a serious and often difficult business. It involves observing nonverbal communication, eye contact, watching for underlying motives, asking the right questions, giving appropriate responses, and knowing when to be silent. It is hard work, but the payoffs for developing closer relationships are worth the price.

Listening is one of the most neglected and least understood of the communication arts. Learning how to listen doesn't require a degree, but it does take training. Anyone can learn to do it right.

Tuning In and Tuning Out

Most of us speak at the rate of 100 to 150 words per minute. A slow speaker may speak only 80 to 90 words per minute, while fast speakers talk at 170 words per minute. (I get gusts of up to 200 words per minute!) But we can listen at the rate of 450 to 600 words per minute. This means we can think five times faster than we can talk. When listening to someone speaking at 100 words per minute while your brain could be taking in 600 words per minute, your mind may wander. The difference between the two speeds is called lag time.[3]

Have you ever asked your husband to do something for you and later he claims he never heard you? You are dumbfounded. "Well, I told you," you say. He replies, "No, you didn't. When did you tell me that?"

This type of problem frequently happens as a result of lag time. The listener's attention was focused on something else, so the listener caught only a portion of what was being said. Other people use lag time to formulate their next response. They fail to recognize that by doing so they are missing information, conveying disinterest, and missing cues that might indicate deeper problems.

Good listening and a productive use of lag time include evaluating what is being said and processing the information, as well as observing nonverbals and acting interested.

Actions Speak Louder Than Words

All body responses and emotional expressions are part of nonverbal communication—they tell the real story. Few people grasp the importance of nonverbals. In normal communication, the words used or the content accounts for only 7 percent of what is conveyed. Tone of voice and gestures amount to 38 percent, and facial expressions alone account for an astonishing 55 percent.[4]

It is difficult for a man to listen to a woman when she is unhappy or disappointed because he feels like a failure.

—John Gray.

Because a total of 93 percent of what is communicated is done without words, understanding nonverbal communication is probably more important than any other listening skill. If you were really angry at your partner, could you reveal nothing on your face or through your body posture, gestures, or tone of voice? It would be difficult, if not impossible, for most of us.

Body postures usually support the verbal message. Sagging shoulders might communicate discouragement; slouching in a chair, disinterest; head in hands, despair; a shrug of the shoulders, "I don't know."

Facial expressions are a part of body language and the strongest silent message sent. Eyes can show the most expression through shiftiness, narrowing, widening, a slow roll, dullness, and rate of blinking. A simple lift of the eyebrows, a wrinkling of the forehead, an uplifted chin, all convey important messages. When you smile, you convey warmth and happiness; when you frown, you show sadness and displeasure.

Gestures are also part of body language. Outstretched arms with palms up demonstrate openness and acceptance; outstretched arms, palms down, indicate closure and distance. The handshake, embrace, clenched fist, slammed door, thrown objects, clasped hands, upturned thumb, and pat on the back all send clear messages.

Nonverbal messages carry more weight than words, but they are restricted in scope. They are more intense and powerful than verbal messages but have a more limited range for expressing concepts and ideas. It is easier to misunderstand nonverbal communication, because of its more ambiguous nature. A listener basing judgment on nonverbal signals alone should be cautious about interpreting these signals. Ask the speaker if what you are understanding them to say is correct.

Your tone of voice carries a lot of weight, too. Words convey information, but how those words are spoken is even more important than the words. Cues in your tone of voice such as teasing, humor, friendliness, happiness, or anger tell the other person whether to come closer or back off.

Style is described in terms of the speed at which one talks, loudness or softness, intonations used, as well as choice of words. When we hear a certain style or tone of voice, we often assume we understand the person's intentions. We think, *She acted interested* or *She attacked me.*

Our style of communicating, which is clear and normal to us, may be perceived by someone else in a totally different way than we intended. Again, it is important to ask if our perceptions are correct.

Paraphrasing: Responding to Content

Paraphrasing is a method of responding to the content and meaning of what another has said. Through paraphrasing, the listener clarifies the statement for accuracy and lets the other person know they have been heard. Paraphrasing deals primarily with content—facts, information, ideas, opinions, or circumstances being described by the speaker. Responses might sound like this:

"I hear you to say that . . ."

"From what I'm hearing, you are saying . . ."

"You mean that . . ."

Paraphrasing deals only with the information shared, not with feelings. The listener works at understanding the information and sends it back, sometimes in question form, for verification.

Wife: "I attended an interesting in-service workshop today for screening applicants through personality testing that could be invaluable to me."

Husband (paraphrasing): "It sounds like this method of testing could be of real help to you as director of personnel."

You show interest in what is being shared but avoid sending back duplicate phrases in parrotlike fashion, which could be irritating to a partner.

Active Listening: Listening for Emotions

We tend to think of listening as a passive activity. However, when the word *ac-*

tive is added, it implies participation by the listener. The active listener tries to grasp emotions often veiled behind the spoken word and attempts to assist the speaker in expressing these emotions. Active listening sounds simple enough in principle but can be extremely tricky when you are hearing criticism, a negative emotion, or something personally threatening or opposed to your values and beliefs.

Active listening is best used when your partner is experiencing a problem such as anger, frustration, resentment, loneliness, discouragement, or hurt. Your first reaction to such feelings may be negative. You may want to argue, defend yourself, withdraw, or fight back. But when you listen actively, you lay aside your personal feelings in order to assist your partner in airing theirs. You lay aside any preconceived ideas about how you think your partner should feel.

Emotions are neither right nor wrong. They are simply transitory feelings that come and go. If at any moment your partner senses a lack of acceptance on your part, they will probably get angry and close down.

The process of venting emotions frees a person to see their own solutions. When you permit and encourage your partner to ventilate pent-up feelings, and you receive them with understanding rather than defensiveness or censure, you ensure a giant leap toward intimacy.

Putting It Into Practice

1. Restate the feeling(s) you hear. Let's say a wife is feeling resentful because her husband is not spending enough time with her. She says, "I am feeling resentful because you are gone almost every night of the week. When you're home you are so tired you watch TV or fall asleep. This is making me feel lonely and unloved. I need more of you than I am getting."

Her husband listens for the feelings. He restates them in his own words. "I hear you saying you feel neglected because I am spending too much time at work and not enough with you." It is important that he restate his wife's statement until she feels he has heard her.

2. Wait for agreement. Her husband might be tempted to say, "What do you mean, I'm not home enough? I was home three nights last week." If he responds like this, he proves he is not listening to her feelings.

The fact is, his wife feels neglected. No counterargument will change this. Arguing will probably only make her more defensive. He may think her unreasonable, but at this point nothing short of listening for feelings and understanding those feelings will do.

The husband may express his own thoughts and feelings later, but not now.

And he should listen without offering any solutions. Far too often, solutions are offered before the problem is understood.

3. Give adequate feedback. The easiest way to ensure you pick up feelings rather than facts is to state the feeling or emotion you just heard expressed, using the words "you feel." For example, you may say something like "You're feeling resentful." This restatement of the feelings will get you into an active listening episode. Here are some examples:

Situation 1: Wife is upset because she feels she is being treated unfairly at work. "I am so angry over this. They can't do this to me. I feel like quitting."

Husband's response (whether or not he agrees): "You are really upset over what is going on in that office. Tell me more" (an invitation to express more feelings).

Situation 2: Husband is despondent over the health of his father. He doesn't verbalize easily, but his astute wife observes his despondency and leads in this way. "Honey, you look troubled over something. Tell me about it."

Husband: "It's just that I'm worried about Dad. He's not getting any better. If it keeps up we'll have to put him in a nursing home."

Begin an active listening response with the words "you feel."

Wife: "You are really feeling upset over what's going on. I'd be interested in having you tell me more about this."

Gear your response level to the mood of your partner. Reveal empathy without overshooting or undershooting. It must come across in a believable way that you care.

Few active listening episodes end with just one response. When a big problem is verbalized, the episode will usually continue for a series of exchanges. Keep listening for feelings and continue to act as an escape valve for the ventilation of feelings. Sometimes it is necessary to prod gently to uncover the true emotion behind the words. When you think you understand, you then say it back, checking for any misunderstanding.[5]

A happy marriage is a long conversation that always seems too short.—**Andre Maurois.**

When Jan says "I'm so tired I could die," Jack could say, "Stop talking about being tired and take some Geritol." But if he's listening actively, Jack would say, "You're really bushed, huh? Any special reason?" This opens the door for Jan to seek understanding from her husband about problems she has had with the children, a run-in with a neighbor, or worries over her career. When she knows Jack cares about her day and duties, it's easier for her to say more, go deeper into her problem, and develop her thoughts further.

Once private feelings are exposed, however, you must restrain the urge to give advice, criticize, blame, or make judgments. This is not the time for that.

Sharing and caring. A great pattern for intimacy!

His and Her Listening Styles: Are They Different?

According to studies conducted on the listening habits of the sexes, women tend to use encouraging comments such as "uhhuh," "mmhmm," and "interesting," and nod their heads more often than men. It's not surprising that women often feel that their husbands aren't listening and men believe their wives are over-listening.[6]

As Archie Bunker from the *All in the Family* hit television series used to say to his wife, Edith, "I talk to you in English, but you listen in Dingbat." No, she just listens like a woman, which is different from a man.

Furthermore, what men and women mean by their listening behaviors differs vastly. When women nod their heads and say "uh-huh," they do so to indicate they are listening and understand what is being said. Men assume that listening noises show agreement.

This complicates the listening process. If a wife listens attentively to her husband, inserting many "ohs," "yeahs," and "un-huhs," which indicate her understanding, he thinks she is agreeing with his comments. If he discovers later that she did not agree with him, but was simply supporting him in his conversation, he might get upset and accuse her of being deceitful.

A woman, misunderstanding a man's response to her comments, may get upset if she shares something with her man and he gives no response, verbally or nonverbally. She thinks he is not paying attention.

A woman needs some kind of listening response from her husband in order to feel heard. She seeks understanding more than a solution. A time will come to search for a solution, but while she is upset she wants to be listened to.

If her husband listens with one eye on the television or gives a string of solutions, she won't feel heard. A woman who feels she cannot be heard soon begins to feel unloved. She'll begin to talk louder and longer in an effort to be heard and feel loved.

Both men and women need to recognize these differences in their listening styles. Neither one is right or wrong. But sensitive partners will adjust their listening styles to encourage their mates to share their thoughts and feelings. This type of communication leads to intimacy.

Six Powerful Listening Rules

If you need to improve your listening skills, merely deciding to try to improve will not work. You must discipline yourself and make a firm commitment to improve this skill. Here are six power-packed ways you can practice listening on a daily basis:

1. Maintain good eye contact. Focus your full attention on your partner. (Turn off the television, put down the newspaper, stop doing dishes.)

2. Sit attentively. For a few minutes, act as if nothing else in the world matters except hearing out your partner. Block all distractions from your mind. Lean forward in your chair as if you are hanging on to every word.

3. Act interested in what you hear. Raise your eyebrows, nod your head in agreement, smile, or laugh when appropriate.

4. Sprinkle your attentive listening with appropriate phrases to show interest and understanding. "I agree," "Is that so?" "Great!" "I hear you." Your partner wants to know you understand the ideas being presented.

5. Ask well-phrased questions. Give encouragement by asking questions that illustrate your interest. However, avoid "why" questions. "Why" questions put the other partner on the defensive.

6. Listen a little longer. Just when you think you are through listening, listen 30 seconds longer!

---

[1] Nancy L. Van Pelt, *How to Talk So Your Mate Will Listen and Listen So Your Mate Will Talk* (Grand Rapids: Fleming H. Revell, 1989), p. 61.

[2] The Communication Inventory, referred to as the CI, is a survey which I developed and administered to over 500 individuals who attended the Compleat Marriage seminars taught by my husband and me. From the 500 anonymous surveys, 149 males and 201 females were tabulated. Those in the survey represent various religions, races, ages, incomes, and educational backgrounds. From the 112 questions on the survey, I derived much pertinent information which has helped form the backbone of this chapter.

[3] Van Pelt, *How to Talk So Your Mate Will Listen and Listen So Your Mate Will Talk,* p. 67.

[4] *Ibid.,* p. 72.

[5] For a more complete description of active listening skills, see Chapter 3 of *How to Talk So Your Mate Will Listen and Listen So Your Mate Will Talk,* especially pages 78-86.

[6] For more about differences in how males and females communicate, see Deborah Tannen, Ph.D., in *That's Not What I Meant: How Conversational Style Makes or Breaks Relationships* (New York: William Morrow and Company, Inc., 1986), p. 145.

Chapter 10

HOW TO TALK
TO THE ONE YOU LOVE

*W*hile we were going together we spent much time talking," Sharon reminisces. "We were best friends. I could tell Ed anything, and he shared everything with me. Now we hardly ever talk, and when we do, we argue."

When couples with communication problems try to talk it out, more talk just brings on more misunderstanding, confusion, and anger. Without realizing it, Ed and Sharon are engaged in a game of mutual aggravation.

The real culprit in Ed and Sharon's case is likely found in *how* they talk to each other. Body language, tone of voice, unstated implications, assumptions, hidden meanings, and resentment from past experiences all influence the message that is sent and received. How a couple talks to each other can either build or destroy a relationship.

Killer Talk: Barriers to Effective Communication

Many of us use alienating messages. We use them so often that we become unaware of how offensive they can be, but they are aptly called "killer talk."

The *solution sender* weights down speech with orders, directions, and commands: "Get over here." "Hurry up." Threats fit here also: "If you ever do that again, I'll . . ."

The *moralizer* acts like a parent and teacher: "Honey, we shouldn't act like that in public" or "You know enough not to . . ." Most of us resent being told we must, should, or had better do something.

The *snub* uses put-downs, criticism, and blame: "Not a bad idea, considering you thought of it" or "That was stupid. Why can't you ever . . . ?"

The *psychoanalyst* interprets and delivers diagnoses: "You say that only because . . ."

The *correction officer* has a compulsion to keep the facts straight and doesn't hesitate to contradict: "No, that's not how it happened . . ."

The *judge* tries to second-guess what will come next: "And like always, you didn't pay attention, did you . . . ? I could see this coming a mile off . . ."

The *topic switcher* changes the subject before meaningful communication can take place, and the *topic overkiller* talks excessively about a subject.

James Dobson tells of a game husbands and wives play. He calls it Assassinate the Spouse. In this destructive game the player (usually a husband, he notes) attempts to punish his wife by ridiculing and embarrassing her in front of their friends. He can hurt her when they are alone, but in front of friends he can really cut her down. If he wants to be exceptionally cruel, he'll let the guests know how stupid and ugly she is—the two areas in which she is the most vulnerable. Bonus points are awarded if he can reduce her to tears.

You cannot control killer messages sent by your partner, but you can stop killer messages *you* are sending. When you do, you will notice you and your mate drawing closer to each other without conscious effort. You will feel closer when you don't have to deal with residual hurt accumulated from killer communication.

The Silent Treatment

The news caption "Talk About a Quiet Marriage: 12 Years Without Speaking" caught my attention. The story told of a husband and wife who maintained a strict code of silence for 12 years! Out of spite, neither would lower themselves to speak, but they did communicate by passing notes. When one partner wrote a note suggesting a divorce, the other wrote back, "Go ahead."

You can send your marriage to an early grave with a series of little digs.

To clam up, withdraw, and refuse to talk about an issue does more to clog communication than any other killer message. Both men and women use the silent treatment as a weapon or form of control, but usually in different ways. When a man is silent, it indicates that strong emotions such as anger or fear are building inside. Or he may be using silence as a power ploy. A silent man cannot be argued with. A woman uses silence more often to get even for some hurt or injustice or when she reaches the stage of total despair and desperation.

The "silent husband," according to some marriage counselors, lies behind half of all troubled marriages.[1] Many women complain that their husbands won't talk to them and cannot be prodded into it. But there are reasons for male silence, and the wise woman will seek to understand her silent partner.

Some men, particularly workaholics, consider only productivity to be of value. Their answer to all of life's problems is action, not talk. Other men are so dogmatic and authoritarian that they refuse to speak further on a subject once they have handed down an edict. Still others dislike discussing what they term "trivia."

Another reason for male silence is that a man under emotional stress usually retreats within himself. He searches for solutions for his problems, and focuses on objective situations such as those presented on the TV or in the newspaper in order to refocus his energies and put his issues in perspective. A wise woman will leave a man who is in retreat alone. She can assure herself that he will be back, when he has reordered his world.

You can't do much about your partner's silence. Begging, pleading, getting angry, or responding in kind is hardly the remedy. Try this approach instead: "There are times when you have trouble talking with me. There must be something I am doing that makes it difficult for you to talk. I'd like to discuss this with you so I can make some changes."

If you ask a question and get no response, try, "What do you think of what I just asked you?" or "Your silence says to me that you are very angry/hurt/upset over something. Is this what you are trying to tell me?"

A woman can remember that a man is more likely to talk after he has had some recover time from the stresses of the day. A man who recognizes his tendencies to be uncommunicative can let his wife know that while he may need space at the moment, he will be willing to talk in a little while. And though he may not feel like talking much, he can show understanding of his wife's need to talk by being a supportive listener.

High-level Talks

So far we have talked about other elements of speaking beyond the actual words. Now let's focus on the message itself. In his book *Why Am I Afraid to Tell You Who I Am?* John Powell describes five levels on which we communicate.

Level 5: Small talk. At this level, shallow conversation takes place: "How are you?" "Whatcha been up to?" "How are things going?" Such conversation borders on the meaningless but is better than embarrassed silence in social situations with those we do not know well. However, if communication remained at such a superficial level in marriage, it would lead to extreme boredom and deep feelings of resentment.

Level 4: Factual conversation. This reads like the evening newscast: Information is shared without personal comment. You talk about the day's events, but you don't tell how you feel about them. Factual conversation is easy because it requires minimal risk. Almost nothing of self is exposed. Men are more likely than women to communicate on this level. They find it logical, factual, and safe. A couple communicating only on this level can never attain intimacy.

Level 3: Ideas and opinions. Real conversation begins here as you freely describe ideas and opinions. As you verbalize personal ideas, your partner has a better chance to get to know you. At this level, you expose personal thoughts. If these are accepted nonjudgmentally, you feel free to move to a deeper level. If not, you stay here or back up to level 4, where it is safe again. When level 3 conversation is met with acceptance, you lay a good foundation for approaching intimacy.

Level 2: Feelings and emotions. At this level you feel secure enough to share feelings that lie underneath the ideas and opinions expressed at level 3. You describe what is going on inside you—how you feel about your partner or a situation. A part of you remains slightly cautious, keeping a watchful eye on your partner's response. Unless you receive the acceptance needed, you will probably say only things you know your partner can handle and will agree with.

Ninety percent of the friction of daily life is caused by the wrong tone of voice.

When a couple can share honestly at this level in a give-and-take manner, with each respecting the other's feelings, their relationship will be greatly enriched. Flashes of insight into your partner's personality will provide a basis for understanding and intimacy. A good combination for daily interaction is to alternate between the levels of ideas/opinions and feelings/emotions.

Level 1: Deep insight. The deepest and rarest level is deep insight, at which complete emotional and personal self-disclosure takes place. You feel secure enough in the relationship to throw yourself open to view. It is risky because you become very vulnerable. Usually some deep personal and emotional experience is shared, perhaps something you've never shared before. Communication on this level usually makes a deep and lasting impression on both partners and enriches the relationship.

Deep insight is the most difficult of all levels to master. It is much easier to stay on the superficial levels of 5, 4, and 3 because of a backlog of rejection and fear. But if you are fighting shy of levels 1 and 2, you will never reach the intimacy possible in your marriage. Take the time to develop the trust you need in each other to talk on these levels. The risks you take in stepping out of your comfort zones and learning to share more of yourselves will be well rewarded in a fulfilling, intimate relationship.

Frankly Speaking: I-Messages

One of the big challenges in marriage is how to talk with your mate about something you don't like or a behavior that irritates you. During the course of any given week, situations arise in which needs and preferences clash. When this happens, rather than blaming and judging, use an I-message.

I-messages express your feelings directly when you are upset, irritated, or annoyed by your partner's behavior. I-messages let your partner know you have negative feelings about the behavior without attacking or ridiculing. You are more likely to be heard because these messages are less threatening. They establish openness and honesty and are an excellent method of venting feelings of irritation.

Compare the different reactions to these two messages sent by wives after their husbands refused to take them out to dinner.

Being married teaches us at least one very valuable lesson—to think before we speak.

Wife Number 1: "You're so inconsiderate! You never think of anybody but yourself. All you want to do is watch TV. You make me sick!"

Wife Number 2: "I feel hurt when you won't take me out to dinner once in a while. I need to be alone with you to communicate on an adult level and feel close to you."

Wife Number 1 blames, judges, and puts down her husband. This gives him ammunition for an argument and will probably cause him to become more stubborn and defensive than before. Wife Number 2 tells only how she feels, a fact her husband can hardly argue with. She selects suitable words to let her husband know she has feelings that, in her opinion, are being ignored.

An effective I-message has three parts.

1. A statement of how your partner's unacceptable behavior makes you feel. "I feel upset/irritated/threatened/angry . . ."

2. A nonblameful description of your partner's behavior. "When you don't take me out to dinner . . ."

3. An explanation regarding the tangible effect of that behavior on you. ". . . because I need to be alone with you in order to talk on an adult level . . ."

Here are some examples of how to use an *I*-message effectively.

• The husband turns on the television during mealtime after the couple has agreed not to watch TV during meals. The wife says, "I feel upset when you break the agreement we had not to watch TV during mealtimes because it is one of the few times during the day when we can communicate with each other."

• The wife gives husband the silent treatment. The husband says, "I feel angry when you close down like this, because I don't even know what I've done to cause it."

• The husband criticizes the wife in a sharp manner. The wife says, "I feel deeply hurt when you criticize me in such an unfair manner, because it makes me feel I am not respected or loved."

I-messages are much more likely to produce positive behavior change because they contain no put-downs and do not tell your partner what to do. Many people, out of love and consideration for a partner, will change an annoying behavior once they understand the impact of that behavior. But that is not the main purpose of an I-message. The major goal is to release your feelings of irritation.

Your partner may or may not change their behavior, but you are staying in touch with your feelings and releasing them by communicating them in a constructive manner, rather than suppressing them. Unattended little resentments and irritations can fester into big, bitter fights. The head of steam that frequently builds up between couples can be let off daily by learning to communicate in this open and direct method.

Here are some suggestions for using I-messages:

1. Use them when you first become irritated. Don't wait until you are boiling mad over a problem.

2. Avoid sending a solution or telling your partner what to do. Telling someone what to do brings defensive reactions.

3. Your tone of voice must match the intensity of your message. Avoid overshooting or undershooting.

4. If your partner does not respond to your first I-message, send another, rephrased in a new manner, until you are heard.

If you really want to have your feelings recognized, you must continually communicate them directly until you are understood. Don't let your partner sidetrack you. And don't give up just because you didn't get the desired response. You simply do not have that many constructive options when you are irritated over something your partner is doing. Even if your partner fails *you*, resolve not to fail your partner.[2]

His and Her Talk Styles: Are They Different?

Is there a difference between the way males and females talk? All you have to do is listen in on any group of males and females to note some of the differences.

Do women really talk more than men? Yes, studies at Harvard show that girls learn to talk earlier than boys, and articulate better. From their earliest years, girls talk more than boys. Even as adults, men never seem to catch up. It is estimated that the average male speaks about 12,500 words per day while the average woman doubles that with more than 25,000! This could explain why many men don't want to talk much after getting home at night. They have already expended their 12,500-word limit. Their wives may have expended 12,500 also, but they have saved as many for their husbands.[3]

Do men and women really talk about different subjects? Yes. She frequently gets bored as he goes on and on about sports, cars, and business. He tunes her out when she rattles on about friends, or people he doesn't even know. It is typical for a woman to talk about people and relationships; it is the natural outpouring of her caring nature. When this kind of sharing is shut off or ignored, a vital element of herself is closed to her husband.

Men consider it normal to talk about sports, politics, cars, jobs, the stock market, and how things work. Women frequently perceive this as a lecture: "I'm the teacher; you're the student. Now learn!"

Does male and female talk function on different channels? Yes. Medical research confirms that males get a chemical bath to their brain that sets the stage for men and women to "specialize" in two different ways of thinking. Men function more in left-brain dominance, which promotes specialization in more logical, factual, analytical, and aggressive thought. Women tend to use the right side of the brain, which is the center for feelings, language, and communication skills. It is the more relational of the two sides.[4]

As a result, women tend to operate on channel E for Emotion, while men tend to operate on channel L for Logic. When Lisa shares a problem with Hal, she is looking for sympathy and support. Hal responds with logical advice, not realizing that is not what she wants.

Do male and female styles of talking differ? Yes. A woman tends to dramatize her story through tone of voice and gestures in an effort to re-create the experience. She relives it as she tells it. A man is more likely to give a *Reader's Digest* version of an event. In brief summary form, devoid of emotion or particulars, he reports the facts. If she presses for details, he feels he is being grilled. He probably can't remember more than he told her anyway.

Do men and women have differing needs to talk things over? Yes. Women have a much stronger need, especially when it comes to their relationships. Men appear bewildered by this need and make such comments as "I want to *do* things with her, and all she wants to do is *talk."*

This tendency doesn't show up until after the wedding because while dating, men are willing to spend time talking in order to build the relationship. After the wedding, the male tendency is to devote more time to work. Women want to talk through difficulties and resolve differences so they can feel close to their husbands, while men will do almost anything to avoid a blowup. Men don't view discussing difficulties as an opportunity to gain intimacy, and feel no burden for constant sharing of thoughts, feelings, and needs. Each sex obtains feelings of connectedness differently.

Do the sexes differ in their use of power and relationship strategies in their talk? Yes, again! For instance, when in a restaurant a man might say, "This food is terrible"—a simple declarative statement. A woman would more likely say, "This food is terrible, isn't it?" tagging a question on the end in search of support for her opinion. This is her attempt at accommodation and politeness, but is often interpreted as a signal of indecision and subordination by males whose goal in conversation is to appear competent.

Men and women just may be marching to different drummers. Women tend to use better grammar and fewer obscenities. Their goal in conversations is to build and nurture relationships. Men tend to take more control of conversations in their search for status and power.

Misunderstandings resulting from a lack of knowledge about male-female talk styles can lead to frustration and misery. Rather than assuming something is wrong with your partner when you come up with different conclusions, why not accept these differences as part of God's marvelous plan for male and female? A change in attitude can bring rich rewards.

---

[1] Van Pelt, *How to Talk So Your Mate Will Listen and Listen So Your Mate Will Talk,* p. 93.

[2] For more about I-messages, see *How to Talk So Your Mate Will Listen and Listen So Your Mate Will Talk,* chapter 4, pages 90-111.

[3] Gary Smalley and John Trent, *The Language of Love* (Pomona, Calif.: Focus on the Family Publishing, 1988), p. 32.

[4] W. Robert Goy and Bruce S. McEwen, *Sexual Differences of the Brain* (Cambridge, Mass.: MIT Press, 1980), p. 64.

Chapter 11

COPING WITH CONFLICT

*W*e really love each other, but we argue and fight so much," sighed a battle-weary wife of 14 years. "We have tried and tried to stop, but we just can't."

Most couples fight over the same issues: money, children, recreation, personalities, in-laws, roles, religion, politics, and sex—in that order. But the frequency of conflict and the issues that cause the most friction do not remain constant over the years. Honeymooners tend to disagree most over personality differences and how to spend leisure time. "Middle marrieds" argue more over money, but such conflicts lessen in time. The least amount of conflict is found among aging couples.[1]

Is It OK to Fight?

You may be one of many who believe it is wrong to argue or engage in conflict. Such a notion has all but collapsed under a barrage of information to the contrary. Couples who say they never fight are deluding themselves or are entirely out of touch with their emotions. Those who refuse to acknowledge the need to fight will suffer from displaced anger such as hostility, emotional instability, depression, a long list of health problems, and a lack of intimacy.

Many psychologists consider occasional conflict a sign of a healthy, fulfilling relationship. It shows warmth and caring. George R. Bach and Peter Wyden, in their classic *The Intimate Enemy: How to Fight Fair in Love and Marriage,* comment: "We have discovered that couples who fight together are couples who stay together—provided they know how to fight properly."[2]

Learning how to fight fair might be the most important communication skill you will ever learn. Fighting between two people who really care about each other does not have to be destructive. It means that you care about each other so much you will negotiate and deal with a problem until you find a mutually satisfying solution. The measure of whether fighting is acceptable for a Christian couple boils down to the methods and style used during disagreement and the end result.

The Share-Care Plan for Resolving Conflict

A few simple rules can lead to constructive conflict resolution:

1. Choose the best time. It is best to keep current when handling conflicts, but if either of you is angry or unreasonable, then postpone the discussion. Just don't delay too long. And if your partner does not bring up the issue again, then you take the initiative to solve the problem. Guard against unnecessary interruptions when discussing major issues. Take the phone off the hook and agree not to answer pagers, cell phones, and doorbells. Explain to your children that you have an important issue to settle and ask not to be disturbed.

Major issues should not be discussed late at night. Decisions made late in the day when the body is mentally, physically, and spiritually exhausted are likely to be emotional ones. A better plan would be to sleep on the problem overnight and arise an hour early or choose an acceptable time on the following day.

2. Select the best location. Neutral territory is the key. The family room, basement, or garage might be right for certain couples. Bedrooms and kitchens may provide psychological hang-ups. Some professionals recommend going to a motel or other such place to handle big problems. A motel provides an atmosphere free of interruptions, with unfamiliar surroundings encouraging the couple to pull together. The expense and effort involved in reserving a motel emphasizes the importance of the occasion.

You might also consider a restaurant. Solving problems in a public arena will ensure that you both control yourselves. Other suggestions include the bathtub, where you sit facing each other. This may sound ridiculous, but it works well. The water has a calming effect, and the position forces you to interface. However, two chairs in any room will do. Just make sure there are ample time and privacy to talk the problem out without interruption.

3. Set time limits. Both minimum and maximum time limits should be set. If an issue is large enough to require the scheduling of a meeting, it undoubtedly will require a minimum of 15 minutes to resolve. A maximum of one hour is reasonable on major issues, although you should remain flexible. If an issue remains unresolved in the allotted time, the meeting can be extended, or another time can be set to continue negotiating.

4. Establish ground rules. Just as a business meeting would crumble rapidly without following Robert's Rules of Order, so disagreements between couples can fall apart for lack of clear guidelines. Establishing a set of your own personal guidelines will greatly improve the atmosphere and promote free negotiation.

Some general ground rules might include no name-calling, no threats of divorce or suicide, no remarks about in-laws or relatives, no put-downs concerning appearance or intelligence, no physical violence, and no yelling, swearing, or interrupting. Both partners can relax when discussion is governed by rules that prevent emotional harm and promote security. If one breaks a rule you can set a consequence such as having to treat the other to a dinner out, pay a fine that is saved toward a romantic getaway, or something similar.

5. *Stay on the subject.* Stick with one problem until you solve it. The more problems brought up at one time, the less likelihood there is that any of them will be solved. Make a rule that additional problems cannot be brought up until the first one has been dealt with. If necessary, prepare an agenda for the next meeting and jot down other issues as they arise. Avoid dragging up old scores and arguments. Agree that if the accusation is more than six months old, it is inadmissible evidence.

6. *Put the share-care plan into use.* The share-care plan includes four steps:

a. *State the problem in I-message form.* A direct statement of your feelings about the problem is needed without put-downs and without telling the other person what to do. An I-message flows as follows: I feel _____ when you _____ because_____.

b. *The other person responds with a care message.* The partner restates the problem and the feelings expressed. The restatement shows the problem has been heard correctly and the feelings involved are understood. This allows your partner to know that you accept their feelings as valid even though you may not agree with their feelings or point of view. To accept does not necessarily mean you agree.

c. *The person with the problem continues to vent in I-message form until there are no more feelings to express.* The other person continues to respond with care messages, restating each new feeling expressed so the partner with the problem feels understood.

d. *Resolution.* Once the problem and feelings have been restated and accepted, you are ready to move to an apology and resolution. Asking for forgiveness is an important part of resolving a problem.

Let's look in on June and Rick.

He (I-message): "I was really upset when you suggested inviting your relatives for my birthday but never mentioned inviting my family. This made me feel that my family was not wanted."

She (care message): "If I hear you correctly, you are upset because you feel I prefer having my family over for your birthday rather than yours."

He (I-message): "Exactly. I like your family, but I resent it when you leave my family off a guest list, especially when it's my birthday. I think my wishes should be considered and my family should be invited too."

She (care message): "You sound as if you have some resentful feelings about this that you've been storing up for a while."

He (I-message): "You bet. Furthermore, I feel . . ."

We have no solution yet, but June has a clearer picture of Rick's feelings. When Rick has no more feelings to express, June can accept his feelings as valid, and they can move to apology and resolution.

She (statement of acceptance): "I have heard your frustration over this situation and accept your feelings as valid." (apology and resolution) "I am sorry for upsetting you by not including your family as often as mine. Sometimes I feel your family has never accepted me, and I'm not comfortable around them. In the future I'll try to be more aware of your feelings and include your family more. Please forgive me."

Shifting gears. Another problem surfaced for June and Rick during the resolution phase. If Rick is a caring partner, he will pick up on this and "shift gears." The shifting of gears does not have to be at this time. A future time can be set. But now June becomes the sender and Rick the receiver.

He (care message): "I accept your apology. If I heard you correctly, you feel unaccepted by my family. I'm concerned about your feelings, and we should talk about this."

She (I-message): "Right. I know you might not understand, but I feel all thumbs around your mother. I feel as if I can't do anything right."

He (care message): "It sounds as though my mom makes you feel inadequate. Tell me more."

She (I-message): "OK. Remember when they were here for Christmas? All I asked her to bring was . . ."

After winning an argument with his wife, the wisest thing a man can do is apologize.

Each time a partner shares a problem, it should be done through I-messages. The one with the problem should be allowed to "dump" as long as there are any feelings, while the other remains in the caring role. Only after enough feelings have been defused will the couple be able to arrive at a mutually satisfying solution.

The skill of shifting gears allows both partners the right and privilege to clearly and completely state their views, feelings, and reasons without interruption. It is an orderly method for airing any troublesome problem. It will not always result in an immediate solution, but each will know exactly where the other stands. Some couples are so busy trying to prove who is right and who is wrong they never hear what the other is saying, and consequently never deal with the real problem.

7. *List in writing all possible solutions.* After all feelings have been aired and are clearly understood by both partners, you will be able to work out more ra-

tional alternatives. Brainstorm every possible solution, regardless of how far-fetched it may seem. List suggestions on paper but do not evaluate them yet.

8. Choose the most acceptable solution. This choice may take a good measure of negotiation and compromise. Solutions can be reached by one partner yielding or by both compromising. Giving in to another in the midst of conflict takes real maturity, because in effect you admit that your analysis of the situation was wrong and you are ready to change your mind.

Make sure that the same one does not always do the yielding. Winning should not be the goal, because where there is a winner there must also be a loser, and no one likes to lose. The most acceptable solution is the one that comes closest to solving the problem and meeting the needs of both.

9. Hang in there! What couples in an argument need to realize is that many times they quit just short of the goal. Anger and frustration mount, and they withdraw or leave prematurely.

Harry and I eventually learned this. We reached an impasse on some issue and began the process of negotiation to an acceptable solution. As our discussion became more heated, I became furious. I wanted to scream about Harry's unfairness and how much I had been hurt. I never wanted to talk with him again. But instead of giving up, I hung in there. Within a couple minutes we both moved off dead center, though I hadn't thought it was possible, and we resolved the issue. I'll never forget the warmth we felt for each other following this incident. I learned through this experience not to bail out of an argument too soon.

Even when you move through all the steps properly, change doesn't take place overnight. Old habits take time to break. Don't expect too much too soon. Pray for patience.

10. Reestablish touch. A simple touch of the hand, a warm hug, or bodies "spooned" as you sleep can melt many hostilities. The closeness of a hug goes deeper than words. The bond may have been stretched while you were in conflict, but now you are one again, and touching reassures you of it. Give your partner an unexpected compliment, a pat on the back, and a big smile, and you'll find that you can draw closer again.

His and Her Fight Styles: Are They Different?

Men are more likely to avoid an argument than women. According to Robert Levenson, who has studied the reactions of couples as they discuss problems in marriage, men react with a greater increase in heart rate than women to the stress of the argument.

Men are also inclined to release anger in spurts rather than in slow-moving negotiations, and withdraw when the conflict is prolonged. It is possible that when a wife thinks her husband is withdrawing from an argument, he is simply reacting to a built-in, health-protecting device. Arguing can be hazardous to a man's health![3]

According to another researcher, Dr. H. G. Whittington, the male thinks solutions should be sought in a manner similar to a game plan that controls sporting events. His game plan dictates that the dispute will take place within certain boundaries, will last for a specific amount of time, and will eventually end. The game is governed by rules that all players respect and remains fair since an umpire or referee limits foul play. [4]

The objective of the game, when viewed from the male perspective, is to display skill and achieve victory. Other opportunities exist for a rematch, if necessary. Sports etiquette demands that aggressive behavior and personal opinions be confined to the game and not be carried off the field into relationships. Consequently, postgame socialization is encouraged among opposing teams.

Women too have a game plan, but it is put through their *emotional filter*. Aggression and skill may be displayed, but they must be modulated to suit the occasion—especially if males are present. A woman is less likely to recognize boundaries, since the "rules" she plays by govern work, play, home, children, and relationships. Because her feelings become involved, she cannot turn them off when the game is over. Blocks of time are usually foreign to women, who tend to see all of life as a whole. Women are less likely to recognize an unseen umpire or referee.

> *Kind words can be short and easy to speak, but their echoes are truly endless.*
>
> —**Mother Teresa.**

Women engaged in conflict have difficulty socializing, even in a group, with someone with whom they have just battled. Their emotions are closer to the surface, and they have easier access to them. They may have difficulty accepting the concept that there is another chance to play the game—a rematch.

With these observations in mind, it's easier to understand how a couple—even a couple who really care about each other—can experience considerable frustration over stalemates in settling their differences. As long as men and women enter into relationships, there will be disagreements between them. Emotions will run high. Resolutions will sometimes prove elusive. Anger, hurt, and guilt will be interwoven with daily life.

No outside force will magically appear to monitor a couple's behavior or call "foul." During a conflict it is just the two of them, standing alone, vulnerable, needing each other but angry with each other, too. How can they hammer out a solution and still remain affectionate?

Unless both have learned appropriate skills so that victory can be attained without either one "winning" or "losing," the conflict will go on. The good news is that hate can be avoided. If you find yourself unable to resolve a conflict on your own, don't allow it to fester. Seek the advice of a counselor who will help you find a solution.

Making the Most of Talk Time

Communication generally peaks during the first year of marriage when a couple spends time exploring inner feelings and setting goals for the future. But after children enter the scene, a couple's focus often moves from their relationship to their home and children. Romance wears off, and the relationship takes on the appearance of a business partnership. Conversation centers on financial problems, managing the household chores, etc.

Husband and wife find themselves pursuing different interests. He works on expanding his business and protecting the family's future. Her life centers on the children, the home, and her career, if she has one. Once the children are launched, couples in their middle years frequently find they have no basis for in-depth communication. They may talk, but only about things and problems—their jobs, the car, the house, chores, the children, the church.

Think back to when you were dating. You were not so concerned with *things* or *problems* as you were with discovering each other. All you wanted then was to be together, talk intimately, and dream big dreams. As you talked, you frequently used the words *I, you, we, us.*

Though couples are slow to recognize it and loath to admit it, after a few years of marriage boredom sets in. Boredom spells death to intimate conversation. The message is clear: A couple who fails to make talking a priority sets the stage for a stale marriage tomorrow.

During all stages of married life, couples need to stay in touch with each other's feelings. There is a great deal couples can do to improve their talk time. The good news is that it is never too late to begin. Here are some fun suggestions:

1. Work at talking. Create time to talk and plan things to talk about. Bring up topics for discussion of particular interest to your partner. Read a book about these topics, clip magazine articles, share a clever cartoon. Introduce topics you wish to discuss. Talking will be fun if you remember to follow certain guidelines: no interrupting, put-downs, criticizing, giving advice, or asking too many questions.

2. Try the walk-talk. If you are not in the habit of exercising regularly, you could begin walking with your mate several times a week. This way you can walk and talk at the same time, getting the physical benefits from exercise as well as benefits to your marriage.

This daily talk time is not for intensive sharing of feelings or deep problem solving. Use it for catching up on everyday life—the kids, jobs, neighbors, the boss, the what-happened-to-me-today type of thing. This swapping of information leads to involvement in each other's life and strengthens the marital bond. If the walk-talk won't work for you, try mealtime or linger at the table after the meal. *When* this daily talk time occurs isn't important, but it should occur daily.

3. Try car talk. Are you commuting to work together, or taking a trip? Utilize time in the car to full advantage by talking. If you can't think of anything to talk about, take this book along. Read sections aloud and discuss some of the topics. Harry and I often use travel time to read to each other, or listen to cassettes and discuss them. Many couples, like us, have rejuvenated their relationships and rekindled closeness—in the car!

4. Play games together. Playing games such as Trivial Pursuit, Uno, Sorry, and Monopoly creates a pleasant, relaxed atmosphere in which a couple can banter without undue pressure to communicate. Games provide an opportunity and reason to talk by creating new situations and life experiences that bring you together.

5. Make the most of mealtimes. Table time can be one of the most pleasant or hated times of the day, depending on the atmosphere. Realistically, we may not be able to gather twice daily simply for titillating discussions or intimate sharing. But mealtimes are a natural gathering time.

Take advantage of this opportunity to establish a tradition of pleasant conversation during meals. Think of it; twice a day, nearly seven days a week, you could talk for 20 minutes or more. And make sure you turn off the TV. It's a conversation killer!

Many people are reluctant to talk to their partners. They worry that it isn't the right time, they don't know what to say, they might say the wrong thing, or they are too angry. But the real risk in refusing to talk is the loss of a relationship. A couple who can't talk to each other has no basis for a relationship. By opening up and sharing, you can turn a stranger into a friend.

A Holy Triangle of Communication

Although this chapter has centered on communication between husband and wife, it would not be complete without mentioning communication with God. Husband, wife, and God form a holy triangle. If communication breaks down between husband and wife, it affects their relationship with God. If the circuits to heaven are jammed, there will be a busy signal between the couple too. One author has said, "A person cannot be genuinely open to God and closed to his mate." When the lines of communication are in working order, God can more easily fulfill His purpose for husband and wife.

No amount of expert communication will make a perfect marriage or create openness and respect where these qualities are not already present. But honest communication does relieve emotional tension, clarify thinking, and provide a release for daily pressures. It allows a couple to work toward common goals and paves the way toward a truly intimate relationship.

---

[1] Reported by Jeanette C. Lauer and Robert H. Lauer in *Till Death Do Us Part* (Binghamton, NY: The Haworth Press, Inc., 1986), pp. 133, 134.

[2] George R. Bach and Peter Wyden, *The Intimate Enemy: How to Fight Fair in Love and Marriage* (New York: William Morrow and Co., Inc., 1969).

[3] Nancy L. Van Pelt, *How to Talk So Your Mate Will Listen and Listen So Your Mate Will Talk*, p. 140.

[4] H. G. Whittington, "When Men and Women Disagree," *Savvy*, September 1981, pp. 46, 47, 51, 54.

Chapter 12

IS SOMETHING REALLY WRONG WITH THE MALE BRAIN?

*M*en and women are very different, and God created the sexes that way. But there has been a distinct tendency in recent years to minimize the difference in order to establish the concept of women's equality to men. The sexes differ markedly in so many ways that it would be a serious mistake to ignore or pretend they do not exist. We need to understand the differences so that we can understand how they affect male and female behavior.

Every cell of the male differs genetically from every cell in a female. Differences in chromosomal patterns dictate maleness and femaleness. As a result of these genetic differences, females generally possess greater physical vitality. The average American woman outlives the typical man.

The female skeletal structure differs from the male skeletal structure. The female has a shorter head and legs, a broader face, a less protruding chin, and a longer trunk. Women seem to lose their teeth earlier than do men. The stomach, kidneys, liver, and appendix are larger in females, but their lungs are smaller.

The thyroid gland, larger and more active in the female than in the male, enlarges even further during pregnancy and menstruation, making females more prone to goiter problems. The larger thyroid provides the female with those elements that we consider important to personal beauty, such as smooth skin, a relatively hair-free body, and a thin layer of subcutaneous fat. The thyroid gland also contributes to a woman's emotional instability—she laughs and cries more easily.

Female blood contains more water and 20 percent fewer red cells. Since these red cells supply oxygen to the body, this may explain why women tire more easily and are more apt to faint. During World War II when the workday in British wartime factories was increased from 10 to 12 hours a day, accidents among women rose 150 percent, while the accident rate among men remained unaffected.[1] Although women tire more easily in a given day, they have the capacity to live more days. Women live longer because men are less likely to limit salt, fat, and cholesterol in their diets, less likely to obey speed limits, less likely to wear a seat belt, more likely to drink too much and to drive after drinking.

A woman's heart rate is more rapid than her counterpart's (80, versus 72 for men). Her blood pressure varies from moment to moment but usually registers about 10 points lower than a man's until after menopause. Women also breathe fewer times per minute (7 for women to 10 for men). Women tolerate high temperatures better than men, which may explain why they are always cold.

Men are larger and stronger than women in all human cultures. The average man is 6 percent taller than the average woman and has 20 percent more body weight. The greater weight comes mainly from larger muscles and bones. Because of the heavier build, men can lift more weight, throw a ball farther, and run faster than most women. Men have a higher metabolic rate and produce more physical energy. Thus they need more food.

Menstruation, pregnancy, and lactation affect female behavior and emotions. Research into suicides shows that 40 to 60 percent of the women were menstruating when they took their own lives. David Levy found that the depth and intensity of the maternal instinct (desire for motherhood) are associated with the duration and amount of the menstrual flow. Absenteeism because of menstrual problems costs the United States millions annually, but the financial toll is secondary to the repercussions in the home resulting from domestic quarrels during this time.[2]

Studies of behavior change show a large portion of crimes committed by women (63 percent in an English study and 84 percent in a French) occurred just prior to the onset of menstruation. Accidents, and a decline in quality of academic attainment and intelligence test scores and in visual clarity and response speed are also markedly affected by menstruation.[3]

This summarizes some of the main physical differences between males and females. But is there also a difference between male and female brains? Shortly after our marriage I suspected there was something different (or the matter) with Harry's brain. During our discussions, Harry would respond with ideas from another planet (most likely Mars!). I joked that there was something drastically wrong with his brain. He thought something was the matter with mine! This drew me into researching brain-sex differences.

Male and Female Brains

The first bit of research I found came from the late Dr. David Hernandez, an obstetrician and gynecologist. Dr. Hernandez confirmed that at three months of life, testosterone is released in male newborns, which assigns brain sex to that particular infant. What is brain sex? It simply means that the male's brain is different—that his brain is "wired" differently and functions differently from that of the female. This differentness is contingent on this surge of testosterone.[4]

It is not known what causes this surge of testosterone, but it is known that without it there is a tendency toward effeminate activity or homosexuality. So it is brain-sex assignment, planned by the Creator, that makes males and females so different. It is a tremendous mistake to minimize these differences. If we don't pay attention to them, we can't understand the differing needs of our partners.

More information about brain-sex differences has since rolled off the presses. One article, "Women Versus Men: Are They Born Different?" by Tim Hackler, confirmed that men and women not only *look* different, but they *act* differently and *think* differently. The article stated that "males and females are born with a different set of 'instructions' built into their genetic code."[5]

For example, female infants are more people-oriented. They recognize individual faces and can distinguish between voices before male babies of the same age. Girls learn to talk earlier than boys, and they articulate better and acquire a more extensive vocabulary than boys of a comparable age. Girls also smile earlier and continue to smile more throughout their lives.

Male infants are more interested in things. A 4-month-old boy will react to a bright mobile hanging over his crib and will babble and respond to it as easily as to his mother. A few months later he will try to take the mobile apart. Boys of pre-elementary school age overwhelmingly outperform girls when asked to manipulate three-dimensional objects. Boys also participate in more rough-and-tumble play and explore away from their mothers earlier and more often.

The simple act of hand-holding can knit hearts and lives together.

Until recently environment was considered the most important determining factor for human behavior. This notion has all but collapsed. Of all the behavioral differences between men and women, aggression presents the most clear-cut case for a biological connection. According to psychologist Janet T. Spence, "the evidence cited in favor of genetically based sex differences is more compelling for aggression than for any other temperamental qualities."[6]

In no human culture ever studied has the female been found more aggressive than the male. It is the genetically determined presence of male or female sex hormones that tends to "wire" the brain for male and female behavior.

According to this same article, one of the most pronounced differences between men and women is that women show verbal superiority, while men show spatial superiority—a quality that shows up in such tasks as map reading, solving mathematical problems, and perceiving depth.

Depth perception is involved in driving and the ability to park a car. Which sex would you suppose has more auto accidents? They actually have about an equal number, but different types of accidents. Men have more major accidents in which cars are totally demolished. Men are aggressive on the roads, as in other areas of life. Women have more fender-bender types of accidents. Because their depth perception isn't usually as accurate as that of males, they have a tendency to misjudge distances and are more apt to crease or dent a fender.

I must emphasize that these tendencies are *generalities*. There is much crossing over that is considered within normal range. There is nothing abnormal about a woman who becomes a pilot, a race-car driver, or a university mathematics instructor.

Left-Brain, Right-Brain Sex Differences

The two cerebral hemispheres of the brain function differently. In a majority of individuals the right hemisphere specializes in verbal tasks, while the left hemisphere specializes in spatial perception. Is there a difference in how men and women use their brains? Definitely! This is part of the reason a man can't act more like a woman and a woman more like a man. Neuropsychologists now report that males and females differ in their use of these hemispheres. Males tend to specialize in the use of the spatially oriented left hemisphere, while females tend to use their left and right hemispheres equally.

This specialization takes place prenatally during fetal development. During the sixteenth to twenty-sixth week androgens are released through the mother and coat the left hemisphere of the male brain. The tiny left hemisphere of the male brain shrinks in size, which "sets" his brain to think more logically.

Connecting the two hemispheres of the brain is the corpus callosum, which is also affected by this bath of hormones. The corpus callosum, which allows lateral transmission between the two hemispheres, loses about 21 percent (or an estimated 25 million neurological fibers that make up the corpus callosum) of its connecting rods between the hemispheres. In other words, males can't talk to themselves across hemispheres as readily as females can.[7]

Because little girls don't get this chemical bath, they have quicker and easier access to both sides of the brain. What occurs during pregnancy sets the stage for men and women to "specialize" in two different ways of thinking. The left-brain dominance permits men to specialize in more logical, factual, analytical, and aggressive thought. Women tend to use the right side of the brain, which is the center for feelings, language, and communication skills. It is the more relational of the two sides.[8]

The two sides of the brain also control how we think. Each side specializes in certain tasks. The left side, being more logical, controls language and reading skills. It gathers information and logistically analyzes it step by step and helps us plan our lives. It processes things such as leaving early to drop books off at the library, where to park to have easy access to the doctor's office, whether to charge or pay cash for an item.

The left side wants to keep us organized, on time, sensible. It helps one read maps, place furniture in a new house, put a puzzle together, pack the trunk of a car, or solve a geometrical problem. The left side is analytical, sequential, concrete, rational, positive, and explicit. This explains why men are more logical and bottom-liners.

The right side is intuitive, spontaneous, emotional, visual, artistic, playful, holistic, and physical. It links facts together and comes up with magical solutions, what some might term intuition.

Those who focus more on plain facts, sound monotonous, and show little emotional expression are more left-brained. Those who ramble when they talk, jump from topic to topic, and rely on their feelings and emotions are more right-brained.

A woman uses her brain differently than a man does. She uses both sides of her brain simultaneously to solve a problem. The two halves work in cooperation. Even as infants, females have larger connectors between the two sides of the brain and can integrate information better than males. Thus they are more in tune with everything going on around them. This may partly explain how a woman can handle five tasks at a time while her husband reads the newspaper, totally oblivious to what is occurring within earshot.

Nothing beats love at first sight except love with insight.

Women tend to be more perceptive and outshine men at reading nonverbal cues. They are more interested in people and are able to pick up on feelings and sense the difference between what someone says and what he means or why she changes her mind so frequently. Women are better at integrating feelings with logic, beliefs with reality, and worship with theological reflection. Women are also better able to perform manual-dexterity tasks involving fine finger coordination, such as crocheting, knitting, embroidery work, and quilting.

Men are usually more curious as to how things work and are more exploratory. They like to examine and take things apart, and they excel in a wide range of skills that require mechanical manipulation. They have superior eye-hand coordination and three-dimensional perception, which may explain their fascination with computer games and video arcades.

This is not to say that a woman can't think logically or a man emotionally—only that the male brain is "wired" to be more analytical. Females are "wired" more globally or with the ability to scan both hemispheres faster. Males can access both hemispheres, but they just have to work harder at it.

Brain-sex differences explain another reason that women are more emotional. Every man is in touch with his emotions, but his emotions are accessed through his right hemisphere. Male emotions are very responsive to stories. Observe a group of males talking, and you'll hear them swapping stories. The stories have a can-you-top-this ring or a joshing quality. These men are still playing king of the mountain. Women rarely sit around swapping stories in the same fashion men do. But this is the way men get into their feelings.

Sex Differences in Spiritual Matters

Ministers need to be alert to how males connect with their feelings in order to affect men in their congregations. Men are called to discipleship through their feelings, not through their logic. Jesus, as Creator of male and female, understood this. This is why the Gospels are filled with stories—stories about Jesus and His healing ministry as well as His parables. Women could melt the hearts of their husbands by telling them stories in soap-opera fashion![9]

A widower is the only man whose wife is an angel.
—**Folk saying.**

In order to be spiritually healthy and strengthen the church, we should use both sides of our brain. Doctrines and dogma are stored more in the logical left hemisphere. But obeying rules and regulations will never save us. We must also live what the Bible teaches and have a personal relationship with the Lord. This is right hemisphere thinking.

The best theologies combine both doctrine and feeling. The charismatic movement is highly right-brained, or emotional, and would be strengthened by more attention to doctrine. Those who follow a highly traditional and more legalistic persuasion need to balance as well. They may prime their right hemisphere through stories or music. Music awakens their emotions and helps them become alive and vibrant.

Balance Translates Into Wholeness

Brain-sex differences make a woman more feeling-oriented and a man more logical. But these two differing perspectives are both needed in marriage in order to live healthy, well-rounded lives. Life would be difficult indeed if we didn't have feelings to balance out logic, or logic to balance feelings. In other words, male and female need each other in order to be whole. This is part of the attraction that holds male and female together.

How incredibly insightful of our Creator to put logical dominance in the male and emotional dominance in the female. God is the only total and truly complete person in the entire universe. Our God has both male and female characteristics in His completeness. When God created humans, I believe He took the more masculine side of His nature and gave it to the male. When He created a woman, He took the more feminine side of His nature and gave it to her. We see the image of God reproduced in marriage when two truly become one in the blending of personalities, thoughts, ideas, and goals, rather than just sexual oneness.

We cannot assume that everyone of the same sex will have identical emotional needs, behavior patterns, or patterns of thinking. But by studying general trends within each sex, we gain insights into how the other half often thinks and responds.

---

[1] James Dobson, *What Wives Wish Their Husbands Knew About Women* (Wheaton, Ill.: Tyndale Press, 1975), p. 133.

[2] *Ibid.,* p. 131.

[3] *Ibid.*

[4] From an interview of Dr. David Hernandez on *Focus on the Family,* "Sex Problems in Marriage," Nov. 4 and 5, 1982, Broadcast 450 (no longer available).

[5] Tim Hackler, "Women vs. Men: Are They Born Different?" *Mainliner,* May 1980, pp. 122-132.

[6] *Ibid.*

[7] Donald M. Joy, *Men Under Construction* (Wheaton, Ill.: Victor Books, 1993), p. 21.

[8] _____, "The Innate Differences Between Males and Females," Cassette CS099. (Radio program in which James C. Dobson, Ph.D., interviewed Dr. Joy, *Focus on the Family,* Colorado Springs, CO 80995-7451.)

[9] *Ibid.*

Chapter 13

What Men Should Understand About Women

A Woman Craves Affection

*A*ffection is central to a woman's relationship with her husband. Without affection, a woman feels distant, disconnected, and eventually totally alienated from her mate. Affection symbolizes emotional security to her. In effect, when a husband showers his wife with affection he says all over again, "You are important to me. I will always take care of you and protect you. You can count on me to be concerned about what concerns you. I'll always be there for you."

A hug—with no sexual overtones—is one way of filling a woman's greatest needs for affection. Most women enjoy a hug—unless it is accompanied by sexual overtones. If the hug includes grasping and grabbing, she begins to think he has sex on his mind, not affection. In his mind the two may be closely connected, but not so for her. Affection must precede sex for her.

The first step to becoming more affectionate is to learn as much as you can about the emotional needs of your wife. Secondly, ask your wife how she would most like to have you show affection. Better than anyone else, she knows what displays of affection would be the most meaningful. Initially she may be surprised by such a request, but unless she is already deeply hurt by a lack of affection, she will probably respond warmly.

The third step is to practice being affectionate. Don't build your wife's hopes with good intentions and then not follow through. Men sometimes think that affection is unnecessary. Demonstrations of "mushy stuff" only embarrass him. "She knows I love her, and I shouldn't have to keep telling her," he says. "She knows I'm not the affectionate type."

So if you aren't naturally an affectionate, demonstrative person, it may take time for affectionate behavior to come naturally or become a habit without conscious thought. Begin with affectionate gestures which are easiest for you and then move to the ones you find a little less natural. Don't give up when a new habit is difficult or makes you feel uncomfortable. Remember that the more you practice, the easier a behavior will become—even one that made you uncomfortable to begin with.

Eventually you will enjoy meeting your wife's needs for affection. You'll be concerned about her needs and about meeting them. She will love and appreciate you more, and you'll both be winners.

Take your wife in your arms and hug her. But before you do, tame and discipline those hands. In case you are out of ideas on how to be affectionate, here are a few winners:

- Write her a love note and tape it to the bathroom mirror.
- Surprise her with a gift for no reason.
- Use a thoughtful message to invite her for a dinner date at a special restaurant.
- Present her with a bouquet of flowers and enclose a card.
- Tell her how nice her hair looks, or how pretty her eyes are, or how lovely . . .
- Give her a hug and kiss before you get out of bed in the morning.
- Smile and wink at her.
- Give her a hug and kiss when you come home at night.
- Ask her to go for a walk with you after dinner.
- Give her a foot rub.

A Woman Needs to Talk to Feel Close

Men would do well to understand the female need to talk—especially about their feelings and problems. When a woman talks, she is usually not seeking advice, solutions, or answers. She is simply exploring her feelings. When this necessary exploration is cut off, it short-circuits the process and she feels alienated from her mate. A woman talks in a search for intimacy, to gain her partner's empathy and understanding, as she would with her women friends. A man can make a real impact by simply listening to her, without interrupting, without offering advice.

A woman talks about problems to feel better. She talks about present problems, problems that may never happen, and unsolvable problems. She finds relief from stress through talking about problems. When she feels that she is heard, she feels validated, listened to, and cared about. Even though the problems are still there, her stress level goes down.

A woman also discusses the problems of her family and friends. *This is normal female behavior.* She is expressing her care and concern. What she is really doing is thinking out loud. Women solve problems by expressing out loud what they are feeling. Putting her thoughts and feelings into words allows her female intuition to kick in.

Men do not understand this phenomenon because when a man brings out a problem for discussion he is searching for a solution. When a woman shares upset feelings or verbalizes problems, a man mistakenly assumes that she is seeking expert advice; and out of love and consideration he tries to help. He has trouble understanding why, after he has tried to solve things for her, she often gets more upset. A woman can appreciate advice given at the right time, but not when she is upset.

Even if a man does not feel it his duty to solve the problem, he may feel she is blaming him for the problem—in which case he may attempt to protect himself from attack. The more defensive he becomes, the more upset she gets.

Another tactic confusing to men is the female tendency to give volumes of detail. His male mind thinks if he has to solve her problem he must listen to all these details to give a logical solution. He struggles to find relevance to the problem, especially when there appears to be no logical order to what she is explaining. As she talks, he searches for the bottom line so he can formulate his best solution—which he can't do until he hears the entire story.

Some women are not beautiful—they only look as though they are.

Her tendency to give extensive detail and to jump from story to story frustrates him. When a woman knows she is married to a bottom-line man, she can give him the outcome first to reduce his frustration level. She can also remind him before she begins that she just needs to talk and doesn't need a solution.

A woman wants to talk about more than the children and bills. She wants to tell her partner all her "secrets" and have him listen to her problems. When a man only listens passively, it isn't enough for her. To get back at him, she may provoke an argument over nothing and blow it all out of proportion. When she gets like this, rather than attempting to straighten her out, just listen.

Sometimes a woman harps on irrelevant points. She may drag up situations that happened five or 10 years ago. Rather than arguing, just listen. In most cases, she doesn't want to win the argument. She only wants to feel that you hear her and care about her.

Your wife's ultimate desire is to have a relationship free enough so she can talk with you about the trivia of life that hurts or pleases her, to talk about everyday happenings, what she did and said, the children's successes and failures, worries over a parent's health, what the boss said, and what happened after she ran out of gas. When a woman gets this type of listening response from her husband, she feels heard. She has her feelings validated and accepted.

When your wife feels free to talk to you about anything, she will feel an intimacy and closeness that goes beyond her wildest dreams. You will be not only her lover, but her dearest friend and companion.

A Woman Needs Honesty, Openness, and Trust

When a woman cannot trust her man implicitly to give her accurate information about what he is doing with his time and money (as well as everything else), she has no basis for a relationship with him. Trust is foundational to a Highly Effective Marriage. Without honesty and trust there can be no openness between the couple, and every conversation will be inhibited. If she discovers he has lied to her, not given her truthful information, or told her only part of the story, this erodes her trust in him. If she senses he is not telling the truth, or not telling all of the story, she puts up her guard.

Some men are born dishonest. Telling "fibs" becomes a part of everyday life. By the time they become adults, lying is deeply entrenched. They fabricate stories about things that never happened, distort the truth, and cannot distinguish truth from fantasy. Such dishonesty radically disrupts a marriage.

Other men tell lies to avoid trouble. Let's say a wife asks her husband if he has paid a certain bill. He hasn't done it yet, but plans to, so he says, "It's taken care of. Don't worry." He means to take care of it but forgets. She finds out later she has been lied to. When he gets caught, he acts repentant and will say and do anything to get her to "forgive and forget." The one who lies to avoid trouble doesn't lie all the time, but only when he is about to get caught under pressure and stress.

Still another lies to "protect" his wife from unpleasant realities—being fired or laid off from his position, borrowing money, a stupid purchase, or being unable to make the house payment—without telling her. He tells her everything is fine to maintain peace, when in fact their lives are coming apart at the seams.

In each case, he feels dishonesty is justified in order to spare his wife. But at what cost? She remains unaware of what her husband is going through. He's irritable, depressed, and moody, and she can't figure out why. What will happen to the marriage when she finds out he lost his job or borrowed money without her knowledge? Then the two will have to face a much larger and potentially disruptive situation. The false sense of security created by protecting a wife from the truth can be shattered in a few seconds and do irreparable damage.

When a man communicates openly and truthfully with his wife, he contributes to her emotional security. If he is always truthful with her about everything, even when a crisis hits, he knows in advance she can handle it. It may be painful for both to hear the truth, but the truth will not drive her away. It enables her, however, to know how to adjust to the situation in order to stand by her husband's side and encourage him as he threads his way through a difficult time.

One man and his wife worked out a signal when total honesty was needed. One would say, "On your word?" That signaled the other that total honesty was required, without game-playing or any evasion of truth. Every couple needs a similar signal so that total honesty can be quickly had when needed. Without the assurance that a wife can totally trust her husband, the relationship will limp along until it eventually staggers into trouble.

When one partner has had an affair, the relationship can be rebuilt only through this type of honesty. The couple will need counseling with a qualified counselor who understands the importance of total honesty once an affair has been confessed. Confession allows for purging for the guilty party and provides the environment needed to rebuild a stable marriage. But the injured party must regain trust once again.

Before asking for total disclosure or delivering it yourself, you need to ask yourself some insightful questions: Do I (or does my partner) really need to hear that? What will be the effect on our relationship if I do tell? For what reasons do I need to tell (or hear) that information? Will total disclosure help or hinder in this situation?[1]

A beautiful lady is an accident of nature. A beautiful old lady is a work of art.—Louis Nizer.

Disclosure of adultery and other personal problems must be approached on an individual basis. The wrong move could throw you into a crushing catastrophe. Seek the advice of a professional Christian marital therapist before making any decisions relative to the future, and do it before too many irreparable choices have been made.

Often a man confesses and immediately demands trust from his wife. Trust cannot be turned on and off like a light. When one has been guilty of an affair, trust can be rebuilt—but not overnight. It takes time. The offending party should provide daily information about his whereabouts, accounting for all activities so they can easily be verified if needed. He might write out a schedule of appointments for her to see daily. Should the schedule change, a phone call would alert her to the change in plans. I also recommend that the guilty party participate in a weekly "accountability group" where accountability for actions and behaviors to godly people who care is required. Accountability partners hold the individual up in prayer, yet exercise a "tough love" approach so it doesn't happen again. In addition to these steps, if a man commits himself to daily Bible study and prayer, it signifies he is on his way to trustworthiness.

A marriage can survive many setbacks and struggles. But the one thing a marriage cannot survive is a lack of honesty.

PMS: The Real Story

PMS (premenstrual syndrome) is a physiological problem affecting a woman's body, which in turn impacts everyone close to her. Some health professionals list PMS as a primary contributor to marital breakdown. Common problems and struggles are complicated and magnified many times over when PMS strikes.

Ongoing marital struggles are difficult enough to endure and survive when a husband understands and supports his wife when PMS strikes. Unfortunately, many men do not understand PMS and often blame their wives. Both need to understand that the wife is not crazy and that it's not all in her head. They also need to understand that there *is* something they can do about PMS.

PMS is defined as a physical and psychological disorder that occurs regularly during the same phase of a woman's menstrual cycle (between ovulation and the onset of menstruation), followed by a symptom-free phase. Common PMS symptoms include fatigue, depression, tension, headaches, and mood swings. Other symptoms related to PMS are both psychological and physical.

Psychological	*Physical*
anger	bloating
sudden mood swings	weight gain
emotional over-responsiveness	acne
unexplained crying	dizziness
irritability	migraines
anxiety	diarrhea
forgetfulness	sweating
decreased concentration	breast tenderness
confusion	joint and muscle pain
withdrawal	backaches
sensitivity to rejection	changes in sex drive
food cravings	depression
constipation	nightmares
suicidal thoughts	shakiness
	seizures

To truly qualify as PMS, symptoms must be severe enough to interfere with some aspect of daily living. They should not be used as a catchall for inexcusable behavior. Genuine PMS sufferers experience their symptoms cyclically and repeatedly in direct relationship to the menstrual cycle and do not experience the same symptoms after the onset of menstruation.

The symptoms occur monthly, generally within seven to 14 days prior to menstruation. Symptoms may seem to worsen as menstruation approaches and subside at the onset or after several days of menstruation. A symptom-free phase usually follows menses. Symptoms can last for a couple days to a couple weeks.

Medical experts estimate that up to 80 percent of all women have had PMS symptoms at some point, but only 8 to 10 percent experience symptoms severe enough to require medical treatment.[2] Although there is no quick fix for PMS, there are several things that can and should be done to help both husband and wife cope:

1. *Chart the menstrual cycle.* This is the best way to get the facts and determine whether you are dealing with true PMS or something else. It's the only way to get objective information and detect a pattern.

2. *Become informed.* Both husband and wife need to find out as much as they can about PMS. Husbands need to accompany their wives to medical appointments, asking questions and gaining information about her specific symptoms. Read brochures and articles about PMS.

3. *Eat healthfully.* For many PMS sufferers, diet makes a big difference. A week or two before the onset of menstruation, adjust your diet in the following ways.

    a. Eliminate sugar (including honey, syrup, and additives such as fructose or sucrose), caffeine (in coffee, chocolate, and cola drinks), artificial sweeteners, cigarettes, and alcohol.

    b. Do include in your diet whole grains (bread, pasta, brown rice), dried beans, nuts, fresh vegetables (especially spinach), and fruit.

    c. Avoid salty and smoked foods, and dairy products. If bloating is a problem, limit fruit and eliminate fruit juices.[3]

4. *Exercise regularly.* Many experts agree that exercise is one of the best treatments for PMS.[4]

5. *Relax.* Meditation, deep breathing, walks, massage, or hot baths also reduce tension.

What Husbands Can Do. Learn what kind of support your wife wants during this time; it differs from woman to woman. Encourage her to walk, and walk with her. Give her a break from household chores. Whip up a healthy meal for her, or take her out to eat. Save earth-shattering news or arguments for a time when she can cope more rationally.

Don't take what happens during her mood swings personally. This only complicates the situation. Recognize that PMS is a normal part of her life and accept it without being devastated by some of the things she says or does. Express your thoughts and feelings without blame or accusations.

Presently there are no specific drugs for treatment of PMS. A new study by the *New England Journal of Medicine* says that "PMS is the result of both hormone level changes and their interaction with central neurotransmitters, such as serotonin." Judith Wortman, Ph.D., is involved in ongoing research to explore the relationship of serotonin to women's mood and eating changes, including those experienced during PMS.

Serotonin is a natural chemical in the brain that regulates mood and appetite. Wortman's research shows that serotonin levels are usually lower than normal during the PMS time frame, causing women to experience the mood swings and appetite changes associated with PMS.[5] PMS doesn't have to tear a family apart. Women need to learn how to communicate their physical and emotional needs to their husbands. And this needs to be done at a time when they are not experiencing PMS. Husbands must also learn how to communicate to their wives how PMS is affecting them.

Shown on the next two pages are two PMS calendar months. The first shows how one woman, using the symbols given, charted her symptoms for January and February. Once symptoms are charted, a pattern can be detected and predicted in advance for the next month. Charting symptoms can be of value to both husband and wife, as well as contributing to the preservation of their relationship during this difficult time.

A Woman Needs Financial Security

Jokes abound about women marrying men for their money. But a shred of truth lies within them. A woman needs her husband to earn enough money to support her. Women have a right to expect financial support from their husbands, since God ordained that the husband provide for the family.

Many women today work outside the home. They claim they want and need a career in order to be happy. But I also hear from many who resent working, especially when forced to do so in order to pay basic living expenses.

Many married women are in the workforce so they can "keep up with the Joneses." The majority of these two-job couples have set a standard of living beyond their needs to be happy. If their standard of living could be reduced to include a smaller but comfortable home—the husband would be able to be home with his family more, and the wife would not have to work outside the home during critical child-rearing years.

Women should be free to choose a career if they want one. But they should be able to depend on their husband's salary to cover basic living expenses to support the family. Families need to learn to live on the husband's salary rather than depending on two salaries to make basic monthly payments. Most families are only a month or two away from financial disaster. If a major crisis hit either wage earner, the family would lose everything.

A couple can live on one salary—maybe not according to the standard to which they might aspire, but it can and should be done. I highly recommend Larry Burkett's book *Debt-free Living,*[6] which certainly changed Harry's and my life. Under Burkett's tutelage we paid off our house in many years' less time,

PMS MENSTRUAL CALENDAR
Month: *January*

Sunday	Monday	Tuesday	Wednesday	Thursday	Friday	Saturday
					1	2
3	4	5	6	7	8	9 BP BLT FT CRY
10 BP FT CRY	11 BP BLT CRY	12 HD CMP BP BLT	13 HD CMP BP CRY	14 HD THIRST BP BLT	15 P	16 P
17 P	18 P	19 P	20	21	22	23
24	25	26	27	28	29	30
31						

PMS MENSTRUAL CALENDAR
Month: *February*

Sunday	Monday	Tuesday	Wednesday	Thursday	Friday	Saturday
	1	2	3	4	5	6
						DP BP
7	8	9	10	11	12	13
DP BP CRY	DP BP CRY	BP BLT ANX	ANX BP BLT	ANX CMP BP BLT	HD CMP BP THIRST	HD THIRST BP CRY
14	15	16	17	18	19	20
P	P	P				
21	22	23	24	25	26	27
28						

KEY:
Breast Pain = BP   Headache = HD   Fighting = FT
Bloatedness = BLT   Depression = DP   Cramps = CMP
Crying = CRY   Anxiety = ANX   Period = P

Chart adapted from Rene L. Witt, *PMS—What Every Woman Should Know About Pre-menstrual Syndrome* (New York: Stein & Day, 1983).

saved thousands of dollars in interest, and actually owned our own home debt-free. We each hold only one credit card, which is paid off monthly. Although we eventually bought a new home, it is our only debt, and we are making extra payments on the principal to pay it off as rapidly as possible.

Men must recognize that a woman's need for financial security goes deep into her soul and is vitally connected to the respect she holds for her husband. A man does not have this need. He finds contentment in providing adequately for the financial needs of his family.

Some men actually resent it or feel threatened when their wives work, especially if their wives earn more than they do. A man usually wants to see himself as the primary wage earner. Regardless of her wage-earning ability, a woman usually wants her husband to earn enough money to support and care for her, and feels it is not her place to support him.

Think through what you really *need* rather than what you *want.* The things we want but don't really need can become our own worst enemy. Men sometimes work themselves into an early grave trying to provide a standard of living that not only doesn't contribute to marital happiness, but actually brings on marital stress and disharmony.

Some men naively think that by working hard to earn more money and provide living on a grander scale, they are proving their love to their wives. But once a woman feels neglected, sensing that her husband puts wealth, status, and his job before her, feelings of resentment build.

When a man's income isn't sufficient to support his family, even after careful evaluation and cutting back unnecessary expenses, he should improve his job skills. Every couple needs to come to grips with what they can afford. A budget helps determine where your money is going and where you can cut back.

A Woman Needs a Commitment to Family

A woman needs her husband to understand how much she needs him to commit time and attention to the family unit. A man should recognize that when he commits himself to spending quality time with his children, he automatically strengthens his marriage. His wife will respect and adore him for his efforts. Quality time involves time spent with a child other than in child-care tasks (such as feeding and dressing) in which positive interaction, and bonds of love and respect are developed.

What activities might a family engage in to enjoy quality time and meet the goal of strengthening bonds of love and respect? Here are some suggestions:

- Bike riding
- Reading aloud to the children before bedtime
- Attending church
- Teaching the children about financial planning
- Family meetings
- Conducting family worship and engaging the children in religious activities
- Board games such as Uno
- Sporting events
- A family project such as building a go-cart

Demonstrate to the children that it is fun to be together as a family. Show them how cooperation, sharing, respect, and encouragement are achieved. Children under the age of 12 can usually be guided into family activities without a problem. But once children enter their teen years, activities with peers usually take precedence. Parents of teens can only *attempt* to interest their children in well-planned events designed to interest them. If you begin family activities when your children are young, they will grow up with the concept.

Perhaps the most important concept that men need to learn is to work *with* their wives and not against them in the discipline and training of the children. When a child wants a privilege, it is granted only when Mom and Dad have discussed it in private and can deliver an agreed-upon answer. When children know that they cannot play one parent against the other, they frequently stop challenging behavior. All privileges should be mutually agreed upon by Mom and Dad, or no action at all should be taken.

Sometimes it is difficult for men to take time for their families. They get involved in careers, church functions, responsibilities, and hobbies because these things are exciting to them. There are times when a man prefers working to going home because it satisfies his ego needs.

Every man needs to sort through his priorities. If changes need to be made, now is the time. The years are slipping by. Children grow up. Do your children really know you, or do they think of you as the man who sleeps here sometimes? Does your wife feel neglected? Unless you make some changes, one day you may wake up to find your children grown and your wife gone. There will be nothing you can to do to bring them back.

A *Godfather* movie ends with a decrepit old man, rich beyond measure in material possessions but devoid of human love, sitting alone in a rocker out in the cold. What good is success and a big empty house?

---

[1] For more information regarding what should and should not be discussed, see *How to Talk So Your Mate Will Listen and Listen So Your Mate Will Talk*, pp. 177, 178.

[2] University of Pennsylvania Health Systems, 1997, http://www.obgyn.upenn.edu/pms/pms.html.

[3] Arnot Ogden Medical Center, "What Women Should Know About Premenstrual Syndrome," http://www.aomc.org/HOD2/general/general-PREMENST.html

[4] *Ibid.*

[5] Stephanie Bender, "The Once-a-Month-Blues," *Focus on the Family Magazine,* May 1996, pp. 9-12.

[6] Larry Burkett, *Debt-Free Living* (Chicago: Moody Press, 1989).

Chapter 14

WHAT WOMEN SHOULD UNDERSTAND ABOUT MEN

Male Ego Strength

don't understand my husband any more," the distressed wife confided. "He never used to mind when I made suggestions about his clothes, but now he flies off the handle if I say anything about what he wears. He used to willingly help me on occasion around the house; but since I've gone back to work and really need his help, it's like pulling teeth to get help out of him."

This woman's husband was suffering from what might be called a damaged ego. Intellectually he agreed that his wife should go back to work. But emotionally he had trouble accepting it. His sensitive ego suffered when he realized he could no longer support the family without his wife's help. He felt inadequate as the family provider and became defensive and critical to every real or imagined threat. Because she did not understand his ego was at stake, this wife made things worse by complaining.

No man is entirely immune to ego problems. Today's highly competitive, complex society continuously subjects men to major assaults on their masculinity. Women have ego problems also, but a man's ego is far more vulnerable. The strength of the male ego strongly affects the health of the marital relationship. The man with a healthy self-image and strong sense of his worth and masculinity is far happier and more competent in coping with life than the male plagued by doubts and feelings of inadequacy.[1]

The strength of a man's ego is subject to frequent fluctuations. Someone has stated that it is like walking a tightrope over an abyss of possible failure every day. Men live an inch from losing all the time. Today's society sets a high standard for its men. The male of yesteryear was considered adequate if he provided for his family. Today providing isn't enough. He must reach the top and be the best in his field. The competition and corresponding tension faced at work can etch great holes in his ego.

Today's world also expects him to be a sensitive husband, a good lover to his wife, an involved father, the life of every party, and excel in some leisure activity as well. It isn't enough for him to *strive* toward these goals; he must *achieve* these goals.

Men return home after a hectic day at work in need of balm for their bruised egos. Far too often they find the opposite. Some women blame their husbands for everything that goes wrong, or undermine them in subtle ways—often without realizing it—by complaining about the income they earn. When a man hears disparaging remarks about his earning capacity, his only tangible measure of success as a breadwinner, his ego suffers. Even worse is the wife who flaunts her own contribution to the family income.

The biggest challenge to the male ego undoubtedly takes place in the bedroom. Today if a man doesn't satisfy his wife every time they make love, he considers himself a failure, even though this goal is unrealistic. When things are going well at work and elsewhere, he can shrug off criticism of his love-making. But when his ego has been dented in some other area, such disapproval can spark days of friction and tension.

Since men still aren't expected to cry or let their emotions hang out, what all this means is that a man can suffer from damaging blows to his ego without appearing to wince. He may only grunt when complimented on his appearance, or shrug when his golf game isn't up to par; but don't think these words haven't gone deep. You can safely assume he's hurting twice as badly as he admits. A man will often disguise feelings of inadequacy by boasting about his accomplishments. This was so embarrassing to one wife that she put down her husband publicly, unaware she'd hit him in his most vulnerable spot—his sagging ego.

One of the most vital services a woman can perform for her husband, her marriage, and herself is to fortify her husband's ego when he is under attack. She can take pressure off him when he's under stress and deal with daily problems quietly by herself. The woman who finds something praiseworthy in her man can help bolster his sagging ego. As long as the praise is genuine, it won't matter what is said.

Express appreciation for everything he has a part in providing—including the children. And encourage him to open up. The more freely he can talk with his wife about himself, the more secure he'll be. Listen with an open, uncritical ear.

The woman who is able to heal her husband's wounded ego becomes the most important person in the world to him. She will earn his undying gratitude and an affection that will pay rich dividends the rest of her married life.

A Man Needs an Organized, Tranquil Home

A group of men were once asked what they most wanted at home. Men did not long for expensive furniture, swimming pools, or a Lexus in the driveway.

What they wanted most was *tranquillity*. Competition in the workplace is fierce. The stress of pleasing a boss, surviving professionally, and beating inflation is so severe that a man needs a haven to which he can return. This puts tranquillity at the top of his list of needs. And who can find tranquillity in the midst of disorganization, clutter, and mess? Just as a woman needs financial security, a man needs an organized, tranquil home environment.

A man has a need and a right to expect that his wife handle household tasks and the children in an organized, efficient manner. So deep is a man's need for a well-managed home that some men fantasize about coming home to an attractive, well-groomed wife who greets him lovingly and pleasantly at the door. The home is orderly and smells wonderful. Dinner is ready.

In the fantasy he joins his wife for a candlelight dinner accompanied by soft music in the background. During the meal she does not hit him with any major crisis. After dinner the entire family goes for a walk. Later he puts the children to bed without hassles. He and his wife relax and watch a little television together, talk a bit, and are off to bed at a reasonable hour.[2]

Many a man feverishly treads water at work, exhausting himself trying to stay one step ahead of the game to meet job pressures. He barely makes it through the day—but to look at him you'd never guess it. He wears a smile, jokes, and is polite. Inside, however, he's coming apart. He can't wait to get out of the office and away from the stress that tears him apart.

He needs a home environment that offers a respite from work pressures. He needs a wife to simplify his life once he walks through the door. This is not to say that he can't contribute to chores at home; but if he is to provide financially for the family, then she needs to supply a home environment that provides the rest and peace he needs.

This is true even in marriages in which the wife works part- or full-time. He may be willing to adjust his schedule to some degree and help with certain tasks, but his need for a peaceful and orderly home doesn't go away.

This presents a dilemma for marriages in which both husband and wife work outside the home to make ends meet. She comes home as exhausted as he is. Who is going to fix the meals, clean the house, care for the children, wash the clothes, and care for the hundreds of other tasks that make families operate?

His logical left hemisphere tells him that she is as tired as he is and can't do it all. He may attempt to help some. Even then, research shows that only about 5 percent of white-collar men help their wives with household tasks.[3] But in doing so, a man shifts into overload. The wife has been operating on overload ever since she went back to work. The result? Endless arguments and angry outbursts. Smoldering issues erupt, resulting in hurt feelings and resentment.

Studies show that marriages are more successful when a woman works no more than 20 hours a week or less when children are small. Divorce rates double when mothers work full-time outside the home. The demands on a woman are too great when she works full-time and attempts to meet her children's needs, her husband's needs, and to care adequately for a home.[4]

And men, just because you need a well-maintained home doesn't let you off the hook entirely. You still have a part to play by pitching in and sharing the load and also by not contributing unnecessarily to clutter, chores, and disorganization.

I am a firm believer that women should learn how to manage a family and home—to cook, clean, and maintain a clutter-free living space (or learn how to delegate these tasks). I've written a book on home management: *Get Organized— Seven Secrets to Sanity for Stressed Women*. But women also need to learn something even more important in creating a tranquil home atmosphere—how to encourage a husband when he's down, how to listen to him, forgive him, laugh with him, play with him, and make his home a happy, contented place.

I wouldn't even venture an estimate regarding the number of marital arguments that focus on clutter and disorganization.

—Nancy Van Pelt.

Over the years many divorced women have whined, "I kept the house spotless and I was a fabulous cook, and the dirty rat left me!" Learning to manage a family effectively comprises a lofty goal for a woman; but a spotless home can never replace the warm, friendly, loving playmate a husband needs.

In an interview Mamie Eisenhower was once asked what she believed was the greatest contribution she made to Ike's career as president of the United States. She felt it was her ability to make his home a haven he could come to after the rigors of the day. Whether her home was in military quarters or the grandeur of the White House, she felt her greatest contribution was to create what was, in the fullest sense of the word, "home."

What matters to a man is not so much polished tables, spotless windows, and perfect decor, but the aura of a home—the degree of restfulness and warmth it offers. To a large degree it is the wife who creates this. And a woman's mood or attitude toward her husband and children is the most important part of this atmosphere.

A Man Appreciates an Attractive Wife

A wife's physical attractiveness is more important to a man than most women recognize. An attractive wife is one who resembles the woman he married, not someone who has allowed excessive weight to pile up. And there is no excuse for letting your hair go or dressing like a bag lady.

Many women do not like hearing this. They refuse to change their eating habits, and add 10 pounds yearly to their ballooning figure. Their husbands are turned off, lose interest in sex, and become less affectionate.

However, men, don't be too hard on your wife if she has gained a few pounds. Men can lose weight more easily than women because their fat is distributed differently. Men also have more muscle than women. The greater the proportion of muscle to fat, the easier it is to burn off fat.

God created men to be stimulated sexually visually. They like to look and enjoy what they see. If a woman lets her appearance go, her husband will not be stimulated to look at her often, and when he does he may be turned off or even repulsed. Suddenly he may notice other women, which may make him feel guilty. Even if he doesn't seek an affair, he becomes vulnerable to one.

A wife can guard against this by making a reasonable effort to remain attractive. A simple test of your attractiveness is how much he enjoys looking at you and what he does after he looks. Sexual stimulation should follow visual stimulation. Even if he doesn't seek a sexual encounter, most husbands fondle or caress their wives when they find them physically attractive.[5]

Women also desire attractiveness in their husbands. But an attractive husband does not rank high on their list of most important needs.

It is possible for a woman to make a dramatic difference in her appearance by applying a little makeup to enhance her God-given natural beauty, especially as she grows older. If you are overweight and cannot or will not lose weight (since I have a weight problem I fully understand how difficult this can be), you will need to pay closer attention to how you dress. A slim, petite woman can throw on most any outfit and look attractive. An overweight woman can look attractive, but she must work harder to achieve that look.

Casual jeans and a T-shirt look cute on a trim woman. But there is nothing cute about an overweight woman with bulging thighs and an oversized shirt draped in useless attempts to hide "love handles." Larger women can be attractive, but only when they pay close attention to the cut and lines of their clothing, along with color and design. Most important of all, dress to be attractive to your husband.

Edie said it had been a long, cold winter, and she had practically lived in her old sweater and jeans. But one afternoon she decided to shower and change into an attractive dress before her husband arrived. When her husband got home, he asked, "Expecting visitors?" Her son came in and asked, "Going somewhere, Mom?" and the small boy from next door, a "regular" in front of their TV, looked up as she passed through the room and asked, "Who was that?" These varying reactions became a valuable lesson to Edie.

In the long run you will find that it feels good to be an attractive woman at all

A man's need

for physical

attractiveness in

a woman is

profound.—Willard

F. Harley.

times. You need not be a startling beauty, but you can do your best with what you have. By making the most of what you have, you can achieve a stunning appearance. To a large degree an attractive woman is not so much born as made.

A woman's attractiveness is vitally important to the success of her marriage. Revitalizing your attractiveness will do wonders for your self-esteem. When you look better, you feel better. And when you see the response of your husband to the "new you," you will feel an inner satisfaction. You'll fulfill a need in him he may never have dared express, and make large deposits in his EBA.

A Man Needs Recreational Companionship

In his book *His Needs, Her Needs* W. F. Harley lists recreational companionship as a man's second most pressing need—second only to his primary need of sexual fulfillment. I concur with Harley's assessment, because it is through sharing activities with a woman that a man finds intimacy.[6]

Little girls generally play with a best friend and share "secrets." After she gets married she expects intimate and meaningful heart-to-heart talks with her husband, whom she wants to be her best friend. She feels tremendous emotional satisfaction from these talks, but he may sense real trouble, since they have to keep discussing things.

In contrast, little boys more frequently play in larger groups, and often outdoors. There is less talk among boys and more "doing" when they get together. Boys enjoy activities. It hardly matters whether the activity is throwing rocks, shooting baskets, kicking a can, or swinging from a tree—males are conditioned from boyhood to enjoy getting together and participating in some activity, with much less "talk." As an adult a man transfers this longing to his wife—he wants to enjoy going places and doing things with her. Sharing an activity with her fulfills his longing to have her join him in what he is doing. He feels close and gains a sense of intimacy.

Women are experts at joining their boyfriends and fiancés for activities during their dating years. But once married and established at home, they no longer feel the need to accompany their husbands in the pursuit of games and recreation. They feel they have "more important things" to do now—such as cleaning the house, cooking, and caring for children.

But women who let opportunities pass to go with their husbands as they pursue leisure-time activities may find that in spite of all their efforts and longings, they may never build an intimate relationship with their husbands. Such women may be quick to point the finger of blame at their husbands; but the deciding finger is pointed in their own direction. These women never considered it important to take time to "play" with their husbands.

When it comes to having fun and pursuing activities, men and women have very different tastes. Men, for the most part, seem to enjoy activities that involve more risk, adventure, and violence than women do. Men enjoy such diverse activities as football, boxing, hunting, fishing, hang gliding, scuba diving, snowmobiling, skydiving, four-wheeling, and motorcycle racing. Their taste in movies differs from women's. Usually they prefer "tough" movies—movies dealing with sports, politics, cars, and violence.

Women usually enjoy more relational activities. A favorite activity for most women is going out to dinner. While a woman sits across the table from her husband, it allows for lots of eye contact and conversation while she talks about people and relationships. To her, this proves involvement, interest, and caring. Sharing this with someone she loves provides closeness and intimacy. It is important to understand how each partner finds closeness and intimacy, for these ways can be very different.

Among the five basic male needs, spending recreational time with his wife is second only to sex for the typical husband. —**Willard F. Harley.**

Unless a woman learns to adapt, and moves with her husband into recreational activities, he'll go alone or with his buddies. He may not leave his wife or stop loving her, but she will certainly cramp his style. It also means that some of the things he enjoys most will never be shared with his wife. If his wife refuses to allow him to pursue his recreational pursuits and forces him to stay home, he may begin to resent the time he is home. She may resent it when he goes on a weekend fishing or hunting trip, thinking he should be spending that time with her and the children.

Men are often fooled during dating days. They think they have found the perfect companion, one who truly shares an interest in what they love. After marriage, when a wife refuses to go with her husband, he's often disappointed. So he goes alone.

For example, perhaps his wife is reluctant to join his bowling league with him. He goes by himself. He meets Bonnie, who loves to bowl. They share some laughs, talk about their bowling scores over a cup of coffee, and before you know it are involved in a full-blown affair. If this scene plays out till its tragic end, the husband will divorce his wife and marry Bonnie—just to satisfy this need.

The husband who follows this course needs to beware of another frequent occurrence. Once married to Bonnie, he may find her interest in bowling lags and she really prefers concerts, picnics, walks in the park, romantic movies, cultural events, and shopping.

Women openly share their desire to have their husbands meet their needs for romantic attention and affection. But women must recognize another side of the coin—a man's need for a companion in his recreational pursuits. A woman who does not recognize or satisfy this need will miss the opportunity of becoming his best friend and having a lot of fun with him.

A Man Needs Stress Relief

Research confirms that stress is more deadly for men than for women.

- Two times as many men die from combined heart disease problems than do women.
- Pneumonia and influenza cause about three times as many male deaths as female.
- Accidents and adverse drug effects kill three times more males than females.
- The ratio of male to female suicides is three males to one female.
- Thirty percent more males die from cancer than females (cancer can be stress-related).
- Men live shorter lives than women by eight years.
- Men exhibit more stress-related health problems such as hypertension, arteriosclerosis, heart attack, and heart failure.[7]

Stress is a result of anything that annoys, threatens, excites, worries, angers, frustrates, or challenges self-esteem. These events, whether pleasant or unpleasant, mobilize a man's body for either flight or fight. The brunt of stress is born by the heart, putting men at risk for heart disease.

Male stress originates in four main areas: (1) body image; (2) career concerns; (3) family concerns; and (4) the inability to share feelings or express emotions.[8]

Both men and women suffer stress, but men have a higher death rate from stress. Women need to understand the unique stresses that men face. If they wish to live a long, happy life with their husbands, they should learn how to minimize that stress.

Heart attacks are more common in men. Male susceptibility is not just physiological but also psychological. The type A personality—the high-achieving, competitive man who pushes himself to the limit—is the most prone to heart attacks. This man rides an endless roller coaster to achieve. He crams his life with more activities to accomplish in less time. His sense of competition is intensely out of balance and follows him from work to leisure activities, his family, and his friendships. Relaxation appears impossible for this man.

Type A male personalities are five times more likely to have heart attacks than type B personalities. Three arterial diseases are believed to be initiated by type A behavior: migraines, high blood pressure, and coronary heart disease.[9]

Another danger to men involves arguing. According to psychologists who have studied the reactions of couples when discussing problems in their marriage, men react with a greater increase in heart rate to the stress of arguments. Therefore, when conflicts become prolonged, men are more likely to avoid them or withdraw in order to protect themselves from increased adrenaline.[10]

Men tend to release anger in spurts rather than in slow-moving negotiations. Such adaptive behavior helps keep stress at a distance. When a wife thinks her husband is withdrawing from an encounter he may be reacting to a built-in, health-protecting device. Heated arguing can be hazardous to a man's health!

While under stress men withdraw and become notoriously quiet. John Gray, in *Men Are From Mars and Women Are From Venus,* refers to this male reaction as "going into his cave."[11] A man's reaction is opposite from his mate's need to *talk* about her problems. When he comes home from a hard day at work he wants to forget about the pressure and finds relief by wrapping the newspaper around himself.

He needs to think about his problems and mull them over in an attempt to find a solution. If he can't find a solution, he'll look for an outlet that will allow him to forget—such as watching TV, going to a ball game, or working out at the gym. By taking his mind off his problems he gradually de-stresses.

When a man is stressed he often becomes so focused on his stress that he loses awareness of other things. He often becomes distant, forgetful, and unresponsive. The larger the problem, the more magnified his absorption by the problem. At such times it is difficult for him to give his wife and family the attention they need. His problems and stress hold him in a vise, and he is powerless to release himself until he finds a solution. Since he won't talk about it, his wife feels left out and ignored and takes this personally—as women tend to do in most issues. Very likely he is not aware of how withdrawn he has become.

A woman will find this male tendency easier to live with when she realizes that his withdrawal does not mean he doesn't love her. A caring wife will give her husband space during times of stress and problem-solving. One wife who was dealing with an extremely withdrawn man began stopping midsentence when she recognized that he was not with her. Without a word of reprimand, she stopped talking until he recognized her quietness and then proceeded when she had his attention again.

Behavioral indications of stress are easier to recognize than medical or psychological ones. Early signals include the following:

1. Verbal abuse or extreme criticism of wife and children.

2. Withdrawal from family conversation or interaction; preoccupation; silent treatment.

3. Overeating and weight gain.

4. More than usual consumption of alcohol or cigarettes.

5. Unusual fatigue and tendency to fall asleep.

6. Overwork or agitated activities.

7. Teeth-grinding, finger-tapping, swinging of feet, or other minor compulsive behaviors.

8. Selective deafness—tuning out what he doesn't want to hear.

9. Reckless driving and a tendency to take chances.

10. Addiction to television, video, or computer.

11. Facial tics, eye blinking, excessive swallowing, etc.

12. Increased spending.

13. Compulsive sex or loss of sexual interest.

Some psychological indicators of stress include defensiveness, depression, disorganization, defiance, dependency, or difficulty in decision-making. Remember that men differ in how they respond to stress and how much stress they can handle.[12]

Women may become alarmed and frightened when observing what is happening to their man. But such behavior will only increase their mate's stress. One of the best things a woman can do is to encourage her husband to talk about his stress and his feelings. But don't be surprised if he rejects your attempts to help. A man frequently rejects advice from his wife, regardless of how "right" she may be, but will frequently take the same suggestions from a physician or some other respected person. A wife's best plan of action might be to encourage her mate to have a good physical examination.

What passes for women's intuition is often nothing more than man's transparency.—George Jean Nathan.

Treatment for stress includes exercise, relaxation techniques, and daily meditation on God's Word. Much of a man's inner stress is self-generated. He might profit from attending a good seminar on stress management and time management skills, and learn to evaluate his life goals.

Seek to Understand

Francis of Assisi prayed, "Lord, grant that I seek more to . . . understand than to be understood." This purpose in a marriage, quickened by the softening influence of the Holy Spirit, could completely transform a couple's misunderstandings. Otherwise, when one becomes preoccupied with merely being understood by his mate, he becomes selfish, demanding, and bitter.

Paul Tournier, a well-known Christian psychiatrist, feels so strongly about the need for mutual understanding between marital partners that he says husband and wife should become preoccupied with it—lost in it—engrossed to the fullest in learning what makes the other tick, what the other likes, dislikes, fears, worries about, dreams of, believes in, and *why* he or she feels that way. Such a purpose would lead a couple directly into the benefits of a highly effective marriage.

Marriage doesn't depend upon how much a couple loves each other as much as how much a couple understands how the opposite sex functions. Scripture recognizes this in 1 Corinthians 11:11: "Remember that in God's plan men and women need each other" (TLB).

---

[1] Peter and Evelyn Blitchington, *Understanding the Male Ego* (Nashville: Thomas Nelson, 1984), p. 242.

[2] W. F. Harley, *His Needs, Her Needs,* pp. 133, 134.

[3] Arlie Hohschild, *The Second Shift* (see page 176 of *Get Organized).*

[4] Carin Rubenstein, "Real Men Don't Earn Less Than Their Wives," *Psychology Today,* November 1982, p. 22.

[5] Willard F. Harley, Jr., *His Needs, Her Needs* (Grand Rapids: Fleming H. Revell), pp. 108, 109.

[6] *Ibid.,* p. 75.

[7] H. Norman Wright, *Understanding the Man In Your Life* (Dallas: Word Publishing, 1987), p. 156.

[8] *Ibid.*

[9] *Ibid.,* p. 165.

[10] Van Pelt, *How to Talk So Your Mate Will Listen and Listen So Your Mate Will Talk,* p. 140.

[11] John Gray, *Men Are From Mars, Women Are From Venus* (New York: HarperCollins Publishers, 1993). See chapter 3.

[12] Wright, pp. 166, 167.

Chapter 15

WHAT'S GOD'S PLAN FOR LEADERSHIP IN MARRIAGE?

Chris and Ben fell in love, married, and had problems from the beginning because they both wanted to be boss. Ben was a farmer, and Chris was captivated by his knowledge of farming. He taught her to drive a tractor, plant crops, and operate an irrigation system. She valued his strength of character and his ability to make a living off the land.

As a pediatrics charge nurse at a local hospital, Chris was used to being in charge of parents and children who thought she knew everything. Ben knew when he married Chris that as a nurse she was a take-charge person, but Ben didn't need anyone to take charge of him. In fact, Ben didn't approve of the way Chris did anything around the house—from paying bills to driving, running errands, or planning meals. Whenever the two of them worked on a project, they ended up battling.

When they were first married, Chris paid the bills, since her paycheck came regularly and Ben's came sporadically. Chris paid bills until their account registered zero. Then they would spend the rest of the month arguing and blaming each other for the problem.

One day Chris decided to surprise Ben by washing the car. Instead of being thrilled, he told her the "right way" to wash a car. Chris got so angry at his criticism that she threw the soapy cloths at Ben and stormed off.

Finally the couple visited a counselor. They both took a personality test that revealed they had the same dominant temperament. This confirmed what they already knew—both of them wanted to boss everything.

The counselor suggested that to minimize the conflicts, they designate in advance who would handle each task. Then each was to agree to follow the leader in that task. When it came to finances, they decided Ben should take charge of paying monthly bills and do the banking. Chris handled balancing the checkbook and preparation of income tax because of her expertise in this area.

Ben was responsible for maintenance of the cars, yard work, grocery shopping, and laundry, while Chris was to oversee holiday and birthday celebrations, housecleaning, and meal preparation. The list evolved over time. It took months to iron out all the issues, but they continued to sublimate their desire to control each other.

Now when they began a new project one would ask, "Who is going to be in charge?" Establishing this up front made each task easier because both understood their roles in advance. All family tasks were divided according to who did what best. This brought peaceful solutions to years of tug-of-war between them. Now they are not only able to appreciate each other's strengths in new ways, but they are more trusting of each other. At last they have learned how to work as a team.

Where's the Balance in Power?

Love, communication, and understanding are all important attributes of a highly effective marriage. Yet they may not be enough if the house is a mess, everyone is hungry, and no one will fix a meal. Who's in charge? And of what? Who will make decisions, and in what area? How are responsibilities handled? Should she work outside the home? If she does, will he help with the meals, household tasks, and the children? Since she has almost as much earning power as he (and sometimes more), should he still make all the decisions?

The accepted pattern for years was for the man to produce the income and the woman to care for the children and keep the house running smoothly. Today that pattern has changed. Nearly 96 percent of all women, when surveyed, expect to have paying jobs when they do not have children or when their children are in school. And more than 60 percent of women do work full- or part-time outside the home.

There is but one just use of power, and it is to serve people.
—George Bush.

This creates tremendous confusion regarding the responsibilities of husband and wife in the home. Distorted views about distribution of leadership for the family continue to emerge. Many fight or argue with God's plan. Some don't understand it. Others don't want to believe it. Some try to get around scriptural passages. Still others ignore it or distort them. But in order to obtain a highly effective marriage, leadership within the family must be reckoned with.

God's Original Plan

God's original plan for marriage was for husband and wife to live together in perfect harmony. Before sin entered, God was the ultimate leader in the home. In their perfect environment, both Adam and Eve willingly submitted to God as a natural part of everyday living.

Many people have misinterpreted the Genesis account of the first marriage. Those who give Genesis a cursory reading or merely listen to what others say without studying the facts conclude that God designated Adam as the leader of the family. Not in the original play. Eve's role as "a helper fit for him" (Genesis 2:18, RSV) was of no less importance than man's position. Shouldering different roles did not mean inferiority or inequality then, nor should it now.

As a result of sin a curse was placed on man, woman, and the serpent involved in the first disobedience to God. Man was to work by the sweat of his brow (Genesis 3:17-19). Woman was to suffer greatly increased pain in childbirth, and her husband was to rule over her (verse 16). The serpent was to crawl on his belly and someday suffer a permanent lethal wound (verses 14, 15).

God created male and female to complement each other. Just as a successful organization depends on each employee's ability to assume the position assigned and produce to the best of their ability, so is a marriage interdependent. Husband and wife are dependent on each other. Although their responsibility and roles differ, they are equal in importance, and both are necessary to the well-being of a healthy society.

The Bible contains several important verses naming men as heads or leaders of the home. One key verse is Ephesians 5:23-25: "For the husband is the head of the wife as Christ is the head of the church. . . . Husbands, love your wives, just as Christ loved the church and gave himself up for her" (NIV). Since few men will literally be called upon to die so their wives can live, what do these verses mean? They bring an almost spiritual, godlike quality to the position of husband. They also imply that husbands are to be to their wives what Christ is to the church.

The overall direction of the entire household falls on the shoulders of the husband. This is literally what the term *husband* means—the male head of the house; one who manages or directs a household. The term *house* comes from the Old English *hus,* which gives us *husband.* The husband is the *houseband,* or the protector of all treasures within the home.

The Authoritarian

Under the guise of "leadership," many men destroy their wives and children. The heavyhanded, commanding, dictatorial, head-of-the-house system has no place in a Christian's life, since it leaves the wife feeling less than an equal partner. The results are destructive to both the husband and wife as individuals and to the marriage as well. Authoritarian men are usually from authoritarian homes where they have seen such behavior modeled. Or they may be weak, insecure males who fear letting anyone usurp their authority. In either case, this becomes the only leadership pattern they know.

But men are not the only ones to demonstrate an authoritarian style of leadership. Any time one partner attempts to control or dominate the other; disregards the other's opinions, desires, activities, and lifestyle; or attempts to force a spouse to do something against their will, a lack of mutuality is demonstrated.

Behaviors that demonstrate a lack of mutuality may not be violent or physically abusive ones; they may be emotionally abusive ones. In one study, 53 percent of a group of couples who were questioned regarding the failure of their marriage said that the downfall was a result of a partner's attempt to control them.[1]

Typical examples of controlling behaviors include making decisions without consulting the other, dictating how the other partner should dress, where they should live, how money should be spent, etc. Some were major decisions, others quite minor. But the common denominator was a lack of consideration for the other's wishes, opinions, and feelings in the decision-making process.

When digression from the authoritarian's agenda occurs, they make immediate attempts to force the other back into line through fear and intimidation. Controllers live in constant fear of losing their position of power and authority. They fear opening up and becoming vulnerable. Submissive partners fear being attacked and overwhelmed by their controlling mate. Such attitudes totally block intimacy.

Because the authoritarian acts alone, he (or she) often isolates and alienates himself from his spouse as well as others in the family. Since he isolates himself, his partner is starved for closeness and intimacy. His controlling nature usually kills his wife's love. In social settings, the controller may express politeness, but such niceties are performed with a purpose—control. Acts of love are without meaning. No real concern exists, which makes their spouse feel used.

The controller's life is regulated by "rules." The more rigid the rules, the happier controllers appear. There is a right way to do everything—their way. They know what is best for everyone in every situation.

Because there is no mutual submission with a controller, regard for the other person or the ability to see the world from their point of view is missing. Empathy means moving into your partner's world and being able to see the world from their point of view without making judgments. A lack of empathy signals a strong message: "You do not count. You are insignificant and unworthy." Such an approach invalidates and discourages the development of a partner's self-esteem. The controller simply does not care about their partner's feelings.

If in the name of leadership a husband totally controls his wife, serious consequences may appear. A continual suppression of her desires will eventually deaden her love for her husband, and she may attempt to get back at him in many insidious ways. She may also develop headaches, ulcers, sleeplessness, or one of many other emotional cover-ups.

A woman needs freedom to operate within her sphere of responsibility. She needs to make decisions and changes when necessary, as well as to receive and enjoy support from a husband who encourages her in her role.

Breaking out of the tenacious grip of a controller isn't easy. But it becomes possible with third-party intervention, since weekly accountability for change is required. But there must be a desire for change in both parties. Change is always possible through the Lord.

The system in which *she* rules has all the drawbacks of the *he*-rules system plus others, such as homosexuality. One of the contributing factors in homosexuality is a dominant mother and an ineffective father. All factors in homosexuality may not yet be determined, but a strong mother figure and weak father figure appear to be contributing factors.[2]

Woe to the house where the hen crows and the rooster keeps still.

—**Spanish proverb.**

This reminds me of the story about two gates leading into heaven. A sign over one gate read "All men who have ever been bossed by their wives, stand here." Several hundred men stood before that gate. Over the other gate a sign read "Men who have never been bossed by their wives, stand here." One bewildered-looking man stood in front of this gate.

Saint Peter approached the lone man and asked why he was standing there alone. "My wife told me to stand here," he replied.

The henpecked husband is the brunt of many jokes, portraying society's ridicule of this state of affairs. Being bossed damages the male ego, and deep resentment results. Don't go this route.

Coleadership

Coleadership sounds good: perfect equality is a worthy goal. Couples who try to be coleaders think they can make decisions together, negotiate, and in an orderly fashion always agree. They assume a time will never come when one must wield power over the other.

Under closer scrutiny, however, numerous drawbacks to this style of leadership come to light. There isn't always time to make decisions together or utilize slow-moving negotiations, especially in emergency situations or when one partner is away.

Even coleaders can't always agree. Two heads are not always better than one, as was reported in a newspaper article concerning the finding of a two-headed snake. "Not only do the heads fight over lunch, but they don't always agree on which way to go," said the amateur herpetologist who found the dual-headed creature and raises mice to feed it. "I have to feed both heads at once or they try to fight," he says. "One head grabs the front of the mouse and the other head the back, and they get nowhere."

Harry and I were riding our bikes side by side one spring evening when we approached an intersection. Neither of us called out a preference regarding which direction to turn. Both of us turned in, and we collided. Sociologists as well as zoologists tell us that humans as well as animals need a leader, and one will take control either by force or appointment. No organization functions on the coleadership principle. Businesses, schools, clubs, churches, and the government all function on the one-leader principle—a place where the buck stops.

The competition that results from the power struggle ends in bitter and resentful partners and confused children. Couples who compete for leadership never approach a supportive relationship. When they observe their parents battling for position, the children take sides, pitting one parent against the other, and copying the same techniques they see their parents act out.

When parents are locked into power struggles, control and authority shift back and forth from one parent to the other. The children feel their loyalties must also be divided and shifted, which makes them hurt and confused. It is vitally important to solve marital problems so that a couple can pull together in their parenting.

A Supportive Relationship

Allow me to introduce a type of relationship that takes into account biblical guidelines yet adapts well for nuclear families. A supportive relationship is based on the concept that marriage partners can work together in an orderly and cooperative manner. Supportive partners willingly give up their power to dictate or control the other. Neither demands that their way is the only way to get things done, nor do they insist on unquestioned obedience.

In a supportive relationship the couple functions more like a successful corporation with well-defined objectives and common goals. The couple works together in attaining these goals, recognizing that each may have different methods or feelings when striving to reach their goals.

In a supportive relationship the husband assumes responsibility for certain tasks because of competence in those areas. The wife manages other areas suited to her capabilities. Both parties agree, however, that an overall leader is needed to direct them when they encounter an impasse—which they are sure to do. In accordance with Scripture, both agree that the husband should assume the role of leader.

Though the husband leads the family, he does not assume the characteristics of a dictator. He behaves more like the president of a well-run organization in which every employee forms a crucial part of the team that makes the company successful.

In our home Harry is president of the Van Pelt Corporation; but like any well-trained executive, he checks out his plans and decisions with his vice president. I, as vice president, have areas of responsibility that I carry out on my own because of my capabilities and inclinations. Others I check out with him before acting. We hold frequent meetings to discuss plans and objectives.

Sometimes Harry will say, "Honey, you know more about this item, so you make the final decision." This doesn't demean his position or ability—it increases his effectiveness in my eyes. He always listens to my opinions, respects my abilities and experiences, and desires my maximum input (well, almost always—and if he didn't get it, he'd know something was drastically wrong).

A supportive relationship has a more even distribution of power where there is a clear division of responsibility and each partner has a balanced sense of control. *It is a mutually submissive complementary relationship.* Both partners think of themselves as competent, which contributes to self-esteem. Both think of their partner as competent, which contributes to the other's self-esteem.

In a supportive relationship the president and vice president consider problems to be enemies who threaten the security of their home. They fight their problems as a unified front.

Clifford Notarius and Howard Markman compare this team approach to problem-solving to a strategy illustrated in the original *Star Trek* series aired years ago. In this particular episode the crew encountered a foreign life-form that drew strength from the crew's anger. The life-form subtly and creatively instigated tiffs to provoke more and more anger, which it fed upon. Wise Captain Kirk realized what was happening and instructed his crew to replace displays of anger with laughter. The foreign life-form continued to provoke quarreling and spats. But once the crew took control over their responses and met the provocations with laughter, the invader lost its power. Had one member of the *Enterprise* crew failed to cooperate with the captain by getting angry and fighting to gain control, the ship would have been overpowered.[3]

Marriage partners need a similar strategy. The only way to beat the enemy is to team up with your partner to protect your marriage from invasion. Recognize that if problems succeed in dividing you, you both lose.

[1] Karen Kayser, *When Love Dies* (New York: Guilford Press, 1993), p. 94.
[2] Nancy L. Van Pelt, *Compleat Marriage,* p. 99.
[3] Clifford I. Notarius and Howard Markman, *We Can Work It Out* (New York: Putnam Books, 1993).

Chapter 16

FAMILY LEADERSHIP

im's problems with his wife and teenagers drove him into counseling. He told the counselor he had a hysterical wife and three undisciplined, rebellious teenagers. According to his story, his wife accused him of failing her and the children, and she cried all the time. She complained she had to do everything alone, that he took no interest in her, the children, or their home. She felt "invisible" and was fed up because he showed no leadership, and she no longer considered him a "man."

Jim was a competent professional who related his story openly. He was baffled by his wife's crazy demands and didn't understand what she wanted, since he earned a good living. He admitted to a rapidly deteriorating relationship. Their fights were marked by bitterness and hostility, followed by days of silence. Jim was at the end of his rope and wanted to know how to straighten out his wife.

The counselor asked him to return for a few visits alone so he could get to know Jim on a personal level. He learned that Jim had a passive father and a controlling, dominant mother. This model from the past taught him that men sit back as silent observers and avoid open conflict. He also learned that women take over and have all the say as well as make all the major decisions in the family.

This pattern had become firmly established, and now he acted out what he had learned during his early years. He was always "there," but he escaped from family encounters by retreating into himself, the television, newspaper, work, or the antique car he was restoring. He rarely entered into family discussions or took an active part in ensuring a smooth-running family.

The running of the home and family was left entirely to his wife, just as his father had done. Rather than arguing with his strong-willed wife regarding any decisions she made, whether he liked it or not, he withdrew. "Peace at any cost" became his motto.

Jim excelled at work and was well liked by everyone. He handled conflicts well and over the years had enjoyed numerous business successes. His counselor pointed out that if he would use at home the same management methods he used at work, his home conflicts would dissipate. Jim listened. The advice made sense.

Over a period of time he worked at asserting himself and taking a more active leadership role at home. Rather than fighting him for control as he feared she would, his wife gratefully gave up control as he stepped in. Evidence of new strength, leadership, and courage showed in little ways at first and eventually in bigger and more important ways.

It became evident to everyone that his feelings of self-worth improved. Gradually his relationship with his wife and teenagers began to change. As he showed more interest in his wife and communicated more openly with her, she became less frantic and hysterical. He made firm demands on his teenagers even when they rebelled. When he stood up to them, they tested him first but then responded positively.

Jim eventually assumed more and more responsibility for total family involvement and supportive leadership. The wife and teenagers who used to fight and challenge him now responded lovingly to him. The family worked through their problems. And it all began when the husband and father recognized that he was at fault and searched for clear answers.

Supportive Leadership

Leadership differs vastly from authoritarianism. An authoritarian represses individual freedom; a leader encourages freedom of thought and action. An authoritarian is uncompromising; a leader is understanding. An authoritarian is unyielding; a leader is adaptable. An authoritarian assumes no willingness to cooperate and therefore dictates; a leader manages, motivates, inspires, and influences in order to obtain willing cooperation toward a mutual goal.

Love keeps the balance in a leadership role, and therefore it demeans no one. It allows for open and honest discussion (even dissenting opinions) and includes a sound system for making decisions, solving problems, and setting goals. When a husband takes seriously the command to love his wife as much as Christ loved the church (Ephesians 5:25), he will establish a supportive partnership in which he never forces his wife to obey but wisely offers tender leadership that encourages her to follow. Such supportive leadership brings harmony and happiness to both and will certainly have God's blessing.

Scripture offers a multiplicity of directions on how to be effective leaders of the home. Authority is granted to the head to meet the needs of his family. But nowhere has any authority been granted for a man to *command* anyone *to meet his own selfish needs.* His leadership is to encompass unselfish love and responsible authority, not tyranny.

Effective Leadership Principles

Current research has uncovered specific principles necessary for successful leadership. While these principles are not hard and fast rules, they certainly can be applied by any man who wishes to lead his family in a loving manner. Let's explore a few of these concepts which have been translated into family terminology.

Principle Number One: In order to look out for the welfare of the family, a family leader must know his wife. After marriage, most men become so wrapped up in supporting a family and pursuing their own interests that getting to know their wives no longer receives priority. But if a man doesn't know his wife, how can he look out for her welfare? Does she need an understanding heart and a listening ear? a few words of appreciation for her contribution to the family? time away from the children? a helping hand with heavy responsibilities within the home? prayer support? time to pursue a hobby or interest? A loving husband must know his wife and then attempt to meet her legitimate needs.

Sometimes a man forgets that working together is the goal. A sign of impending marital problems is one or both partners feeling so strongly about protecting their own views and interests that they can't consider or hear their partner's views. But a supportive husband puts himself in his wife's shoes and views her concerns through her eyes, not only his own. He recognizes that her desire for a successful relationship usually exceeds his. Yet she is more or less dependent upon him—his understanding, wisdom, and cooperation—to accomplish her goals.

> *If a woman is not asking for support, a man assumes he is giving enough.*
> —**John Gray.**

Principle Number Two: A responsible family leader must consult with his wife and keep the channels of communication open and clear. It is hurtful for one partner to discover that a major decision or purchase has been made without their being consulted. When decisions are made together, equality and self-respect are reinforced.

A husband should take his wife into his confidence, ask for her opinions on family matters, and listen attentively as she presents them. He needs her to advise, not just to second his ideas and opinions. He needs to recognize her as a partner who possesses a respected grasp of situations that he may not see or comprehend. Her knowledge regarding the facts of a problem may be limited, but her assessment may be more reliable than his because of her intuitive reflection on the issue. He should provide her full opportunity to express herself, while observing her facial expressions, body movement, and tone of voice.

When goals are being determined, it is a good idea to take a weekend away from the children and all responsibilities and spend time alone talking over goals and objectives for your life together. The family leader needs to plan a strategy for discussion, not forcing his ideas, but giving direction—similar to planning an agenda for a business meeting.

The weekend should be accompanied by prayer for direction as you plan your future. Discussions should also include how you can manifest the fruits of the Spirit—love, joy, peace, long-suffering, gentleness, goodness, meekness, self-control, and faith (Galatians 5:22, 23)—in your everyday life.

Principle Number Three: A family leader sets a consistent example. How can a man who wants to be considered a responsible leader of his family require something from his wife and children that he doesn't consider important enough to do himself? He needs to set a consistent example of godly qualities, which include integrity, morality, and responsibility.

Principle Number Four: The successful family leader oversees family policies and division of tasks and makes sound and timely decisions. Successful leadership also includes overseeing family policies and division of tasks. Any president who tries to run the show alone without delegating authority and responsibility will soon find himself working alone. A careful division of responsibility is necessary in a well-organized home so that each person may function in their area to the fullest potential.

A supportive husband will not make unreasonable demands on his wife but instead be sensitive to the multiple demands on her time and position, just as he expects her to be understanding of his position. He will practice mutual submission, not always giving in to her requests or opinions, but always listening to her with respect and dealing fairly with her. He will consider her feelings and recognize her rights in each issue, dealing with them respectfully, fairly, and kindly.

The making of sound and timely decisions takes much thought, work, and prayer. One of the tremendous advantages of putting yourself under God's control is that you have the entire resources of heaven at your disposal. God's Word promises that He will instruct and guide us in the way we should go. Making sound decisions means that the leader will not only listen to his wife, but that he must then search for a compromise on each issue that meets both their needs.

Whenever the couple is caught in an impasse, he must ask, "What should we do to serve the best interests of the relationship?" not "What can my partner do to serve my interests?" A leader must be open to negotiation and compromise. This includes common problems revolving around spending styles (which may differ widely from the other partner's), priorities in use of time, in-law problems, different parenting styles, and sexual problems. The responsibility lies with the husband, as the over-all leader of the home, to be alert to problems and ensure discussion regarding them.

Principle Number Five: A family leader recognizes his wife's gifts and capa-

bilities and encourages her to utilize them. Some men have no difficulty delegating housekeeping tasks, care of the children, and meal planning to their wives. But many are intimidated when their wive's talents overlap theirs or when their wive's earning capacity exceeds their own.

For years both Harry and I have had two demanding careers. In recent years mine has had a higher profile because of the public nature of my publications and speaking appointments. However, we aren't in competition, nor does one strive to outshine the other. Harry believes God has equipped me for a special ministry to families, and he encourages and supports me every step of the way. From early in our marriage he has encouraged me to use my abilities, even when it was inconvenient for him.

We keep our marriage supportive by communicating. We discuss everything—from everyday events to our dreams for the future. Much of our discussion takes place in the spa, where we allow the hot water to soak away our stress and tiredness and we get in touch with each other's lives again.

God did not intend husband and wife to compete with each other but to complete each other. A considerate leader will consider his wife's talents and abilities and encourage her accordingly.

Principle Number Six: A family leader takes responsibility for his mistakes. Many men have abdicated their position in the family, and women have taken up the slack by taking control themselves. But a man needs to assume responsibility—not just demand submission! And after assuming responsibility, he must also take responsibility for his own actions.

Sometimes leaders make mistakes, calculate incorrectly, and react hastily. Even outrageously successful business leaders make mistakes. There will be times you, too, are 100 percent wrong. When this happens, rather than trying to cover it up or refusing to admit it, go to your wife and tell her you blew it. Tell her you are sorry and ask for forgiveness. Then discuss the next steps you need to take to resolve the situation. Rather than thinking less of you, she will respect and love you more.

Every couple must decide who is going to lead. In our marriage, over time, we have distributed responsibility. Harry decides the make and model of the family car. I get more say in cost and color. When something in the house breaks down, I go to Harry. He decides if he can fix it or if it's worth repairing. In matters of furniture styles and decorating, Harry allows me more sway. (This works well, because his ability to distinguish color got buried with the Loch Ness monster!) The social calendar at home is usually left to me, but I keep Harry up to speed on engagements. I write the checks, but he balances bank statements and pays taxes.

How we manage our internal affairs may not be of interest to you, yet it provides a glimpse of how real people make the nitty-gritty aspects of marriage work. Getting these responsibilities fairly divided and functioning faithfully gives life to a marriage.

When a family leader functions effectively, a wife knows she can trust him implicitly because she is valued. And there is no limit to her love and respect or her willingness to submit and support his leadership because he has proved himself to be all she could ever ask for in a husband.

Leadership a Woman Really Wants From a Man

What a woman wants when it comes to leadership is a combination of both tough and tender qualities. How can a man be both tough and tender? Such traits sound as if they conflict with each other. But there are men who can maintain a precision-like balance between being strongly decisive when making hard decisions that keep a family operating and communicating this lovingly to their families.

Govern a family as you would cook small fish—very gently.—Chinese proverb.

A woman, regardless of how traditional or liberated she may claim to be, most often desires a politely aggressive male who radiates masculinity, yet is sensitive to her needs and evokes positive feelings. This kind of man can provide the type of tender leadership a woman longs for only when he determines to become God's man—deliberately, intensely, and faithfully.

If a man is going to lead his family effectively and survive the crises of life, he must ask God to come into his life, forgive his past sins and failures, and make him into the kind of leader needed to guide his family. Remember, positive change never comes through nagging and critical wives bent on reforming their husbands. Change proceeds from a desire within, strengthened by the Holy Spirit's power. On his desk, Harry has the following quote from Scripture: "Therefore, if anyone is in Christ, he is a new creation; old things have passed away; behold, all things have become new" (2 Corinthians 5:17, NKJV).

Common Objections to Leadership

"My husband isn't worthy of respect!" Some women argue that their husbands are mean, unfair, wishy-washy, ornery, cantankerous, thoughtless, or dis-

honest, and so they can't respect them. A woman who finds it difficult to respect her husband can learn to differentiate between her husband's personality and his position. It is possible to respect his position while recognizing personal deficiencies that need correction.

Let's say a police officer gives you a traffic ticket for a speeding violation. I seriously doubt you will ignore the ticket because you didn't like the personality the officer demonstrated while writing the ticket! Their position as a police officer stands for law and order. Their uniform carries authority. You must respect their position even though you do not respect the person.

This same principle can be applied in marriage. You may not approve of or respect everything your husband does. All leaders have deficiencies of one kind or another, but God can work through them. God will not hold a wife accountable for her husband's deficiencies, but He will hold her accountable for her response to him, for the way she chooses to react. God is able to work through even defective persons to accomplish good.

"My husband is weak and has no leadership abilities!" How can a woman trust leadership to a weak man, one who is wimpy, passive? Generally when the husband is a weak leader his wife possesses strong control qualities. She unconsciously chooses a weak or passive partner who complements her strong abilities. She may have seen this modeled in her childhood home, or her husband may not be strong enough to fight her. Eventually such husbands settle for allowing their strong-willed wives to handle everything rather than fighting them on every matter.

Something happens to a woman over time, even the fiercely independent type. Eventually she begins to realize she needs someone she can lean on during stressful periods. She doesn't want to do all the controlling, leading, and initiating. If her husband began leading at this point, she would probably still fight for control. But yet she longs for her man to be just a little stronger than she is. Oh, that men could understand this about strong-willed women and stand their ground when challenged!

When a woman thinks of her husband as the "weaker" partner, one who won't pull his share of the load in responsibility, her respect for him deteriorates. Deep feelings of resentment surface for the one who should be assuming responsibility, even though she bucks his attempts to assume leadership.

One of the great mysteries about a woman is that she feels secure when functioning under her husband's leadership. She wants and needs his leadership. In the Garden of Eden, God Himself spoke to this matter when He said to Eve, "Your desire will be for your husband" (Genesis 3:16, NIV). The Hebrew word for *desire* means to run after or to violently crave something, which indicates the strongest possible yearning for it.

Often men accept responsibility when their wives stop assuming it, when they are allowed to feel the full weight of leadership. Sometimes all a wife needs to do is let go and let her husband take over. A supportive wife will encourage even feeble attempts at leadership by showing appreciation.

When her husband makes a suggestion, she can accept it graciously even if she doesn't feel like it. Chances are she would act that way if someone other than her husband had made it. If a wife's attention and appreciation reinforce her husband's attempts at leadership, he will be encouraged to try again.

"My husband has failed repeatedly!" One of the most difficult tests of submission for a woman is to step out of the way and let a man fail without interference. Since opposites often attract, this can be extremely difficult for a dominant wife to do, especially when she thinks that *she* would not fail.

Frequently a woman may say she wishes her husband would succeed, but she may unconsciously not allow him to do so. She may buck every idea or criticize his faltering attempts to exert leadership. Or she may destroy his efforts by saying "I told you so" when he fails. Again, she needs to let go, not try to rescue him, and let him feel the full burden of his failures. She may also need to test her willingness to go to the full limits of submission.

"My husband isn't a Christian!" Since a wife's spiritual awareness often runs deeper than her husband's, she may use this as a pious excuse for not submitting to her husband's wishes. She feels entitled to counter his wishes in matters of Christian education, church attendance, baptism, Bible study, discipline of the children, and many other matters.

Rather than helping a difficult situation, ignoring a husband's wishes frequently worsens it. He begins to resent the God who forces his wife to disregard his wishes. This lessens the chance of winning him to the Lord. In effect, the husband becomes jealous of the very God his wife serves!

The Living Bible sheds some light on this subject: "Wives, fit in with your husbands' plans, for then if they refuse to listen when you talk to them about the Lord, they will be won by your respectful, pure behavior. Your godly lives will speak to them better than any words" (1 Peter 3:1).

This godly counsel was taken literally in Brazil by a church group during a great religious revival. Large numbers of women were coming to the faith without their husbands. Some men were only indifferent about their wives' newfound faith, but others were openly hostile and forbade their wives to attend church or take part in church activities. Church leaders wisely advised the women to accept this and trust God to change their husbands' hearts. A number of men have thus been won to the faith.

The Limits of Submission

Submission has its limits. A woman should not bow to every evil desire and idea of a depraved man. God has given every wife a conscience and a mind of her own to use, and she must draw the line between what she believes is morally correct and incorrect according to the Word of God. This very subtle and delicate matter will not always mean the same decision for each wife, even on identical issues, and will frequently require the intervention of a Christian counselor.

A mother must certainly protect her children from moral and physical harm. Should the father give a child illicit drugs or alcohol, or should he physically or sexually abuse the child, the mother must step in to shield the child. Even then she should make every effort to preserve respect between the child and father.

She might explain that Daddy does not always see things as we see them and that we must be patient with him, just as Jesus is patient with us when we fail Him. By word and example she can teach her child to love and respect Daddy through difficult situations.

Women are frequently confronted with moral dilemmas. Suppose a husband wants his wife to accompany him to places of amusement she does not condone, watch offensive movies or videos, or engage in objectionable practices. What can she do in such cases? She should draw the line according to the principles found in Galatians 5:19-21. She has no obligation to obey her husband when he attempts to lead her into evil practices.

She must, however, leave all condemnation to the Holy Spirit. When she must say no, she should do so with love and respect. If she wants to go to church and he doesn't, she should go. But she should leave with the same attitude she might have when going to the supermarket—kiss him goodbye without attempts to make him feel guilty for not attending with her. Whether she should take children with her is another issue, since the children are not hers alone to educate. Neither should she "church" him to death with meetings that constantly take her away from home, leaving him alone.

If he refuses to take charge of family devotions, she should do it. Should an opportunity present itself to invite him to join, she might say "Honey, let's tuck the children in and hear their prayers" or "Would you read the children their Bible story tonight? They love to sit in Daddy's lap and listen to you read." If he declines, she should carry on alone.

She may ask one of the children to bless the food at the table if he isn't interested. Should he tell the children there is no God, she should later explain why she believes differently, always modeling respect for their father's right to believe as he wishes.

A woman facing such difficult situations will need to spend extra time with God seeking divine guidance and strength. A supportive relationship is difficult enough to attain when both partners work together to achieve mutual goals. But when the husband opposes her spiritual beliefs, a wife has an even greater need to prayerfully maintain harmony in the home.

She need not parade her prayer and devotional time before him as evidence of her spirituality. Rather, her life should be a silent witness. A daily time for Bible study and prayer will provide the wisdom needed to know how to make the best of the difficult circumstances facing her. A faithful prayer partner and counselor who can guide her through the most trying times will be most helpful.

A continued attitude of respect and willingness to submit to her husband, even when it goes contrary to a woman's thinking, allows God to work matters out. A woman's submission often softens a husband's negative attitudes toward Christianity, for he cannot help respecting a faith that leads his wife to give so much of herself to him.

Chapter 17

Submission—What It Is and What It Isn't

*D*onna and Brad had been married five years when the discussion of when to have their first child became an issue. Brad wanted to have a baby someday, but not now. Donna wanted a baby now. The issue became so heated that they sought advice from a professional counselor.

After several months of counseling, another impasse surfaced—where to spend the Christmas holidays. Brad wished to stay home, and Donna wished to visit her parents in the East. Attempts to reach a mutually satisfying decision on either issue appeared impossible. This couple had not yet learned that in long-term relationships each partner must make a sacrifice at one time or another.

Finally Donna and Brad were asked to look at the two issues from the other's point of view. An amazing transformation occurred. Donna began arguing to stay home for the holidays, and Brad began arguing to visit her parents in the East! Once they saw the problem from the other's viewpoint they reentered the problem-solving stage and sought more creative solutions.

Ultimately they decided to stay home and work on their relationship. A trip to Donna's parents was planned for the next year. And they even began talking about trying to get pregnant over the holidays.*

Mutual Submission

With a little help, this couple learned about mutual submission. Submission is more than just something women do for their husbands. It should permeate the life of every Christian on a daily basis.

Christ is our example in this process of submission. Our first loyalty is to God. Then Christlike servants are to obey and honor spiritual leaders, the government, parents, elders, and each other. "Submit to one another," Ephesians

5:21, NIV, says. This statement refers as much to the marriage relationship as it does to brothers and sisters in the faith.

Mutual submission, then, when put to use in everyday life, means *there are times when each partner yields or defers to the ideas or wishes of the other.* Supportive partners recognize individual competencies. Each partner operates with a willingness to adapt when a conflict of interest occurs.

Obviously mutual submission functions only when both partners consider each other as equals. Domination and submission occur when an inferior surrenders to a superior person. The supreme example of mutual submission occurred between God the Father and Jesus. Jesus was perfectly submissive to the will of His Father, but He did not become inferior when He submitted. He always remained equal with His Father. Couples should aim for this type of mutual submission.

The Missing Link

This is what I call "the missing link" in the discussion of "who's in charge." It is not a matter of submission and domination. It isn't a master-slave relationship or a dictator-robot obedience that is necessary, but one of mutual submission.

Note: this verse precedes the famous "wives-submit-yourselves-to-your-husband" quote—not by accident but by God's design. Mutual submission implies that the marriage is not dominated by a "ruler"—that the husband commands and his wife submits (or vice versa). Such an interpretation leaves out the mutuality described in Ephesians 5:21.

Mutual submission simply means there are times when each partner defers to the right of the other. Each person has specific areas of expertise in which his or her views have greater weight than the other's; but because of the balance of power, this is not threatening. Both partners have the freedom to initiate action and give advice, but their behaviors are not competitive. Neither vies for the dominant position. Each operates with a willingness to adapt during times of conflict.

Marriage requires endless mutual submission or give and take. Harry and I certainly had to learn it. He prefers classical music; I am strictly a soft pop fan. I'm an early-to-bed, early-to-rise person; he's a night owl who can begin his best work after 11 p.m. He's a pessimist; I'm the eternal optimist. He's a spender; I'm a saver. He's a procrastinator; I'm the efficiency expert. He prefers comedy; I prefer drama. He's a couch potato; I'm an active outdoor person. How do such opposites find each other? Without mutual submission these differences would be nearly impossible to work out.

What Submission Isn't

The word *submit* in our culture connotes groveling, losing one's identity, servility, blind obedience, and passivity. But it does not have to mean that. According to the New Testament, submission is at the core of every Christian relationship and is modeled after Christ's willing submission to His Father. He was never forced to obey, but rather voluntarily complied. In this context, submission is a willingness on the part of one to adapt their rights to those of the other.

Doormat servility on the wife's part is just as far from God's ideal as is the henpecked husband. Nor is marriage enhanced by a helpless, dependent wife who refuses to accept responsibility or make decisions within her realm of responsibility. A wife has her own responsibilities and obligations that must be carried out in order for the relationship to thrive. If her husband is not available to consult, she acts in accordance with her best judgment.

A wife who perceives her husband's judgment or decision as wrong or disastrous to the family's welfare should tell him so—firmly, honestly, but respectfully. If an issue arises and a wife says "Go ahead and do whatever you want" without offering an opinion even when she sees the decision oozes with trouble, she is not being submissive, but foolishly servile.

The man who marries for money earns it.—Talmud.

A woman who echoes "yes dears" to every whim an unwise husband expresses willingly acts inferior to her husband and rapidly loses his respect and devotion. She lacks a sense of self-worth, since she will not allow herself to offer an opinion even when she thinks it necessary.

The extremes of silence, helpless dependency, doormat servility, and blind obedience are not qualities found in a supportive wife.

A Supportive Wife

The thought of a husband leading the family bothers many women. The word *submission* raises hair on the back of their necks. Yet if a husband loves his wife enough to die for her, suffers ridicule and pain for her, and provides the kind of love Christ suffered for the church, I'll show you a wife who will gratefully and lovingly submit.

What woman in her right mind wouldn't give herself wholeheartedly to a man who loved her like Christ loves the church? This wife is no downtrodden shadow of a woman, ignorant of the world around her. She is independently strong, fully aware and concerned about the world of hurts within her church and community.

Whether she has a bubbly, outgoing personality or a quiet and retiring temperament, she walks with quiet confidence because she safely trusts her husband.

When Harry and I married, I had to grapple with the question of submission. Could I and would I submit when necessary? This question wasn't a joke. Could a strong-willed, independent person such as I become a mutually submissive partner? In my young adult years I had been leader, team captain, director, manager, and supervisor of everything there was to supervise. Could I submit to a husband's leadership?

I considered myself to be God's woman and open to His plans for my life. I had not missed the biblical injunction regarding a woman's place in the home. I recognized that when two people marry, one of them has to make final decisions—a designated spot where the buck stops. If I could trust God to forgive my sins and save me for eternity, couldn't I then trust His word on who was to head the family? With difficulty I proceeded to try, but with an I'm-going-to-regret-this attitude.

The most important thing a father can do for his children is to love their mother.

Since then, I have learned that *submission* isn't a dirty word. Even though Harry is the head of our home, he has a tender, loving attitude toward me and a willingness to have a submissive spirit. He expects the same from me but never demands it from me.

Submission is mine to give or withhold, because I am a freewill agent. And there is nothing in Scripture that suggests he should remind me to be submissive should I have a rebellious spirit. Should I refuse to be submissive to my husband, I am not disobeying Harry but disobeying God's command to women—a spirit I must reckon with God about when my name comes up for judgment.

A woman who thoroughly understands the principle of mutual submission will willingly adapt her own rights to those of her husband *at the point of conflict*. How does this idea actually work?

Let's say that Harry wants to accept a job offer in another state, which means a major move for me and the children. He allows me full freedom to express my doubts and opinions. He listens attentively to my reasons but remains convinced we must move.

I might wait a few days and bring the matter up again, especially if I think he hasn't considered all the angles. We might go back and forth in this manner, always listening with respect to the issues that concern the other. But when all has been said and done, a decision must be made. Whether I can accept his final decision, even when I am hesitant or opposed, is the test of submission.

Whenever he gives me a flat No, I do my best to accept it. At other times I might be so outspoken as to say, "You may think you are right from your point of view, but I'm right from mine!" We may never agree on some decisions, but I feel better because I have expressed my opinions. This freedom of expression is part of a supportive relationship too.

Acceptance of a decision that goes contrary to one's own desires isn't always easy. We are all a bit selfish when it comes to getting our way. Sometimes we need time to adapt to decisions that go contrary to what we want. If a man at this point would lovingly take his wife in his arms and assure her of his love and concern for her, while explaining that he must follow his own conscience in the matter, it would go a long way. She needs time to adjust to a decision with which she does not agree.

Imagine the stress of being ultimately responsible for the outcome of all decisions. Picture the pressure this puts on a man. What if his final decision becomes a disastrous flop? What if he goes out on a limb with a decision, only to find he has sawed off the branch he perched himself on? Can you encourage him even after he's made an error in judgment?

This is when the for-better-or-worse clause from the wedding vows is tested big-time. When a husband fails, his wife goes down with him too. She must be willing to accept her part of his failures because the two have become as one. It takes courage on both her part and his. But Ephesians 5 spells out his responsibility as well as hers. And it clearly defines ultimate responsibility.

In the final analysis, then, a supportive wife possesses dignity, opinions, and spunk; but she also respectfully responds to her husband's supportive leadership and yields and adapts to a decision that goes contrary to her thinking at the point of conflict.

Submission Is an Attitude

The adapting and yielding required through submission starts as an *attitude*. A wife might bend to every wish of her husband; but if it isn't done willingly, it isn't true submission. Underneath a woman's apparent compliance, she might be nursing insidious hurts and resentments that are stockpiling into a major case of bitterness and rebellion that will soon burst into the open.

Respect is at the heart of true submission. When a woman doesn't respect her husband, it shows in everything she says and does. She may say, "Dad is boss," but deep in her heart she knows this is not true. Whenever there is a conflict of wills, she does what she wants.

Children quickly notice when their mother fails to practice what she preaches.

However, if children see Mom always treating Dad with respect, such an example cannot fail to influence them. Every child needs a hero. A mother can and should help her children to think of their father in this light.

A respectful, submissive attitude will not stifle a woman's personality but instead will provide the best atmosphere for the wholesome expression of creativity and individuality. God wants us to fully express His gifts to us of intelligence, insight, and common sense. Everyone's personhood in a highly effective marriage must be preserved at all costs.

---

*Clifford Notarius and Howard Markman, *We Can Work It Out* (New York: Putnam, 1992), p. 234.

Chapter 18

Spiritual Leadership

Imperfect Situations

Men sometimes think of spiritual guidance as being as much woman's work as having babies and cooking the evening meal. Many women have tearfully confided to me that they would give anything if their husbands would only assume spiritual leadership for the family. Yet women are going to their spiritual deaths because their husbands are not willing to be the priests of their homes.

Some men plead their case by saying they attend church every week (at their wife's insistence), or serve on the church board, and say grace at the table. But such Christianity won't hold the family together when a major crisis arises or when children hit their teen years.

When it comes to spiritual leadership, Joshua challenges my heart and mind. In chapter 23 of his book Joshua tells the leaders of Israel that he is an old man. Then he traces what God's hand has done for his people during his life as their leader. He gives some practical instruction about marriage, warning people not to intermarry or they will not have God's protection.

In chapter 24 he begins his favorite and most eloquent theme. He tells Israel that serving God should be the highest priority of all. He then asks each to choose that very day whom they will serve. "But as for me and my family," he declares, "we will serve the Lord" (verse 15, TLB).

Joshua didn't say "I will serve the Lord." He assumed responsibility for his entire family. He announced to the entire nation, once and for all, his unyielding decision that he and his entire household would serve God. He didn't leave the spiritual chores to Mrs. Joshua.

Women of the world cry with me in asking their beloved husbands to take on the spiritual challenges of the home. It is the husband's responsibility to give spiritual security to his family unit. Husband and wife need each other emotionally and physically, but spiritually we need each other desperately!

Three Secrets That Will Build Spiritual Oneness

1. Attend church together. A recent study showed that couples who attend church together, even as little as one time a month, increase their chance of staying married for life. Churchgoing couples feel better about their marriages than those who do not worship together.[1]

Mixed-faith marriages experience trouble sooner than marriages in which both partners are of the same faith. One reason is that while dating, a couple finds it difficult to think realistically about marriage. It is easy to minimize the difficulties likely to be encountered. The four most common causes of conflict in mixed-faith marriages are summarized below.[2]

> a. Conflict over what religion the children will follow. *In homes in which children are taken alternately to both religious services in two faiths, one study showed that six out of 10 children end up rejecting all religion.*
>
> b. Conflict over church attendance.
>
> c. Conflict over interference by in-laws in religious matters.
>
> d. Conflict over size of family and/or spacing of children.

For Harry and me, worshiping together has been an experience of rest, peace, and renewal. We dedicate our day of worship to liberating ourselves from the tyranny of productivity that fills the rest of the week. Dedicating one day per week to worshiping our God strengthens our relationship as well as providing renewed energy to tackle the week before us. Worshiping together nurtures the very soul of our relationship.

Worshiping together automatically draws a couple closer. In addition to a physical bonding, a spiritual bonding takes place that promotes humility, sharing, compassion, and intimacy. Spiritual truths help couples transcend selfish desires and become part of a larger plan.

2. Become engaged in a service ministry. Hundreds of ways exist to incorporate service to others in your marriage. The key is to find something that fits your personal lifestyle.

Harry and I enjoy inviting friends and strangers to our home after the worship service. We have tried to make our home a center of friendship and encouragement. Sometimes our hospitality is spontaneous and casual, sometimes planned and elegant, but we always try to make it a special time.

It's through hospitality that I met Harry in the first place. My parents had a beautiful waterfront home with a terrific view of the bay in Tacoma, Washington. During my young adult years, my mother and I always thought it our patriotic duty to invite home for dinner after church all the tallest, most handsome unat-

o man is able of
mself to do all
ings.—**Homer.**

tached servicemen stationed at Fort Lewis. Harry came to dinner and never left.

Today hospitality to others has become a team service ministry that has provided us with endless opportunities for fun and the occasion to meet new people and add to our list of friends. If this sounds like something you'd enjoy, you will find more about it in my book *Creative Hospitality—How to Turn Home Entertaining Into a Real Ministry.*

The following list has service ideas that have worked for other couples and their families.

- Adopt an elderly person with no family to visit and take them a treat.
- Volunteer to serve at a soup kitchen for the homeless.
- Visit a nursing home and sing or read stories to the elderly.
- Visit the ill in the hospital.
- Deliver food baskets to the needy.
- Make up a friendship basket of goodies and deliver it to someone new in your community.

Working together in a service ministry helps blend spiritual oneness. As you become involved in a ministry outside yourselves, you'll learn about selflessness. It will create opportunities to spend more time together, as well as provide new topics for conversation.

3. Pray together. How often do you and your mate pray out loud—together? The story is told of a young couple on their honeymoon who wished to start their marriage out right by praying together before retiring each evening. At their bedside that first night together, the bride couldn't suppress the giggles as she heard her new husband pray, "For what we are about to receive, may the Lord make us truly thankful."

Humor aside, research shows that couples who pray together are happier than couples who do not. And couples who pray together frequently are more likely to rate their marriages as being highly romantic as those who pray together infrequently. And get this—married couples who pray together report higher satisfaction with their sex lives than are couples who don't pray together![3] Because prayer makes one vulnerable, it draws a couple closer.

At first, Harry and I had a hard time praying together. For one thing, we were too uncomfortable and embarrassed to pray out loud together! On the few occasions when we did pray at night, Harry would fall asleep while I prayed. And while Harry prayed I mentally wrote chapters for a new book, redecorated the family room, or allowed my mind to wander to any number of tasks the morrow held. We soon lost interest in praying together.

Then we were introduced to "share prayer," which has become one of the most enriching experiences of our lives. The idea is to take turns at being the prayer leader and introducing requests. The first night it was my turn, and in one sentence I introduced and prayed conversationally for the first request on my heart. Then Harry prayed a short sentence prayer for that same request. Next I introduced and prayed my second request, and Harry followed.

We repeated the process until I had covered all the topics that burdened my heart. Harry admitted that this was a vast improvement over our previous attempts to "pray together." This method not only kept him awake but made it interesting. It was like having a three-way conversation with God. We both lost track of time. The next night it was Harry's turn to introduce the requests of his heart.

Within a week several strange things began happening. Because I now knew what was near and dear to Harry's heart, I began praying for his requests, almost making them mine. He did the same with my requests. Our bonds of love deepened when we saw the other remembering, caring, and praying for our requests.

Once while traveling from Fresno to Brazil I was detained in Miami because of visa problems. Officials at the Brazilian embassy had warned it was impossible to obtain a visa in one day. I found myself alone at the Sheraton Hotel in the center of Miami at 1:30 a.m making phone calls to Brazil to alert my contact there that I would not be arriving in time to meet my speaking obligations.

Frazzled, I phoned my husband next, and broke into a running disaster report. While we were still on the phone, Harry prayed for me. "Dear Lord, my wife is 3,000 miles from here on her way to Brazil. She's frightened, and there isn't much I can do to help her get out of the situation. But I ask You to take care of her and calm her.

"Give her the peace that only You can provide. You can perform the miracle necessary for her to obtain the necessary documentation so she can continue on her way tomorrow and then return safely home. Thank You, Lord, for beginning Your work right now. Amen."

Even before Harry finished his prayer, my hysteria left. My confidence in my Lord, my ministry plans, and my husband had been restored as he prayed out loud for me. I slept peacefully until morning. I got the visa the next day and continued on to São Paulo.

The longer I continue in my ministry to families, the more convinced I become that the depth of relationship that comes from worshiping together, engaging in a service ministry, and praying together can prevent many marital problems that trouble relationships today.

The Benefits of a Mutually Supportive Relationship

The marriage that functions in a mutually supportive manner has fewer arguments and less fighting or contention. A natural peace and harmony settles over the family once power struggles vanish. A closeness and intimacy result that would not be possible any other way.

The husband will grow in self-confidence as he practices supportive leadership. The wife will notice an improvement in her attitudes toward herself and her marriage as she responds and adapts to his leadership. Together, backing each other up, their supportive attitudes will enrich their relationship and make their marriage more cohesive and enjoyable.

The children will learn a natural respect for family organization. This respect will be transferred from home to the school, church, and society. Our homes are the basic unit of society, and only when a home functions successfully is a house in order. When a home is in order, the community, church, and the nation can function as they should.

Success Is Just Around the Corner

Randy and Raylene, married nine years, had a relationship plagued with power struggles about money, parenting issues, and sex. Neither approved of the manner in which the other disciplined their two sons. They had constant battles over money and how it should be spent and saved. Randy felt Raylene was so critical and demanding that repairing the marriage was hopeless. Raylene was ready to give up because she thought Randy would never change.

Our prayer life never needs a bridle, but sometimes it needs a spur.

At home their fights were so volatile that they avoided each other. They had not had sex in more than a year. Although they attended church together, as well as required social functions, they spent no free time together. Randy and Raylene were held hostage by the fight for control of their marriage.

Since both were physical therapists, their counselor personalized the *Star Trek* concept and had them envision their destructive behavior through medical terminology. The couple were to imagine that a deadly virus was attacking their marriage. The only way to survive was to team up in their search to find a cure. As long as they fought each other, all available energy and resources were directed toward simply surviving their self-induced, destructive ordeals. No reserves were left to fight the enemy.

Once Randy and Raylene grasped this analogy, they agreed to work on saving their marriage. Each agreed they wanted less fighting, better parenting, and increased closeness. They worked on basic marriage skills like filling each other's EBA. They learned to accept personality differences and control their thoughts and actions. Next they worked on communication skills so they could speak respectfully through I-messages and listen effectively.

Within a few short weeks this couple contained the spread of their "disease." A short time later they expressed confidence in their ability to manage disagreements without fighting for their own way. Approval, support, and validation began to replace criticism, put-downs, and angry outbursts. Their positive interaction was reflected in how they thought of and related to each other. Now they began to recapture the closeness and intimacy that had gotten lost in the swirl of conflict and the struggle for power and control.[3]

Has your marriage been plagued with power struggles? You too can banish the monsters threatening your relationship and become the warm, intimate partners you were meant to be.

---

[1] Les and Leslie Parrott, "Soul Mates," *Virtue,* May/June 1995, pp. 28, 29.

[2] Paul H. Landis, *Making the Most of Marriage* (New York: Appleton-Century-Crofts, 1965), p. 260.

[3] Clifford Notarius and Howard Markman, *We Can Work It Out* (New York: Putnam, 1992), p. 154.

Chapter 19

How Good Sex Happens

Too Tired for Sex?

*H*aving sexual energy available is necessary for sexual desire to occur. Sexual desire is different from sexual arousal. Arousal occurs when the body has been stimulated, but sexual desire shows up in our sex drive or libido.

Some use all their sexual energy on other absorbing projects—establishing a new business, caring for a new baby, participating in sports, or managing several school-age children. When extensive amounts of creative energy are expended on other tasks, there is little energy left to fuel the sex drive. Consequently this person will have less desire for sex. This may be desirable for a single person engrossed in a career, but detrimental to a marriage.

Sexual desire is an outgrowth of the energy derived from proper nutrition, exercise, and sleep. All these affect the energy available for sexual involvement. If you want to enhance your levels of sexual desire, make sure that you eat properly and get enough exercise and sleep.

For those who live complicated, busy lives, there may never be enough time or energy to feel sexual desire. To correct this problem, begin by clearing away distractions. The first and easiest thing to do is turn off the TV. Spend a few quiet moments together. Eliminate outside commitments that keep you from having enough time to nurture your relationship. Even church commitments may need to be curtailed.

Children can be a distraction, particularly for mothers of preschoolers. A child with health or behavioral problems can consume so much energy that parents find themselves having little sexual interest in each other. Such couples can remedy the situation only by going away overnight without the children.

Sexual fulfillment is more likely to happen when you know yourselves and each other intimately, behave lovingly toward each other, are both trustworthy and trusting, and anticipate and plan for sexual times, allotting time to connect physically on a daily, weekly, monthly, and quarterly basis.

"Not Tonight, Dear!"

A couple arrives home late after a night on the town. She is sitting at her dressing table removing makeup and getting ready for bed. He places two aspirin and a glass of water in front of her.

She asks, "What's that for?"

"Your headache," he says.

"But I don't have a headache!"

"Gotcha!"

A common problem in marriage arises when one mate desires sexual relations more frequently than the other. Although men most frequently make this complaint, more recently women, particularly in the over-40 age bracket, also wish for more frequent sexual intercourse. Statistics on frequency tend to make us preoccupied with numbers; but studies show that couples in their 20s and 30s have sex on the average of one to three times per week. Couples 45 years of age or older report on the average one time per week.[1]

> *The typical wife doesn't understand her husband's deep need for sex any more than the typical husband understands his wife's deep need for affection.*
>
> —Willard F. Harley, Jr.

Frequency of sexual encounters between couples depends on a number of factors such as age, health, social and business pressures, emotional readiness, the ability to communicate about sex, and many other variables. Averages tend to be misleading. Each couple must find a frequency comfortable for their levels of desire and lifestyle without worrying about numbers. Even then their individual patterns will vary from time to time, depending on circumstances.

While both sexes exhibit variations of desire, not only from person to person but from occasion to occasion, studies done around the world show that most men think about sex more often, are more easily aroused, and want to have sex more frequently than their partners do.

Researchers now know that men and women have the same half-dozen sex hormones, only in differing amounts. It is testosterone that fuels the sex drive in both genders. The fact that men have 10 to 20 times more testosterone than women is one of the primary reasons they experience greater desire. One researcher found that women who were given a testosterone additive had a dramatically higher level of desire and arousal. They also had more energy and a greater sense of well-being.[2]

Men also experience an ebb and flow of hormones. A man's testosterone level can double in the morning hours, which may explain why he wakes up in the middle of the night or early in the morning desiring sex. This is something that tends to decrease with age, however. Life events—something as minor as winning or losing at sports—can also affect a man's testosterone. In a study of tennis players, the winners of a match consistently experienced a rise in testosterone while the losers experienced a decline.[3]

Another reason men hunger for sexual release more consistently than women is a physiological one. The prostate gland contains a small sac that acts as a reservoir for semen. As this sac fills, men feel the need for sexual relief because of the overabundance of semen in the seminal vesicles. When the reservoir is emptied, the pressure is relieved.

One expert has concluded that most men operate on a 48-hour cycle—that is, they need sex that often to keep them on an even keel. Another writer has reckoned that a healthy man's semen builds up every 42 to 78 hours and produces a pressure that needs release.[4]

The male's desire for frequency sharply contrasts with the female's. Not only do men and women differ vastly in desire, but there are also enormous differences between women. Approximately 20 to 25 percent of adult females might be termed "inhibited," which means that they express negative or lukewarm attitudes toward sex. Two percent are totally unresponsive to sex, and another 2 percent possess a high sex drive. However, 20 to 25 percent of women demonstrate an excited attitude—that is, they desire sex, seek it, and initiate it frequently. The remaining 40 to 50 percent register only average sexual interest.[5]

Studies show that some women are more interested in sex during ovulation, when their bodies produce the most testosterone. Other women, particularly those with high testosterone levels, feel sexier just before or during menstruation. Finally, some women appear to be more interested in sex during the first half of the menstrual cycle, which may be caused by the surge of well-being that accompanies the monthly rise in estrogen.[6] Both men and women need to be conscious of this cyclical change in a woman's sexual interests.

Some studies suggest that a third of all women rarely have enough spontaneous interest in sex to initiate lovemaking. They may enjoy sex and be orgasmic, but they don't experience a pressing physical need to make love as men do.[7]

Anyone with an unusually low level of sexual desire should get a complete physical exam. If blood tests indicate a hormone deficiency, the individual should be referred to an endocrinologist for further testing and treatment.

Problems arise when there is a marked difference between the needs and desires of a husband and wife. Compromise is necessary in order for both to be happy. When a husband's needs are stronger than his wife's, he does not have to demand intercourse at his every whim. For her part, she should be willing to go out of her way to meet his needs as an expression of her love for him. A sexually satisfied person is far easier to live with than one who is not.

Good sex doesn't seem to be happening much anymore. Whether it's *Newsweek* reporting on the yuppie syndrome of decreased sexual activity or a *US News & World Report* on sexual desire, it's apparent that millions of people are unhappy with the sexual side of their relationship.

In Hart's study on Christian men, although 72 percent of the men rated their current sexual experience as excellent or good, one out of three reported their sex life as fair or not good. One in 12 had a major complaint about his sexual needs not being met. Since the current divorce rate is about one out of two marriages, having one out of three married men dissatisfied with their sex lives spells problems for marital stability.[8]

Fortunately, according to the "Sex in America" survey, the best sex is happening between monogamous couples.[9] The epidemic of dissatisfaction may be the result of our complex and busy lifestyles as well as the belief that good sex just happens.

The myth that "good sex just happens" may be perpetuated by watching what happens on television or in the movies. A couple find themselves irresistibly attracted and within moments are having passionate sex. Every couple wants to have that kind of gut-grabbing sex.

If you believe that "good sex just happens," then you may also believe that when it doesn't happen or it ceases being irresistible, you are no longer in love. But maintaining a fulfilling, nurturing sexual experience that will last for decades of loving together requires deliberate action and energy.

Understanding Female Sexuality

Most men do not fully appreciate or understand the complexity of a woman's sexuality because it is so different from their own. They would be willing to pledge a year's salary to learn the secret of how to get their wives to be more sexually responsive. Female sexuality is related to the quality of the relationship a woman has with significant males in her life.

Dr. Seymour Fisher investigated the differences between women who were high and low in sexual responsiveness. He investigated his subjects' social and psychological makeup, traits, attitudes, and values. This thorough and well documented study demonstrated that the answers to a woman's sexual issues usually lie in what is happening between her and her sexual partner, not in what is happening in her mind.[10]

Two major insights were reported. "In the first place, orgasm capacity in a woman is very strongly tied to her perceptions and feelings concerning the dependability of her relationships with the significant people in her life. The study indicated that the highly orgasmic woman has the ability to trust the people in her life in general and the men in particular. The men will be there when they are needed. They are dependable. They are seen to be the kind of men that look after a woman's best interests. In contrast, the woman who is low in orgasm capacity is characterized by a fear of loss of significant relationships." [11]

The low orgasmic woman instinctively feels that significant people in her life will either go away or let her down. She finds it difficult to trust, to relax, to abandon herself into the arms of her husband, and her apprehension robs her body of its ability to fully respond sexually.

The second major finding of Dr. Fisher's study has to do with the quality of the relationship the woman had with her father. "The lower a woman's orgasm capacity the more likely she is to describe her father as having treated her 'casually,' without elaborate attempts at control or enforcing his will, as having been easygoing rather than expecting conformity to well-defined rules. To put it another way, the greater a woman's orgasm capacity, the less permissive and the more controlling she perceives her father to be." [12]

> *The best way to hold a man is in your arms.*
>
> —Mae West.

It is apparent that a woman's relationship to her father influences her sexual responsiveness to her husband during her married years. If her father was involved and interested in her upbringing, if he invested himself in caring about what happened to her, she learned to work, perform, and respond to him. She became accustomed to responding to a man.

Men, if your wife is a great sex partner, perhaps you might thank your father-in-law! And don't forget your own responsibilities in staying active and involved in your wife's spiritual, social, emotional, and intellectual interests. Your wife needs you to be aware of her needs, her wants, and her goals as a person.

The Four Phases of Sexual Response

Today more and more Christian couples understand that God designed sex to be a blessing in their lives and to create pleasure. They want a good marriage in every area, including their sex life. But their marriage will remain incomplete and unfulfilled if they do not fully understand how their own bodies were designed to function as well as how to pleasure their partners.

Masters and Johnson in their classic but highly technical book *Human Sexual*

Response identified four distinct phases in sexual encounters: (1) excitement, (2) plateau, (3) orgasm, and (4) resolution.

Phase 1: Excitement. Kissing, embracing, petting, and fondling mark the beginning phase of love play between a couple. The caressing of each other should be done slowly and lovingly and should include all areas of the body, not only areas directly related to sexual excitement. For both husband and wife, it should include caressing of the inner thighs, lower back and buttocks, earlobes, and back of the neck. This demonstrates interest in the entire person, not just their genitals.

The first sign of arousal in the husband is the erection of the penis. This occurs within a few seconds after an erotic thought, a stimulating sight, or a caress. From this initial stage of excitement, he progresses rapidly into the next phase if effective stimulation continues.

The penis, like the clitoris, consists of three parts—the glans, the shaft, and the base. The penis is wrapped in a resilient, expandable sheet of skin. The glans, located at the tip of the penis, is the most sensitive and responsive part of the male genitals and is the part he prefers to have stroked. When the brain receives a sexually arousing message, involuntarily blood vessels in the penis widen, and blood rushes in. Special valves in the penile veins close, thus trapping the blood and keeping the penis erect.

Eighty to 90 percent of a man's sexuality centers in his penis and the nerve endings there. He enjoys a gentle massaging of the genital region, also, for his second most sensitive area is the scrotum, a sacklike pocket of skin that hangs outside the body behind the penis. The woman must be careful not to apply excessive pressure to the testicles, however, since it causes a man as much pain as when he puts too much pressure on her clitoris. Most of her caressing should center on the top shaft of the penis. Fondling the shaft, the head of the penis, and the frenulum on the underside of the penile shaft will greatly increase his excitement.

During this phase the skin of the scrotum thickens, thus forcing the testicles up closer to the body. This is believed to occur in order to increase slightly the temperature of the seminal fluid as it is prepared for expulsion and fertilization of the egg. About 60 percent of men also experience nipple erection; but since a man's breasts are less prominent, this usually isn't noticeable. As this happens he will want to "hurry" just when she wants to take her time. A successful sex life depends on a couple's ability to understand and adjust their different timing needs.

The first evidence of sexual arousal for the female will be lubrication of the vagina. This lubrication takes place within seconds of sexual arousal but is only a beginning sign of arousal and *does not signify that she is ready for or desires intercourse.*

The clitoris is the center of a woman's sexual desire. Male attention during lovemaking most often centers on the breasts and on the vagina, for these areas bring him much pleasure, and they are erogenous zones for the female as well. But the clitoris brings a woman her greatest sexual pleasure. It is located about one inch above the entrance to the vagina and is composed of a glans, a shaft, and a hood. When stimulated, it engorges with blood, much as the penis does, and throbs pleasurably.

According to the research of Masters and Johnson, the clitoris has no other function than to produce sexual pleasure. Termed "the trigger of female desire," it is the most sensitive point for female sexual arousal. Yet it is not necessary for intercourse. Only a vagina and penis are essential. God placed something additional in a woman's anatomy in order that she might experience the same supreme sexual pleasure that her husband does.

The vulva is the second most important component. The vulva is the fleshy area that surrounds the vaginal opening. It is made up of outer lips (the labia majora) and inner lips (labia minora). The outer lips consist of two rounded puffy folds of skin that protect the other parts and preserve the mucus needed to lubricate the vaginal canal during intercourse. The inner lips are inside and parallel to the outer lips. They join at the top of the vulva and serve as a covering for the clitoris. The vulva is the most visibly responsive to sexual stimulation, since it fills with blood much like the penis when it becomes excited. It is the vulva and the clitoris that are the center of a woman's physical sexuality, not her vagina!

The vagina was designed for two purposes: to receive the erect penis during intercourse and as a channel for the birth of a child. But neither of those purposes brings her sexual excitement. While the insertion of the penis into the vagina is most pleasurable for him, this is not necessarily true for her.

The vaginal barrel has very few nerve endings and as a result is basically insensitive to sexual stimulation. This is why so many husbands "lose" their wives when they insist on insertion too early. When this occurs, sexual arousal for the wife is basically over. All that is left is orgasm—and usually she is not ready. What pleasures her more is the caressing of her vulva and the outer edges of the vagina.

Since the area to be filled with blood in a woman is much more extensive than the penis on a man, the excitement phase takes longer and *cannot be hurried*. As a woman is stimulated, the outer lips fill with blood and separate. The inner lips may increase two to three times in size. The inner two thirds of the vagina expands and extends in anticipation of the insertion of the penis. It is now that she may demonstrate other physical reactions—the sex flush, nipple erection, and increase in pulse and respiration.

Phase 2: Plateau. Relatively few changes take place in the male during the early plateau phase. The "head" or glans of the penis deepens in color, because of greater engorgement, and enlarges slightly in preparation for orgasm. During extended love play a small amount of preejaculatory fluid seeps from the penis. This fluid contains live sperm that can impregnate a woman. The skin of the scrotum continues to thicken, and the right testicle pulls in closer to the body. There is also a significant increase in the size of the testicles.

At the end of the plateau phase he reaches "the point of no return"—a point in his sexual arousal when he cannot stop ejaculation. There's no turning back. To a man, it feels like a full balloon ready to burst. When a man reaches the point of no return, he will ejaculate. Nothing can stop it—a ringing phone, falling out of bed—he will still ejaculate.

Men need to become skillful in learning to delay this "point of no return" as long as necessary to satisfy their wives. Most often what pushes a man beyond this point is continued pressure on the glans and shaft of the penis. With practice he can learn to pause prior to the point of no return and relax before crossing over the line. Often just a few seconds' pause will lessen the pressure. With practice a man can come closer and closer to this point without ejaculation. The longer he can wait (up to a point), the more likely he is to pleasure his wife.

In both men and women the heart rate increases, blood pressure often rises, and breathing intensifies. But once again, more extensive changes take place in her than in him. During this phase a saclike area forms when the vaginal barrel becomes larger. A pocket is formed where the semen will be deposited. At the same time the outer one third of the vagina actually becomes smaller. What is created is an ideal repository for the sperm to have the best chance for fertilization.

The Bartholin's glands located in the inner lips of the vulva secrete a mucous substance designed to create the alkaline environment necessary for sperm to live long enough to achieve impregnation. Without this secretion, the vaginal canal would be too acidic and the sperm would not survive. God in His infinite wisdom leaves nothing to chance!

The Song of Solomon describes a position ideal for this time of increasing excitement: "Let his left hand be under my head, and his right hand embrace me," the bride says (Song of Solomon 2:6 and 8:3, NASB). The word *embrace* in the original Hebrew usually means to fondle or stimulate with gentle stroking. In this description, then, the husband lies on his left side, to the right of his wife's body. The wife lies on her back with her legs extended. He places his left arm under her neck. From this position he can kiss her lips, neck, and breasts, and his right hand is still free to caress her genitals.

At this stage a husband's caresses and kisses will likely be just as exciting for her as for him. As he kisses and caresses the nipple area, her nipples will become more firm and will stand out from the breast. As excitement increases, the nipple may appear to disappear as the breasts and surrounding tissue swell. The breasts may become more sensitive to touch during this stage.

Gentle, creative, loving touches to a woman's genitalia will be more welcome than a rough, demanding approach. The clitoris continues to enlarge but draws up under the hood as arousal continues, and becomes more difficult to locate. Often the sensitivity is so extreme it cannot be touched directly.

Normally, during intercourse the penis does not touch the clitoris. Consequently the loving husband should gently massage the clitoral area until his wife indicates that she is ready for entry. The clitoris is so sensitive that a husband needs to use caution as he explores its potential. Guernsey likens stimulation of the clitoris to the sensitivity of the cornea of the eye. If something flew into your eye, you would close your eyelid and rub it, using your eyelid as protection. This is similar to the sensitivity of the clitoris to direct touch.

It is better to bring indirect pressure by a gentle massaging of its hood. Heavy manual rubbing brings pain and irritation. Gentle stimulation with indirect pressure is what is needed to bring most women to orgasm.

During this period of foreplay, a husband must not suspend stimulation of the clitoris, for a woman requires continuous stimulation to orgasm as opposed to the interrupted stimulation that serves adequately for most men. A man can, with practice, learn to insert the penis while continuing to massage the clitoral area.

During this phase it is critical that a wife concentrate on her physical sensations and communicate her progress verbally or nonverbally to her husband. This is necessary so he can decipher her level of excitement.

A couple might wish to include oral sex if both enjoy it and find it pleasant. However, if either partner has any hesitancy about it, it should be discontinued. One of the purposes of lovemaking is to build a delightful trove of memorable experiences. Helen Singer Kaplan, M.D., Ph.D., one of the most recognized authorities on sexuality, states: "You should never do anything sexually which is physically painful or morally or emotionally repugnant to you. If you don't like oral sex, there are plenty of other pleasurable things you and your partner can do."[13]

Medically the practice is generally safe unless there are infectious genital lesions. However, anal sex is not sterile and should be avoided. There is no clear biblical directive, although some verses in the Song of Solomon seem to suggest oral sex. The Levitical laws, which give explicit sexual prohibitions, do not mention it.

A couple should engage in love play that both enjoy. Usually the husband is the more willing to initiate a greater variety of lovemaking experiences, but he should not force these upon an unwilling partner. The key here is mutual enjoyment, and a couple can experiment with a great variety of pleasurable lovemaking experiences if they so choose.

A man needs to keep in mind through the entire process, that his wife is a whole person—not just a vulva or a clitoris—and pleasure all of her. Kissing, breast play, and caressing and fondling of the vulva and clitoris are what foreplay is all about.

Phase 3: Orgasm. In the male the sphincter muscle from the bladder closes off so that no urine escapes during ejaculation. It is nearly impossible for a man to urinate immediately before or after ejaculation. Orgasm for the male takes place in two phases. When the blood in his sexual organs has filled every available space, the muscles at the base of the penis contract, thus spurting about one half teaspoon of seminal fluid out the end of the penis. In younger men the force comes out in great spurts, but this decreases with age. His orgasm is complete when he has expelled the semen.

Semen is primarily protein, similar to the white of an egg, and is neither dirty nor unsanitary, although it has a distinctive odor. The seminal fluid expelled contains some 250 to 500 million sperm, which stay active in the vagina for up to 10 hours.

Men usually experience five or six contractions centered in the penis, prostate, and seminal vesicles. The second and third contractions are usually the most intense. Once the ejaculatory experience has been initiated by contractions, it cannot be stopped or delayed until the seminal fluid has been expelled. Although the woman can easily be distracted or interrupted in the midst of her orgasm, the man will carry out his two-phase experience—contraction and ejaculation—regardless of external stimuli.

Men are usually limited to one release per experience and must have a rest period of 20 to 30 minutes, or more likely several hours, before they can become rearoused. Men who experience release without ejaculation can maintain their erections after release and continue lovemaking with repeated releases.

Should the husband climax first, he should immediately begin manual stimulation of his wife's clitoris so that she can have repeated orgasms if she so desires. This is the way God designed her body. She should not have to ask for this, since sex is something we engage in to please each other. It should be the natural desire for a husband to provide for his wife every pleasure. However, a better plan might be for him to bring her to orgasm first. Observing her responses will heighten his response, and then he can seek release.

Orgasm for the female begins with what has been described as a sensation of "suspension," probably caused by uterine contractions, followed by a wave of warmth that sweeps through her body. The muscle contractions and rushing out of fluids create the sensation of orgasm and an immense sense of pleasure and relief. Since the female has a greater area of congestion and more fluid that must be removed, she usually has more contractions.

Three to five contractions mark a mild orgasm, and eight to 12 contractions, an intense orgasm. These contractions occur at intervals of less than a second. Climax is a wonderful physical sensation designed by the Creator, a high point best described as "ecstasy," which is why so many people seek it so often.

Should a woman not achieve orgasm, she is left in an extremely uncomfortable state. Her body has been prepared for sexual release; but when orgasm does not occur, there are no contractions to force the fluids from her genitalia. The sexual excitement turns to irritation, because of genuine discomfort. For a male it would be like trying to go through the day with an erection that wouldn't go away! The blood that could have emptied in less than 15 minutes following orgasmic release now takes up to 12 hours to empty. Should this happen to her repeatedly, she will feel sexually discouraged and will eventually avoid sexual encounters.

Phase 4: Resolution. Following sexual satisfaction the couple enters a phase of calm when body functions return to normal levels. At this point another pointed difference between male and female sexual response occurs. Men's bodies typically return to normal abruptly. The blood that once filled the penile area empties quickly. Erection diminishes; the testes decrease in size and once again descend to their original position. Once the congestion diminishes, if a man follows his natural inclinations he will probably turn over and fall asleep.

Because of the greater body area involved in the female sexual processes, resolution takes longer for the female than the male. Usually 10 to 15 minutes is required, whereas only a minute or two is needed for the male. Orgasm for women does not signal the end of lovemaking but merely an entry into another phase—the afterglow.

Following orgasm a woman seems to have a subconscious need to remain in touch with her husband. He may wish to pull away and get some much-needed rest, but women feel rejected and used by such actions. This is the time to caress and kiss her. Talk to her. Shower her with tender hugs and kisses.

A couple should lie close in each other's arms and just enjoy closeness. This ensures a smooth transition to complete relaxation together. Following orgasm for the male, some men report that the head of the penis becomes very sensitive to touch. Because of this, they wish to withdraw immediately. A woman may take this as a sign of rejection. A loving husband must tell his wife that he feels postejaculation discomfort so that she can be understanding and sympathetic rather than feel rejected.

Note that each phase can be more quickly achieved and completed in the male than in the female. This is why he needs to be extremely patient with her and take his time, never rushing through the act! To a woman, sex isn't an act but rather an event.

The following books have contributed greatly to my understanding of male and female sexual responses and are the sources from which I have drawn most of my knowledge:

William H. Masters and Virginia E. Johnson, *Human Sexual Response.*

Clifford and Joyce Penner, *The Gift of Sex.* Waco, Tex.: Word Books, 1981.

Ed and Gaye Wheat, *Intended for Pleasure.* Old Tappan, N.J.: Fleming H. Revell Co., 1977.

---

[1] Timothy La Haye and Beverly La Haye, *The Act of Marriage* (Grand Rapids: Zondervan, 1976), p. 252.

[2] Patricia Love and Jo Robinson, "Not Tonight, Dear," *Ladies' Home Journal,* March, 1994, p. 64.

[3] *Ibid.*

[4] La Haye, *The Act of Marriage,* p. 22.

[5] James Dobson, *What Wives Wish Their Husbands Knew About Women* (Wheaton, Ill.: Tyndale House, 1975), p. 119.

[6] Patricia Love and Jo Robinson, "Not Tonight, Dear," *Ladies' Home Journal,* March 1994, p. 64.

[7] *Ibid.*

[8] Archibald D. Hart, *The Sexual Man* (Dallas: Word Books, Inc., 1994), pp.126, 127.

[9] Note: *Sex in America* is a 290-page report of the most scientifically accurate sexual study ever conducted in America. Nearly 3,500 adults were randomly selected and interviewed in depth.

[10] Seymour Fisher, *Understanding the Female Orgasm* (New York: Bantam Books, 1973).

[11] Dennis Guernsey, *Thoroughly Married* (Waco, Tex: Word Books, Inc., 1975), p. 47.

[12] *Ibid.,* p. 49.

[13] Helen Singer Kaplan, *The New Sex Therapy* (New York: Brunner/Mazel Publishers, 1974), p. 54.

Chapter 20

Understanding Sexual Climax

*S*ome couples think that the main goal in intercourse is to reach orgasm simultaneously. Since only about 17 percent of all couples experience a simultaneous orgasm—and even then only on occasion—this leaves many couples wondering whether their sexual experiences are lacking. The Janus Report showed that 24 percent of men and 14 percent of women felt a simultaneous orgasm was a must.[1]

Trying to achieve orgasm at the same time can actually make sex less fulfilling. When a couple achieves orgasm together, each is so absorbed with their own intense pleasure that all attention is concentrated on self. One minute she enjoys the full extent of his attention; the next minute he is absorbed in himself. In the same way, he will miss experiencing the full extent of her pleasure because he is too caught up in the intensity of his own experience.

If he times it so that she has her orgasm first, he can then help to intensify her orgasm and can fully enjoy her pleasure. Then she is free to experience his. It's almost like having two orgasms instead of just one. Both partners fully experience her orgasm, and then both experience his. Should he have his orgasm first, she is distracted from her own arousal. Even if she eventually does achieve orgasm he is less interested since he is no longer fully aroused.

Please note that even though a woman does not always achieve orgasm, she can feel quite fulfilled when not burdened by her husband's expectations. Sometimes men measure their sexual prowess by their wife's orgasm (which appeared to be the case in the Janus Report). If she doesn't achieve orgasm, he pouts. This produces pressure for her to perform to satisfy him even when she doesn't feel like it. Once a woman feels she has to perform or fake orgasms, it can prevent her from having real orgasms.

A requirement for great sex is that a woman feel no pressure to perform. A great sex life means that sometimes sex will be fantastic, and other times it may be only ordinary or not so ordinary. But whatever the intensity, it should always be loving. This usually means that the man gets his orgasm and the woman gets the physical affection she wants. Then they both win.

Clitoral Versus Vaginal Orgasm

Confusion has resulted because of the vaginal-orgasm versus the clitoral-orgasm theory. A vaginal orgasm, according to the old school of thought, supposedly indicated emotional maturity and resulted from penile thrusting with no added stimulation of the clitoris. A clitoral orgasm supposedly resulted from manual manipulation of the clitoris. A woman who experienced only clitoral orgasms was regarded as psychologically flawed and immature.

To date, no major study has ever proved a clitoral orgasm inferior to a vaginal orgasm. Indeed, it is now well documented that an orgasm is an orgasm. The brain and the sex organs work together to produce a climax. Whether they originate in the vagina or clitoris, all orgasms produce the same response—the formation of the orgasmic platform, the contractions in the outer third of the vagina, and the contractions of the uterus.

Women have two centers of orgasmic response. The orgasm is experienced not only in the vagina but also in the uterus. The uterus undergoes contractions similar to the first stages of labor. These contractions are a normal response, and women learn to enjoy the sensation.

God not only created the pleasurable drives within us but also the proper context for their complete expression and fulfillment.—H. Norman Wright.

While the center of response is in the vagina and uterus, the sensations include the entire body. Clifford and Joyce Penner describe the sensation as analogous to dropping a rock into a pool of water. The most intense reaction is at the center where the rock is dropped, but the reaction continues to move out in wider and wider circles. This is true regardless of the source of stimulation.

Some women report increased emotional satisfaction brought about while the penis is in the vagina, but this is strictly a matter of personal preference. There is nothing the matter with having an orgasm as a result of external stimulation. In fact, some women report more intense orgasms when the penis is not in the vagina.

The Hite Report found that only 30 percent of the 300,000 women studied could achieve orgasm regularly without clitoral stimulation. This means that for approximately 60 to 70 percent of the female population, penile thrusting alone does not lead to regular orgasm.

The reluctance of loving partners to incorporate clitoral stimulation as a meaningful part of foreplay has cheated more women out of orgasmic fulfillment than any other single factor. Couples must not confuse manual stimulation of the clitoris with masturbation. Masturbation involves the manipulation of one's own genitals. It is basically selfish and excludes the happiness of the other person. Not so with clitoral stimulation during intercourse. God designed the clitoris to be used in sexual expression. It constitutes acceptable love play between husbands and wives, and for a majority of women it offers the only path to sexual fulfillment.

Multiple Orgasms

New research into female sexuality has shown that some women can experience many orgasms in a brief period of time. Men sometimes find this difficult to comprehend, since they are powerless in most cases to regain their capacity without a rest period. But a continuously stimulated woman is capable of five or more orgasms, often each one increasing in intensity. Most woman in the Hite Report did not know this fact.

Because a woman can experience repeated climaxes, a thoughtful man will often, after ejaculation, immediately stimulate the clitoral area so that she can repeat the experience. It is the natural response of a loving husband to provide his wife with every pleasure. *But multiple orgasms should not be forced upon a woman or expected during every sexual encounter.* Most women prefer the experience on those special occasions when the circumstances, mood, and all the other factors work together. The single orgasm is still the most frequent response for a woman, and in the Hite survey the majority of women reported a desire for only one orgasm.

Tips for Increasing Pleasure

Five practices can increase the intensity of pleasure for the male: (1) waiting 24 hours after the previous orgasm to allow a greater amount of seminal fluid to store; (2) lengthening foreplay and excitement so the penis is erect 20 minutes or longer; (3) increasing the imagination by seeing and feeling his wife's ecstatic response to his skillful stimulation; (4) voluntarily contracting the anal sphincter muscles during orgasm; (5) increasing the force of thrusting while orgasm is in progress.

A woman can increase the intensity of her physical sensations by voluntarily strengthening her muscle contractions and adding her pelvic movements to his as she abandons herself to seeking release.

Problems That Can Ruin Your Sex Life

Sexual problems are common in the population at large. A host of organic factors (such as illness and drugs), psychological factors (anger and performance anxieties), and cultural influences (shame and guilt) can intervene and sometimes derail the delicate sexual mechanism entirely.

The assumption that happily married couples are free of sexual problems is not necessarily a valid one. Nor can it be assumed that a sexual problem is synonymous with an unhappy marriage. A most significant truth is that very few people have trouble-free sex lives, even when their marriages are happy.

Sex problems can be dealt with very effectively through simple education and behavioral techniques. As researchers have helped us come to a clearer understanding of what can go wrong during various phases of the sex response cycle, specific methods have emerged for dealing with a variety of problems.

Premature Ejaculation. Premature ejaculation (PE) means a man lacks adequate voluntary ejaculatory control and climaxes involuntarily before he wishes to do so. Ejaculatory control should be natural, easy, and voluntary. PE can be a source of distress for both a man and his wife. Unless both are very understanding and mature, this condition can have a destructive impact on a couple's sex life and may eventually threaten their entire relationship.

A sexually healthy man can usually choose whether to stay aroused for a while or to climax rapidly. But the premature ejaculator has no voluntary ejaculatory control. He peaks quickly and moves right through the "plateau" stage to orgasm, which puts an end to the sexual experience before he wishes.

Premature ejaculation is divided into a primary and a secondary form. Primary PE has always been present and is usually associated with early sexual experience such as masturbation. When he has only himself to please, he usually ejaculates in one to two minutes. With repetition this timing becomes imprinted in his subconscious. Other early sexual encounters requiring haste can also be contributing factors. But since this is a learned behavior, it can be unlearned.

Secondary PE is brought about by physical causes. After years of normal ejaculation, the duration of intercourse grows progressively shorter. Some men with severe PE will ejaculate during foreplay, even before penetration.

Although PE is essentially a male problem, it requires teamwork to rectify. The husband needs to admit his problem, and the wife must exhibit patient understanding. At times she may become so frustrated that she may lash out at her "quick" husband, but such reactions will only heighten his feelings of inadequacy and complicate the situation.

Fortunately, treatment for this devastating dysfunction has dramatically improved the outlook for men who climax too fast. Now the cure rate approaches 100 percent within an average of 14 weeks of treatment. Unhappy couples can enjoy a much more gratifying sex life in just a few months.

There are two main methods of treatment for PE: (1) Masters and Johnson's "squeeze technique" and (2) the "stop-start" procedure. We shall explore the latter method here. It involves several steps.

1. *Bring the wife to orgasm first.* Since a premature ejaculator cannot concentrate on solving his problem while he is bringing his wife to orgasm, he should help her reach a climax first so that he can concentrate completely on his own sensations later. The husband can help his wife achieve orgasm by manual stimulation of the clitoris or another agreed-upon approach.

2. *Spend time in loving foreplay.* Recognizing that increased fondling heightens a man's excitement, a wife will often eliminate touching her husband's penis. In their effort to short-circuit excessive sexual tension, they proceed directly to intercourse. However, when penetration of that warm, familiar environment occurs without prior stimulation, a husband may actually thrust and ejaculate more quickly because of the shock to his system. Therefore, the wife should lovingly fondle her husband's genitals—especially caressing the underside or head of the penis—but not to the point that he ejaculates.

3. *Entering and withdrawing.* During this state the husband inserts his penis (from the man-above position in which he maintains better control) *slowly* into the vagina—stopping penetration or withdrawing whenever he feels the desire to ejaculate. The friction of total withdrawal may trigger ejaculation, so it is preferable for the penis to remain in the vagina if possible.

Suspension of motion will not cause the erection to subside but will only curb the desire to ejaculate. When he feels in control, he can slowly begin entering or penetrating again. If the desire to ejaculate increases once more, he should stop movement or withdraw immediately. The objective during this phase is to penetrate until he senses imminent ejaculation. A man with a severe problem may not be able to insert more than the head of his penis before stopping to gain control.

4. *Controlling "the point of no return."* Sooner or later every man reaches "the point of no return" when he continues to thrust till ejaculation is completed. There is no turning back. During this part of the treatment, the man should approach the point of no return but maintain control by suspending motion. After deferring ejaculation, he then should rest from 15 seconds to two minutes or more, depending on his problem—carefully timing himself by means of a clock with a sweep second hand.

Although this sounds unromantic and clinical, it is important to time himself until he can consistently recognize the sensation preceding ejaculation. During the time of suspension, he does not thrust, and she does not move, cough, sneeze, or wink, because the slightest movement could signal "the end" for him.

5. *Extending the act of intercourse.* Once the husband learns the feeling that occurs just prior to the point of no return, he can begin *light* thrusting motions. The ob-

jective is to tolerate gradually increasing amounts of momentum. At first he will have difficulty controlling his movements because his instincts and excitement motivate him toward deep thrusting. However, such deep thrusting does not usually produce the greatest amount of female satisfaction and can actually produce discomfort.

Concentrating the motion closer to the vaginal opening is more advantageous for both husband and wife than deep penetration. It is better for her because only the first two or three inches of the vagina contain primary sensitive tissue, and it will reduce his excitement and thus assist him in learning ejaculatory control.

6. *Lasting ejaculatory control.* Once a man learns the sensations that precede ejaculation and can tolerate light thrusting with periods of rest, he is well on his way to ejaculatory control. After he can control ejaculation for 15 seconds, he should increase the time to four 15-second periods. If he can learn to add one minute, he can eventually add two. And if he can add two minutes, he can add three.

Soon he can engage in light thrusting, approach the point of no return, stop thrusting, and lose the desire for immediate ejaculation. After extensive practice, he will be able to maintain intercourse as long as he and his wife desire. A man attains complete ejaculatory control when he can select the time when his orgasm should occur.

Remind me, O Creator, that sex comes from You and not from the devil, no matter what the prudes may say.

—**Harry Hollis, Jr.**

The stop-start training sessions can produce increased pleasure for any couple. The husband can increase his ability to delay ejaculation and thus prolong the pleasures of intercourse, and the wife may begin to experience sexual arousal unknown to her before. If she has not had climaxes, she may now do so. If she has already reached this plateau, she may go on to enjoy multiple orgasms.

Many couples also find that stop-start training frees them to experiment with various positions—an option never open to them previously, because of the shortness of time before ejaculation. Through teamwork they will have developed valuable verbal and nonverbal communication skills as well as a new awareness of their interdependence in bringing each other sexual fulfillment.

Erectile Dysfunction. Impotence or erectile dysfunction is defined as the inability to achieve or maintain an erection sufficient for satisfactory sexual performance. Between 10 and 20 million American men suffer impotence at some point in their lives. When individuals with partial erectile dysfunction are included, the number increases to about 30 million.[2] The likelihood of erectile dysfunction increases with age but is not an inevitable consequence of aging.

For elderly persons and for others, erectile dysfunction may occur as a consequence of specific illnesses or of medical treatment for certain illnesses, resulting in fear, loss of self-confidence, and depression. About 5 percent erectile dysfunction is observed about age 40, increasing to 15-25 percent at age 65 and older. It is treatable in all age groups, however.[3]

Impotence is not all in a man's head. About 85 percent is caused by disease, particularly diabetes and heart conditions that restrict blood flow. The most common causes include vascular disease, diabetes, neurologic impairment, pelvic injury, prescription drugs, hormonal imbalance, and Peyronie's disease.

Psychological aspects of self-confidence, anxiety, and partner communication and conflict are often important contributing factors. The problem is also associated with depression, loss of self-esteem, poor self-image, increased anxiety or tension with one's sexual partner, and/or fear and anxiety associated with contracting sexually transmitted diseases, including AIDS. Other factors, such as obesity, poor physical fitness, as well as heavy smoking and drinking, can contribute to erectile dysfunction.

For many men, erectile dysfunction creates mental stress that affects their interaction with family and associates. Virility and self-esteem are so tightly intertwined for some that discussion can be difficult and embarrassing even with people they trust, such as their partner or doctor. Even though 85 percent of impotence is a result of physical causes, once erection troubles are perceived, emotional factors often compound the problem.

It should be recognized that desire, orgasmic capability, and ejaculatory capacity may be intact even in the presence of erectile dysfunction or may be deficient to some extent and thus contribute to the sense of inadequate sexual function.

Many advances have occurred in both diagnosis and treatment of erectile dysfunction. The four most frequently prescribed treatments include vacuum therapy, self-injection, penile implants, and intraurethral pellets. Other treatments are available. New pills promise to restore sexual function without the discomfort and embarrassment of traditional therapies. Specific antihypertensive, antidepressant, and antipsychotic drugs can be chosen to lessen the risk of erectile failure. Many patients and health-care providers are unaware of these treatments, and the dysfunction often remains untreated, compounded by its psychological impact.

Erectile dysfunction is not permanent. About 95 percent of all cases can be successfully treated once the cause has been determined. Erectile dysfunction is not just a man's problem. Because it can disrupt marriages, relationships, and the way sufferers feel about themselves, it becomes a couple's problem. Treatment success rates are higher when both partners are involved.

The biggest hurdle might be mental attitudes toward the problem. The more a man thinks he is sexually finished, the more real the possibility becomes. When a man first encounters erectile dysfunction, he should have a complete physical examination, making certain the physician is aware of his impotence. If there is no physical malady, he can thus adjust his attitudes in a more positive manner toward success. The first step to recovery is admitting a problem exists and asking for help.

Pornography. Many men use pornography as a sexual stimulant even after marriage. A regular sex partner does not remove their need for pornography nor for masturbation. Once these habits are established, they continue for a long time.

The Janus Report on Sexual Behavior, a 1993 survey of 2,765 adults nationwide, states that 24 to 32 percent of males actively masturbate, but it is not clear what percentage of these are married men.[4] Archibald Hart's study shows that 15.5 percent of married men and 6.8 percent of married clergymen continue to masturbate to pornography while married.[5]

Pornography's popularity results from early conditioning, a way of satisfying curiosity, a desire to improve sexual performance, and a tendency to become habituated to its stimulation. Some men turn to erotica to restore lost interest or to revitalize a sagging sex life.

One man turned to erotica after 10 years of marriage and what he called a "boring" sex life. He began by visiting sleazy X-rated movie houses and purchasing a few erotic videos and magazines. He got his hormones pumping, and declared himself fully alive again. But this improvement was short-lived. He became dependent on the erotica. Without it he couldn't perform. Soon he found himself turning to "S and M" (sadomasochism, meaning that pain and suffering are inflicted). It wasn't until he found himself drawn to kiddie porn that he recognized the deeply coarsening effect pornography was having upon his life.

Unfortunately, the Internet has opened a new era of pornography and sex addiction. No longer must seekers cruise the seedy side of town. Now they can cruise the "net" and indulge in pornography, "cybersex," or even have an affair on-line. Addiction counselors say that sexual addiction via the Internet is the fastest-growing addiction today. The accessibility to inappropriate sexual activities creates problems for many. Struggling Christians, weak and susceptible to its pull, are becoming more deeply entrenched at home and at work, even with filtering software. Wives are calling addiction counselors in anguish, not knowing what to do about their husbands' continued involvement with Internet porn. Many people say they don't see anything wrong with what they are doing as long as the relationship is not physically consummated. Indulging in forms of pornography, as well as other sex addictions, is not considered adultery by them. Let's remember that infidelity begins at the point of making a strong emotional connection. This means it doesn't take a physical act to betray your marriage vows.

Pornography destroys intimacy because, by definition, it introduces a third person into the relationship. Dependency on it is not only detrimental to the husband and to the couple's sex life, but is devastating to the wife's self-esteem. It undermines her sense of safety within the marriage and damages her trust in him. Sex addictions such as this can be broken, but only when a man admits his problem and gets into a program designed to break the addiction. (See Appendix.)

A Word to Preorgasmic Women

Not many years ago the sexually unfulfilled wife was left to rot in her own sexual frustration. But that day is over, and research has proved that all married women are capable of achieving orgasm. The word "frigid" is no longer used for women who are sexually unresponsive. "Preorgasmic" is more descriptive, since orgasm for females is a learned experience. A woman who is not achieving orgasm has simply not yet learned how. Certainly no Christian wife should settle for less, for she owes it to both herself and her husband.

A woman's orgasmic response is closely connected to her feelings about herself. Resentment, bitterness, misinformation, and tired attitudes erect sexual barriers for a woman that make it difficult, if not impossible, for her to respond to her husband. And since our most important sex organ is the brain, it must say "OK, go ahead" for her to be sexually satisfied.

A woman who finds such attitudes blocking a satisfying sexual experience can help herself by adopting more positive attitudes. Such books as *The Gift of Sex,* by Clifford and Joyce Penner, may offer insight into her problems. If such efforts fail to help, she should contact a trusted physician or ask for a referral if necessary.

Another method of increasing sexual pleasure, as well as teaching women how to achieve orgasm, comes as a result of strengthening the pubococcygeus (PC) muscle. In 1940 Dr. Arnold H. Kegel, a specialist in female disorders, inadvertently discovered that an exercise to strengthen a weakened bladder muscle also increased sexual satisfaction for women. Not only did the Kegel exercise cure the patient's urinary problem, but also she experienced orgasm for the first time in 15 years of marriage.

Widespread reports now confirm Dr. Kegel's original discovery. The Kegel exercises have since been adopted by many physicians to improve the sexual response of patients, for perhaps as many as two thirds of all American women suffer from a PC muscle weakness severe enough to interfere with sexual functioning.

The PC muscle runs between the legs from front to back like a sling. It supports the bladder neck, the lower part of the rectum, the birth canal, and the lower vagina. In two out of every three women, this wide muscle is weak and sags, interfering with sexual functioning.

The Kegel exercises to strengthen the PC consist of a series of contractions first utilized when urine is voided. If urination can be interrupted, the PC has been contracted. Once control of the muscle is learned, the exercise can be practiced any time. Women should begin with five to ten contractions six times daily for the first week. Over a six week period they should increase the number of contractions during the six daily sessions to 50. Most women note changes in their sexual performance within three weeks of time, and after six to eight weeks a small amount of exercise will maintain the muscle tone.

Strengthening the PC muscle can tighten a vagina stretched by having children. A stretched vagina can result in significantly reduced sensation for both partners. Squeezing these muscles during intercourse (and adding her pelvic movements to his) is another way to intensify pleasure.

Let's Talk About It

Why is it that the most fascinating subject known to humankind is the most difficult for a couple to talk about? A couple who can pore over house plans by the hour fall silent when faced with talking about their sex lives.

People can revert to the most childish ways of sending indirect messages when sex is involved. Tantrums, silence, pouting, irritability, name-calling, and threats are some tactics used in dealing with sexual issues. It seems a couple will resort to anything but open, honest talking and listening

A study conducted by Jessie Potter, a sex educator, therapist, and director of the National Institute for Human Relationships in Chicago, showed that 87 percent of sexually active adults don't tell each other what they like in bed.[6] And my guess is that even those who say they can talk with their partners would admit that there is a limit to what they can talk about.

Good listeners make good lovers.

When a sexual problem is not addressed, it does anything but disappear. It tends to grow in its dimension and impact. Since open communication on sexual preferences produces a happier sex life, it's worth a try.

A sexual problem can separate a couple or it can bring them together, depending on their response to it. If they are willing to trust each other and share their fears, they can more firmly cement their relationship. Sex is like that: it can rip a couple apart or bond them together more securely.

For more information on how a couple can talk about sex more freely, see chapter 7 of my book *How to Talk So Your Mate Will Listen:* "Sexually Speaking: Strangers in the Night."

Does Sexual Desire Decline With Age?

Sex, over the years, invariably changes. But that doesn't mean sex dies. One study at the University of Chicago found that women in their 20s are the least likely of all age groups to achieve orgasm during intercourse, while those in their early 40s are the likeliest. As one woman explained, "I finally got my body figured out and my mate trained. Lovemaking isn't all silent hoping and frantic squirming anymore."[7]

Women in their 30s start taking more sexual initiative. These women feel a marked increase in the need for orgasm. One reason is a shift in hormonal balance that gives testosterone more of a say in their body chemistry—which translates into increased assertiveness, self-confidence, and interest in orgasm. When women manifest a new interest in sex, it can be the worst or best in a couple's sex life. Some men find their wives' new attitudes downright frightening, and many relationships don't weather the storm.

As forty-something women complete the reproductive years, there is a tremendous freedom in realizing more fulfilling sex. Both men and women in their 40s have usually achieved a certain measure of sexual and emotional maturity and compatibility. There is a renewed sense of fun, balance, and respect. The children are older and spend more time out of the house, which has a liberating effect. The sense of intimacy couples feel during these years finally allows them to experiment with new techniques they may have been too inhibited to try in their younger years.

The 50s can be even more relaxed, romantic, and intimate. This is when partners are most likely to be perfectly matched sexually and emotionally. Their careers are under control, and they have more time, less pressure, and fewer worries than they did a decade earlier. Sometimes men greet their 50s with trepidation, however, since the frequency of erections drops slightly and it takes more than visual stimulation to produce an erection. What men don't realize is that the erections they do get will last longer and may even be fuller than in the earlier years.

The Janus Report found that men 51 to 64 described sex as "more deeply gratifying" and "unhurried" than in their younger years. They had plenty of time to spend on foreplay and reported more warmth and intimacy after intercourse, with less compulsion to ejaculate. Arousal becomes the focus. And because fewer erections arise purely from visual stimuli, it means an increased need for touching, which produces greater intimacy.

Believe it or not, after 60 can be the sexiest time of life. Most women have frequent if not multiple orgasms now, and men have learned that age does not equal impotence. The Janus Report noted that those 70 and over said sex was as gratifying as ever. Some said it was the best. Even those in their 90s who had partners and were in good enough health said sex was still good.

When growth and intimacy take place on every level of a relationship, sexual intimacy continues over the years. When this happens, the changes that occur over time will be welcome ones.

---

[1] Samuel S. Janus and Cynthia L. Janus, *The Janus Report on Sexual Behavior* (New York: Wiley and Sons, 1993), pp. 80, 81.

[2] Institutes of Health Consensus Development Conference Statement, Dec. 7-9, 1991, p. 3, http://text.nlm.nih.gov/nig/cdc/www/91txt.html

[3] *Ibid.*

[4] Samuel and Cynthia Janus, *The Janus Report on Sexual Behavior* (New York: Wiley and Sons, 1993).

[5] Archibold D. Hart, *The Sexual Man* (Dallas: Word, 1994), p. 95.

[6] Ronald M. Deutsch, *The Key to Feminine Response in Marriage* (New York: Ballantine Books, 1968), pp. 58-61.

[7] Jesse Potter, as quoted in *Ladies' Home Journal,* "Problems That threaten Your Marriage," by Carol Lynn Mithers, p. 80, Nov. 1993.

[8] Alison Glock, "Love Always," *American Health,* Dec. 1996, pp. 50, 51.

Chapter 21

His and Her Tips for Great Sex

 t is one thing to have knowledge about why and how your partner responds differently and another thing to accept the differences and change your behavior accordingly. To a large degree, a woman can make her husband feel either great about himself sexually or inadequate. When a wife makes her husband feel like a sexual king, he is much more likely to fulfill that role and make her feel like a queen.

Likewise, by failing to create an atmosphere in which his wife can respond, a man can deprive himself of the sexual pleasure that is important to his happiness. He may wonder how she can say that she still loves him and yet deny him what he wants and needs most. But when things are out of balance in the sexual department, the husband might well look at himself, for where you find a lukewarm wife, you will most likely find a husband who fails to meet her needs.

How to Satisfy a Woman Sexually

Although men today are much more sexually aware than in any previous generations, there is much to learn about satisfying a woman.

1. *Romance her outside the bedroom first.* Lovemaking is a deeply emotional experience for a woman. She is stimulated by the amount of romantic love her husband has shown for her throughout the day and considers each romantic encounter a moment of profound love and a deeply important part of her life.

If her husband seems to take their sex life for granted, she can feel deeply hurt and offended. She withdraws instinctively from sexual encounters devoid of love and adoration. Repeated assurances may seem unnecessary and theatrical to him, but not so to her. She does not need reassurances because she is vain or seeking flattery. She needs reassurances because they feed a deep and constant yearning for a romantic relationship.

Romance her with loving touches, pats, and hugs throughout the day. Hold hands with her while riding in the car, or while you are out walking. If you touch her only when you want sex, she'll learn that every hug or touch means a trip to the bedroom and will resent it.

A woman needs to hear words and to experience feelings before she can respond in the bedroom. When asked what one change she would like to make in her mate's lovemaking ability, one woman replied, "Have him realize that the lovemaking atmosphere starts when he jumps out of bed in the morning—not when he jumps in at night. Little attentions, kind words, concern for me, touching, set the mood for me." Any husband who thinks he can merely walk into the bedroom and expect his wife to "turn on" with no preparation doesn't understand female sexuality.

Two things arouse a woman most—touch and words. A great lover knows how to romance his wife with words. "You mean everything to me." "The best day of my life was when I found you." "I'm the luckiest guy in the world to have you for a wife." Such words arouse a woman's love feelings and prepare her for lovemaking. Beware of using crude sex words or terms while making love to your wife. They may be stimulating to you, but most women find them offensive.

Now through words and touch you have prepared her for lovemaking.

2. *Spend time in loving foreplay*. Men tend to concentrate on intercourse. It's what you want, and you want it *now*. But what's good for a man is often not good for his wife. Many men are hurry-up lovers. And hurry-up lovers are rarely good lovers. They are often insecure males who need an orgasm fast. The most important thing to remember is that it takes 15 to 20 minutes on the average to prepare a woman for the sexual experience, and an inexperienced bride or a woman with a sexual problem might require 30 minutes or longer.

> *Four hugs a day are necessary for survival, eight for maintenance, and 12 for growth.*
> —**Virginia Satir.**

Just because she's slower does not mean there is anything wrong with her. Again, this happens by God's design. If it took the male as long as the female, we wouldn't be as fruitful or multiply as fast, according to God's command. If both sexes achieved satisfaction as quickly as the male, it would take much of the loving foreplay from the act. When a man has to slow down, laying his own urgent needs aside to woo and prepare his wife, it takes what could be a purely selfish act and turns it into an act of unselfish love. When a man is patient with his wife, he can move her along so both can enjoy the experience.

3. *Understand female pleasure zones*. It is important that a man understand the interrelationship between the three separate components of his wife's sexual apparatus: the pleasure zones of her body, the vulva, and the clitoris. Most sexual focus for the male is centered in his penis, but the female has many areas on

her body that are potentially erogenous. Her breasts, ears, mouth, and vagina are all responsive to sexual exploration, depending on the individual woman. The creative husband is not afraid to use his hands and mouth to explore her body, looking for areas in which she is most sexually responsive.

To make it more complicated for males, what is sexually pleasurable for her on one occasion may be distasteful on another! A skilled husband will locate the areas that excite her and explore them in ways that are appropriate and pleasing to her. Ideally the two will be able to talk about what she needs from him so that he is able to vary his approach to suit her mood.

Routine and monotony are as deadly to a woman's sexual responsiveness as they are to a male's. The creative husband needs to vary the tempo and pressure of his touch, always keeping in mind that his goal is to pleasure her.

4. *Learn to extend love play.* Sooner or later while thrusting, the male approaches "the point of no return." Once a man learns the sensations that precede ejaculation, he can learn to control ejaculation and extend love play. When a man learns this kind of control, he is well on his way to being a great lover. And he just may begin to pleasure his wife so that she enjoys lovemaking more than ever. If she has had orgasms only on occasion, she may begin to have them frequently and consistently. If she has never had an orgasm, she may now begin to have them and with fervor. Or she may begin to experience multiple orgasms.

5. *Enter by invitation.* Prior to orgasm the husband places his penis into his wife's body. Even though a woman may have shown certain physical signs of readiness, such as vaginal lubrication, the husband should wait until her emotional response matches her physical response before he enters her. Termed "entry by invitation," such an approach gives her control over when and how her body is to be entered.

If someone were to enter your home without an invitation, you would feel that they had invaded your privacy, and they would not be a welcome guest. So it is with a woman. When she is ready she can ask for entry. If he wants to feel welcome, the husband should wait for an invitation. We all feel more welcome when someone has invited us into their home. The same is true for a woman's body. The invitation might be nonverbal, or it might be through a pet word you both know and understand.

When a woman feels adored, she wants her husband closer. Song of Solomon 4:16 puts it this way:

> Awake, O north wind,
> And come, wind of the south;
> Make my garden breathe out fragrance,
> Let its spices be wafted abroad.
> May my beloved come into his garden
> And eat its choice fruits! (NASB).

At her pace, she invites him to taste the sexual fruits of her body.

An accomplished lover will enter his wife slowly, all the time remembering that the vagina has next to no nerve endings after the first inch or two. He will concentrate his efforts around the entrance to the vagina, where she experiences the greatest sensation outside of the clitoris.

6. *Sexual pleasure and enjoyment without demands.* A woman does not have to achieve an orgasm every time in order to enjoy sex. Many women can participate in sexual relations, not achieve orgasm, and yet feel fully satisfied. Never should a husband *demand* that his wife achieve an orgasm, for such a demand would put her in an unresolvable bind. She might lose interest in sex altogether, or she might begin to fake orgasm.

Most men despise the farce, and as Dr. James Dobson points out, "Once a woman begins to bluff in bed, there is no place to stop. Forever after she must make her husband think she's on a prolonged pleasure trip when in fact her car is still in the garage."[1]

A man who insists on a brief nighttime romp regardless of his wife's mood or her state of health will always end up disappointed in the quality of their sex life. A highly sexed, egocentric, selfish man may experience maximum relief but minimum fulfillment, since he has never learned the meaning of genuine love.

Men are the pursuers, to a great extent, and women the responders. But women must have something to respond to. Even an inhibited woman can be responsive if her husband woos her gently, slowly, patiently, and creatively. What could be more exciting or challenging for a man than improving his sex life? Any man can become a better lover or even a great one, if he works at it.

How to Satisfy a Man Sexually

Most women have been taught that when it comes to lovemaking, their husbands are to take the initiative. It is he who is supposed to make love to her. Therefore most women expect their husbands to make love to them, and be sensitive to their needs and desires. But making love should not be a one-way street, with only the husband satisfying his wife. He needs and wants a partner who knows how to make love to him. Most women have never thought of lovemaking this way.

Let's say you sense you should make some changes. How would you begin?

1. *Make him feel sexually attractive.* A woman needs to feel loved before she can respond to her husband's sexual needs, but the opposite is true for him. He needs to know she finds him sexually attractive before he can respond to her emotional needs.

A *Ladies' Home Journal* survey of more than 4,000 men listed an unresponsive woman as the biggest turnoff. During the initial phases of foreplay, a woman's body responds automatically to effective stimulation. But she must *learn* how to move toward and actively seek orgasmic release. She cannot achieve it through passivity, regardless of how skillful her husband's techniques may be. She must surrender, not only to her husband, but to her own drive toward the release of sexual tension. This takes active participation during lovemaking.

A man wants to feel wanted, not endured. Some women go through the motions of sex as if they were paying compulsory dues to an organization. If a wife wants a happy husband, one who will love and romance her, she must tell him how much she wants him and what a great lover he is!

A woman in a marriage seminar told me how much she enjoyed a sexual experience with her husband one night. Since she had just attended my seminar, she wanted to practice in a creative way what she had learned. Immediately following her orgasm, she popped out of bed and began applauding. He never forgot his standing ovation!

2. *Understand what turns a man on.* What turns men on is not what turns women on. A glimpse of her in a breezy nightie may be all it takes to flip his switch, and his thoughts race with excitement as he imagines what lies ahead. But she is wired differently. Although she may admire his masculine build and enjoy seeing him dressed in a racy sports outfit, this will rarely sexually arouse her. Similarly, a passionate kiss arouses him far more than it does her.

God created the male to be sexually responsive to external stimuli. His genitals are on the outside, and so is his sexuality. He is extremely vulnerable to visual stimulation and tactile movement. Men love to look at the female body, and they turn on at the glimpse of a nude or partially nude female.

One woman imagined her husband to be a "dirty old man" simply because he became aroused when she undressed before him at night. This frustrated both of them until she learned that his ready attitude did not constitute depravity on his part. Instead, he reacted this way because God designed his body to do so.

Think about what is in the bureau drawer where you keep your night clothes. Is it full of stained bathrobes, flannel pajamas, and ragbag nighties? It's time to shed those old rags and treat yourself to some new nighties in attractive colors, pretty styles and lengths. I've never yet heard a man complain about this expenditure!

Sometimes women are troubled by Matthew 5:28, which reads, "Whosoever looketh on a woman to lust after her hath committed adultery with her already in his heart." A man's viewing of another woman's body won't tempt him to go to bed with her if everything is right at home. The first seeds of dissatisfaction usually begin with anger, bitterness, and resentment rather than with lust.

A normal, healthy, virile man responds naturally to what he sees and touches. For example, the more a wife wants to cuddle at night, the more this excites his sexual pursuit. A ready-to-go-at-any-time attitude isn't the result of a man's depravity. It's the way he was created by God.

3. *Romance him with touch.* Generally speaking, men respond to touch differently than women do. Women see a hug or caress as a form of affection and warmth. Men see the same hug or caress as a prelude to sexual activity. To a large degree, men equate touching with a goal. That goal is usually sexual.

For a man, nonsexual touching is a series of steps he progresses through to get to genital touching. A woman is more likely to want genital touching only in the later stages, and she likes gentle caresses. A man, however, usually wants direct and immediate genital stimulation, using a firmer and stronger touch, and he tends to want it early, during the first stage of lovemaking. But his wife should also introduce him to the erogenous zones all over his body such as the ears, neck, nipples, buttocks, and inner thighs (especially near the genitals).

4. *Extend lovemaking.* Women have the idea that a man should reach his orgasm rather quickly. But it takes an extended amount of time for a man to reach an intense orgasm. And an intense orgasm is what differentiates lovemaking from routine sex. The more stimulation a man has had, the more intense his orgasm will be. If he has 15 to 20 minutes of stimulation prior to intercourse, it will provide greater intensity.

A man can be stimulated to a point just short of ejaculation, stop for a few seconds, then begin again. This buildup of sexual tension and slow-down process give extraordinary intensity to his orgasm. Most men can handle two, three, four, or more of these cycles. You can tell when orgasm is near. The scrotum becomes compact and ascends up into the body. You can stop ejaculation by stopping your movements. With experimentation you can provide an experience for your husband that he'll talk about for a long time.

5. *Feel good about yourself and your body.* Most women aren't comfortable with their own bodies. Take Rowena, for example. She's an attractive 37-year-old teacher with gorgeous eyes and the kind of skin most women dream about. But if you asked her how she feels about her body she'd say, "As long as I have clothes on I'm OK. But the minute I take my clothes off I want to hide. My husband says I'm beautiful, but I don't think so."

Many women are like Rowena. They have to have the lights off or at least down low while making love. They are afraid to show too much flesh. But if you don't think of yourself as sexy, you can't be sexy. A woman doesn't need to be a beauty queen, but she must feel good about herself and her body. If you feel comfortable with your body and feel you are sexy, your husband will feel that way too. When you feel good about yourself, you'll be much more confident in the bedroom.

Do what you need to do to help yourself feel attractive. Exercise. Wear the clothes that make you—and him—feel sexy. Pamper yourself in the bath. Enjoy the oils, lotion, facials, and sessions in the beauty parlor that give you confidence about your attractiveness and appeal in the bedroom. Often it's just little things that boost your self-confidence! Learn what they are, and use them to good advantage.

Trust your husband's response to you. Believe yourself attractive as he demonstrates his attraction to you. Often it takes seeing yourself through your husband's eyes to recognize what an alluring person you can be. Build on this knowledge of what he appreciates as sexy in you. It may mean stepping outside your comfort zone, risking embarrassment as you try out new movements, ways of speaking and dressing, but trust your husband's enjoyment of a sexy you. As you learn to enhance this side of your nature, you will delight in delighting your husband.

6. *Make sex a priority*. One of the main hindrances to a woman's interest in sex is fatigue. After she has struggled through an 18-hour day, sex can be the last item on her mind—and whatever gets done last probably gets done poorly. A loving wife will sort out priorities so that sex doesn't languish in last place. When 9:00 p.m. comes around, she will fight the urge to begin one final project before bed. The wife who considers the sexual aspect of her marriage to be important will reserve time and energy for it.

The Joy of Quick Sex

What is generally referred to as a "quickie" can be for one or the other or both partners. A quickie can include intercourse, orgasm or ejaculation, or none of the above. It is engaged in only by mutual agreement.

Quickies can be fun. They can be a before-breakfast treat, a middle-of-the-night special, or an afternoon rhapsody. They are a quick way to stir up the passion of marriage. However, they should never be the staple of your sexual diet. You might survive on quickies, but you will stagnate. Occasionally engaging in them will add spark and variety to your sexual diet.

Maintaining Fidelity

One of the key factors in achieving a great sex life is remaining committed to one partner. It's called fidelity. Confining sex exclusively to one's partner for a lifetime is the only way to build an emotionally healthy, stable relationship. Choosing to restrict one's sexual focus to a lifetime partner is basic to character building. Your character defines who you are. Paul wrote, "That each one of you should know how to possess (control, manage) his own body in consecration (purity, separated from things profane), and in honor" (1 Thessalonians 4:4, Amplified).

Self-control is a key ingredient in all sexual expression. Without it, not only does society disintegrate, but a person becomes unpredictable and dangerous.

When two divorced people get married, four get into bed.—Folk saying.

Married Lovers. Husbands and wives should aim to be imaginative, creative, and willing lovers. God designed that sex—unhampered by selfishness—be exciting, enjoyable, and fulfilling. Good sex, then, comes as the end result of a satisfying relationship. Should there be sex problems, including time pressures and sexual energy, ask God for help in solving the problems. Pray also that you might prioritize your life in such a way that you can give the energy, time, and creativity needed to enjoy a superior sex life. Remember, good sex doesn't just happen.

Thank God for Sex!

Lord, it's hard to know what sex really is—
Is it some demon put here to torment me?
Or some delicious seducer from reality?
It is neither of these, Lord.

I know what sex is—
    It is body and spirit,
    It is passion and tenderness,
    It is strong embrace and gentle hand-holding.
    It is open nakedness and hidden mystery.
    It is joyful tears on honeymoon faces, and
    It is tears on wrinkled faces at a golden wedding anniversary.

Sex is a quiet look across the room,
    A love note on a pillow,
    A rose laid on a breakfast plate,
    Laughter in the night.

Sex is life—not all of life—
    But wrapped up in the meaning of life.

Sex is your good gift, O God,
    To enrich life,
    To continue the race,
    To communicate,
    To show me who I am,
    To reveal my mate,
    To cleanse through "one flesh."

Lord, some people say
    Sex and religion don't mix;
But Your Word says sex is good.
    Help me to keep it good in my life.
Help me to be open about sex
    And still protect its mystery.
Help me to see that sex
    Is neither demon nor deity.
Help me not to climb into a fantasy world
    Of imaginary sexual partners;
Keep me in the real world
    To love the people You have created.

Teach me that my soul does not have to frown at sex
    For me to be a Christian.
It's hard for many people to say,
    "Thank God for sex!"
Because for them sex is more a problem
    Than a gift.
They need to know that sex and gospel
    Can be linked together again.
They need to hear the good news about sex.
Show me how I can help them.

Thank You, Lord, for making me a sexual being.
Thank You for showing me how to treat others
    With trust and love.
Thank You for letting me talk to You about sex.
Thank You that I feel free to say:
    "Thank God for sex!"

—Harry Hollis, Jr.[2]

---

[1] James Dobson, *What Wives Wish Their Husbands Knew About Women* (Wheaton, Ill.: Tyndale House, 1975), p. 125.

[2] Harry Hollis, Jr., *Thank God for Sex* (Nashville: Broadman Press, 1975), pp. 109-111.

Chapter 22

MAKE LOVE LAST A LIFETIME

Creative Ways to Keep Romance Alive

Carol and Philip met, fell in love, got married, and had three children. But on their way to building a family, their marriage started to fray at the seams. Their dreams got lost somewhere between starry-eyed illusions and the stark reality of rearing children. What this real-life couple discovered was that babies can be a real workout for the parents' relationship. The humdrum details of domestic life become emotional land mines.

Frequently parents become so involved in their children's lives that they forget to make their marriage a priority. If this pattern continues, their children become the only glue that holds them together. A couple usually do not realize that they have put their marriage on hold. It begins with a subtle shifting of priorities and often continues unrecognized until the children are older. Midlife markers such as a fortieth birthday or a high school graduation become rude awakeners. Once children are launched, these partners look at each other and wonder about the stranger who sits across the breakfast table.

It's not easy to keep a marriage on track romantically. Lori explains it this way: "I was shocked, after we went on a vacation to celebrate our tenth anniversary, to realize it had been seven years since we'd had more than a weekend away together. I wasn't holding a grudge about never having a vacation, but it was heavenly to be able to do *what* we wanted, *when* we wanted, *where* we wanted, without children. It was like wearing a beeper for nine years and suddenly taking it off and leaving it somewhere for a whole week. I was so free! I never relaxed that much at home. It was like our honeymoon before we had kids."

After we've been married awhile, the tendency is to give work and children our freshest energy. Marriage gets what's left over. But if a couple is going to maintain a healthy marriage over the long haul, romance and fun activities must become part of the delicate balancing act. Without taking time for this, patience with each other wears thin.

As the second law of thermodynamics notes: "Everything left unattended will tend toward disorder." Living in the same house, practicing the same faith, parenting the same children, sharing the same bed, isn't enough anymore.

Note that the couples mentioned were not considering divorce. They probably had a better relationship than many. But they weren't happy. Being married was not satisfying to them. This happens in many marriages. Newlyweds become disenchanted with married life when their marriage is no longer like television sitcoms with a happy ending in 30 minutes. Routine, sameness, boredom, and child-centeredness settle in. Such couples stand perched on the brink of what might be termed "marital burnout."

Couples unprepared for changes in romance will eventually begin to question whether or not they are really in love in the first place.—
H. Norman Wright.

Marital burnout is a state of complete physical, emotional, and mental exhaustion in marriage. It afflicts those who expect marriage to give meaning to life and finally realize that, in spite of all their efforts, their marriage isn't providing what they want.

Marital burnout doesn't happen overnight. Instead it's a gradual process, a growing awareness that things are no longer as good as they once were, that one's spouse is not as exciting as he or she once was.

Creative Ways to Keep Romance Alive

- Try a 20-second romantic recharge. Kiss each other for at least 20 seconds two times a day, rather than the usual pecks on the lips or cheek.
- Tape a note to the mirror that reads, "Hello, Favorite Person. You are looking at the person I love with all my heart."
- Prepare a homemade booklet of coupons that your partner can redeem at will. The coupons might say "This entitles you to two hours of my undivided attention. You choose what we do" or "This entitles you to an afternoon of antiquing at your favorite location."
- When you know your partner has had a really tough day, give him/her an all over soothing massage.
- Write out a list of all the things you love about your partner. Seal the list in an envelope and leave it on her pillow.
- When your mate enters a room, do a full body turn and let out a long, low whistle.
- Invite your partner to a hug party. Call yourself a hug therapist who gives great hugs, and tell her it wouldn't be a party without her.
- Move your kids' bedtime up by 30 minutes and spend the extra time with your mate. The kids may complain, but stand your ground.
- Every day, grab five or 10 minutes when you can touch base with each other. For example, share a cup of tea before the kids get up in the morning.
- Turn the television off and lie in bed in each other's arms talking until you fall asleep.
- Call your mate in the middle of the afternoon, just to touch base.

Chapter 23

DATE YOUR MATE

chedule time for romantic attention. Scheduling time for romance and special activities together is essential to a highly effective marriage. The amount of time you spend will be reflected in the overall quality of your marriage. Counselor Willard F. Harley recommends that if your marriage is healthy and both husband and wife are highly satisfied with the marriage, a minimum of 15 hours a week of undivided attention is usually enough to sustain a romantic marriage. Note, this is the least amount of time necessary to do so. He recommends this time be evenly distributed during the week rather than overdoing time on weekends.*

But when couples are experiencing marital trouble, recovering from the aftermath of an affair or other serious marital conflict, even more time is recommended. Twenty to 30 hours a week is necessary in order to restore the love couples once had for each other. In cases like this, Harley recommends that in order to salvage the marriage, the couple may need to go on vacation, where they can spend the entire time restoring the intimacy between them that has been lost. Usually two to three weeks of giving each other undivided attention brings a couple to the point where they can make an intelligent decision regarding their future.

Many couples say they simply don't have this kind of time to put into their relationships. But if either of them were carrying on a clandestine affair, they would find the time. It is simply a matter of priorities. The real problem is they don't want to spend time together, because they are getting so little from their relationship. But if this troubled couple can learn to re-create the type of romantic occasions they had while dating, there is hope for restoring the love they once had for each other.

Give focused attention when on a marital date. Perhaps a reminder is needed regarding what focused attention means—time spent paying close attention to each other. This time spent together must not include children, friends, or relatives. Romance can only blossom in privacy. Some couples think they can be romantic with their children present. No. Romance and children just don't go together. Intimacy is destroyed.

Remember, it is next to impossible to create intimacy between husband and wife with little ones crawling on you, a toddler wailing from another room, or a preteen checking on you. But as parents you do have a responsibility to keep your children inspired regarding the possibilities that lie within marriage. A romantic relationship between the two of you will do the trick.

Agree you will not discuss upcoming dental procedures, strange diaper rashes, soccer practice, schedule changes, or transmission problems. Time spent in going to the movies, watching television, attending sporting events, concerts, and plays doesn't count either, because you are being entertained by an outside source and there is little or no time for intimate conversation or focused attention.

It is essential that couples create activities that meet their greatest emotional needs. Romance, for most women, means intimate conversational sharing and affection; for men it means sharing a recreational activity and sex.

Dress up a little. On a date night both partners need to dress to look different. A woman dressed like she's about to clean the oven will not delight her husband's eye. Don a dress with a cut that will make your husband look twice. Fix your hair, spritz on perfume, and slip into a pair of heels that make your legs look great. If the children cry and the baby-sitter gasps when they see you, you'll know you've succeeded.

The best way for you and your spouse to guarantee some time without the kids is to do the dinner dishes together.

While dressing for the occasion, men also need to clean up their acts. Beer bellies, holey T-shirts, and a face covered with unshaven stubble fail to pass the dreamboat test. Ragged jeans, dirty fingernails, and halitosis won't make it either. But a fellow with a fresh shave and aftershave lotion, a clean, pressed shirt, a pair of slack pants, and polished shoes, is sure to make a hit impression. Most important of all, wear a smile!

It makes a woman feel special when you take time to dress nicely for her. When you make the extra effort to prepare yourself for her, she takes it as proof you love her. When you don't, she assumes you don't. Being appealing to her was an important part of your courtship. She needs the same kind of thoughtfulness now.

One man spoke from his heart: "You're right. I get dressed up to go to the office every day. But after work and on weekends, all I wear is a favorite old pair of jeans and a ragged T-shirt. I try to love her up a little and she pushes me away, saying I need a shave. The only time I turn her on is when I'm going out the door in the morning. Now I know why."

Try meeting at your destination rather than leaving the house together once in a while. This creates the feeling that you are about to rendezvous with someone exciting. Week nights lend themselves better to this strategy. There is something special about walking into a room full of people and allowing your partner to get an eyeful before settling into your seat.

Flirt with each other. It isn't difficult when you are out to distinguish dating couples from married ones. While a dating couple caresses each other with their hands and eyes, what's a married couple doing? Eating. There's no touching, no intimate lingering looks, no teasing smiles. If the couple does talk, the conversation goes like this: "Careful, you're going to spill." When the food arrives, they hunker down and concentrate on moving fork to mouth. There's nothing to say because they already know everything about each other and don't attempt to discover anything new.

While couples who have been married a few years are well past the early discovery dates, there yet remain a few subtle, changing mysteries about the other person that need to be peeled back gently. That's what marriage really is—an ongoing discovery process. And that's what dating after you're married is all about. Where you go and what you do don't matter as much as that you make plans to be alone and do not lapse into habitual ruts.

Husbands and wives need to learn to flirt with each other all over again. A whisper in the ear, a playful hug, a note tucked into a briefcase, or a kiss for no reason at all can help couples stay connected during the day. Pleasing glances, complimentary phrases, a sidelong glance, a charming smile, a hand laid lightly on your partner's arm when laughing at a remark, all produce a momentary lift.

Get over any hang-ups you have about displaying affection for your mate publicly. You can show good taste and still lay your hand on your partner's leg, play a little footsie under the table, or subtly invade your partner's personal space. If you are having dinner together, regard dinner as a tempting type of foreplay. Smiling, eye contact, suggestive touches, and intimate conversation go a long way.

It's impossible to develop a close, intimate relationship without spending meaningful time together. I recommend a couple hours one time per week, or every other week if you can't manage weekly dates.

Creative Date Ideas

1. Kidnap your partner for a mini vacation—an afternoon or evening of something he/she has been wanting to do.

2. Drive through a new housing development and tour a model home.

3. Check out new furniture in a furniture store. (It doesn't cost anything to look.)

4. Take a stroll through the park. Try out the swings and see who can swing the highest.

5. Take a tour of yesteryear—build a fire in the fireplace; sip a hot drink; or spend an hour going through family albums together, reminiscing about fun times shared in the past.

6. Take a late-evening walk. Talk about what's on your hearts.

7. Go exploring—any place your mate would like to go (within reason)—to a mountain hide-away or a ghost town you've heard about. Check out a quaint shop on a side street.

8. Buy a couple bottles of bubble-blowing liquid. Go to the top of the tallest place around—a building, a mountain, the roof of your house. Blow bubbles and watch them drift out of sight.

9. Go to the nearest pond or lake to feed the ducks. Toss leftover bread to the ducks while you watch them dive and fight for lunch.

10. Try a hot-tub date. If you don't have a hot tub, use a friend's. Let the hot, bubbling water soak away your stress. Talk about something fun.

11. Visit the Golden Arches. Dress up in your best clothes, and then go to eat—at McDonald's! Your formal attire in an informal place will be fun! Play footsie with each other under the table.

No marriage is all sunshine, but two people can share one umbrella if they huddle close.

12. Create a treasure hunt for your mate. Begin with a note directing him to a specific drawer in the kitchen, where he'll find another note telling him to go to the car, where there will be a bouquet of flowers with a note saying that he must drive to a certain spot for further instructions. At the end of the trail (you can make it as long as you like), you be there with a picnic on the beach or a reservation at a favorite restaurant.

13. While one of you is at a board meeting and the other is driving the kids to music lessons, rendezvous someplace and share a bag of M & M's.

14. Take turns asking each other out on a date. The one who asks has to make all the plans for the evening, choosing the restaurant, making reservations, arranging for baby-sitting, etc.

15. Be adventurous. Climb a mountain together; go white-water rafting; travel to a foreign country.

16. Take a night class together—cooking, photography, landscaping, a foreign language, or craft. This provides something new to talk about.

17. Meet for lunch one day a week. This gives you both something to look forward to and breaks the monotony of the week.

18. Plan an afternoon of biking in a favorite neighborhood, in the country, or in an interesting area. Over a picnic lunch, share ideas for building your dream home. Take memory pictures.

19. If you have a sick child or lack a sitter, plan a date in front of the fire-place or in a cozy bath converted into a luxury spa for two. Light the candles, play your favorite romantic music, and read love letters you wrote each other long ago. Add a cup of tea and homemade cookies, and you've got an interesting evening.

20. Make a list of six activities you would like to do with your mate. At least once a month take turns picking one activity from your partner's list and joining in with gusto. Whether it's horseback riding, scuba diving, or in-line skating, par-ticipate graciously just as you would if you were dating and not married.

---

*Willard F. Harley, Jr., *Love Busters* (Grand Rapids: Fleming H. Revell, 1992), pp. 220-223.

Chapter 24

PLAY WITH YOUR MATE

*O*ne of the reasons we love to be with our children is that they are so much fun. They tell silly jokes, giggle, share new experiences, and dream about the future. When was the last time you did that with your partner?

Kids are masters at playing together and enjoying simple activities with sheer abandoned joy. Adults don't lose the ability to play; they just get distracted by the pressures of life. And society doesn't emphasize the importance of play for adults. Instead, work and achievement are glorified, while leisure pursuits are classified as time-wasters. But those who are the most satisfied with life are those who balance work and play.

Play helps us achieve a sense of connectedness with those we love. And couples who enjoy playing together count playtime as a significant strength to their relationship. Couples who lack a sense of playfulness in their marriages are unhappy that it is missing from their lives.[1]

The importance of playfulness is underscored by the research of R. William Betcher, a clinical psychologist, who found that playfulness stabilizes a marriage. It enhances communication and strengthens the marital bond, because we highly value our most playful relationships. When play disappears from a relationship it is a symptom that the marriage is disintegrating. When play resumes, it indicates that a troubled relationship is healing.[2]

Play is a way of demonstrating you are happy. Communicating this in a relationship says to your partner, "I enjoy being with you and sharing fun times together. You make me happy, and I want to make you happy."

Play is even more important when a relationship is stressed. It helps couples plow through the rough times, because it relieves tension and helps one keep a sense of proportion when struggling with problems. When a couple is irritated over something but get caught up in a game or some form of play and begin laughing, they will like each other again.

Play is a powerful mode of communication because, to a large degree, it is a nonverbal language. With few words you can express keen thoughts and feelings in a playful manner.

Because of their more demanding roles, adults have a harder time being play-ful than children do. Responsibilities make it more difficult to behave sponta-neously in a childlike manner. In order to regain this sense of playfulness, you'll probably have to plan for it. One suggestion is to turn the television off one night a week and play games with your partner. And instead of trying to win, learn to enjoy the game; banter back and forth, tease, flirt, converse, and laugh, like you did when you were going together.

When Adam was lonely, God created for him not 10 friends, but one wife.

Harry and I play together frequently. I call him names, chase him around the house; we have pillow fights and snap towels at each other. Harry spurs me on to be more creative when I get my attacks of playfulness and silliness. He gives me positive feedback, which en-courages me to keep on being playful.

Creative Play Ideas

There's no better time to start playing together than today! Here are some fun ideas:

- Wash the car together and have a water fight afterward.
- Toss socks or pillows at each other.
- Sing badly in the car together.
- Without warning, pull your partner into the hall closet and plant a kiss on his or her lips that will leave him or her breathless.
- Paint the bathroom together while blasting old romantic favorites on the stereo.
- Keep the surprises coming. Try a stuffed animal that growls, "Guess who cares about you, baby."
- Create traditions just for the two of you that only you know about.
- Develop a "you-are-special" signal that can be delivered across the room without embarrassment and anyone else's knowledge.
- Share a silly fantasy about owning an island or the palace you'll build and live in someday.

---

[1] Gini Kopecky, "For Play," *American Health,* May 1996, p. 66.
[2] R. William Betcher, "Intimate Play and Marital Adaptation," *Psychiatry,* February 1981, pp. 13-33.

Chapter 25

LAUGH WITH YOUR MATE

*H*appily married couples laugh together far more frequently than those who are unhappy. Nearly three-fourths of the happily married respondents in one study said they laugh together once a day or more.[1] Shared humor is high up on a list of why happily-married couples believe their relationship has endured. Humor keeps variety and enjoyment in a relationship. Couples who laugh together are obviously not suffering from the rut of boredom.

The funny guys at the Gelotology (the science of mirth) Institute of Stanford University Medical School tell couples to laugh out loud. Double over and roll on the floor, they say, because laughter releases endorphins and enkephalins (those natural painkillers, chemical cousins to opiates such as morphine). Laughter turns you into a human vibrator that massages practically every organ in the body.[2]

Laughter has been likened to an aerobic workout. The average laugh comes out at about 70 miles an hour and provides the same benefits as 10 minutes of rowing. It strengthens the immune system, lightens pain, eases stress, and improves circulation and breathing.[3]

Humor and laughter relieve tension. That's what telling jokes is all about. You create tension and build it; then you pop the balloon by delivering the punch line. Some couples are afraid of humor because it exposes one's vulnerability, and they see that as threatening to their relationship. Rather than seeing the humor in their own real-life situations, their tendency is to turn on the TV and follow the passive humor dictated by the laugh track of a sitcom.

One night a pastor visited Bob and Sue, a newly married couple attending his church. Bob greeted the pastor and motioned for him to be seated in the living room while explaining that Sue was taking a shower. The men were engrossed in some serious discussion of a recent sporting event when the bathroom door opened. Sue, not realizing her husband had company, came bounding out of the bathroom—stark naked—to surprise her husband with a kiss.

Astonishment registered on her face as she realized her husband was not alone. With a shriek, she spun around and raced to the bedroom. The mortified pastor left as graciously as possible, while the new husband struggled unsuccessfully to suppress his mirth.

The next week, after the church service, Sue marched up to the pastor and said with a twinkle in her eye, "Hi. I'm Sue. I didn't think you'd recognize me with my clothes on!" They were both able to laugh at the ridiculous situation, and an awkward moment passed.

Humor strips away our self-righteous veneers. It eases tension. Heated discussions are defused by shared laughter. Someone has said that laughter is like having a God's-eye view of a situation. It helps us gain perspective on petty annoyances and heals a thousand hurts.

Laughter is to life what shock absorbers are to automobiles. It won't take the potholes out of the road, but it sure makes the ride smoother.—Barbara Johnson.

Even a simple smile can improve health as well as your state of mind. Smiling stimulates the thymus gland, which aids the body's immune system. One physician who treated chronic pain sufferers recommended to his patients that they smile at themselves in the mirror twice a day. Studies show that even when a smile is faked, the mind dwells on more pleasant things.[4]

Beware, however, of trying to laugh all your troubles away or trivializing serious problems. This could be extremely annoying to a concerned partner. Some situations are never funny.

You and your mate may have very different tastes in humor. Harry prefers cornball humor and silly jokes. I like quick wit and spontaneous humor with powerful punch lines. Nevertheless, humor and laughing together have given our marriage strength and spontaneity. Love and laughter build intimacy. Ruth Bell Graham in *It's My Turn* writes, "It is impossible to love someone at whom you cannot laugh."[5]

One researcher found that couples who agreed on what was funny were more likely to like, love, and marry each other than those whose humor preferences differed. Those who had similar humor likes had also been together longer than those with dissimilar tastes. Humor obviously contributes to closeness, because it indicates similar values, interests, intelligence, imagination, and needs.[6]

Creative Humor Ideas

If you wish to up your quota of laughs, here are some tips:

- Learn what humor appeals to your mate. Clip a cartoon from a magazine or newspaper and share it with your partner.
- Share a funny story. Embellish a real story to get a laugh; or make up a funny one about your day.
- Share private nicknames that make you smile.
- Make funny faces or noises that will let your comic side show.
- Tell a joke. A bad joke is better than no joke at all. The goal is to laugh, not earn tips as a comedian. You can laugh at something that is silly.
- If something doesn't go just the way you want it to go, try laughing it off rather than coming unglued. It will reduce stress and put a smile on your face.
- Have a giggle fit over something silly.
- Share private jokes and nicknames. Create private traditions shared by just the two of you.
- Share a silly fantasy or dream. Playful communication creates a sense of confidentiality.

If you and your mate aren't laughing together, it's time to begin. As Scripture tells us; "A merry heart doeth good like a medicine" (Proverbs 17:22).

The Romantic Getaway

I recommend a romantic getaway every three months—an overnight stay in a hotel or motel. Some of you may question my sanity at this point. You're asking, What about the children? Don't you know what this would cost? We don't have time for such craziness!

Think of it this way: It just might be the best investment you ever made in your marriage. Isn't it wiser to spend some time, effort, and money building a romantic, healthy relationship now? If you don't, the chances are high that you'll spend the same amount of money later on—but on some very different things, such as counseling, divorce lawyers, court costs, and spouse and child support.

And yes, it must be overnight in a hotel. Let me explain why. What is "home" to a man? It's his castle! This is where he comes after a hard day at work to spend his free time, to relax, to tank up his energy so he can go out and fight the world again.

What is "home" to a woman? Whether she works outside the home or not, "home" represents WORK, WORK, and more WORK. It doesn't matter what room she is in. There is something screaming, "Pick me up," "Put me away," or "Clean me." Within the confines of home with so many tasks demanding her attention, it is difficult for her to let go and relax and play the role of "lover" with abandon.

When a woman is away in a motel or resort, she can forget all the work and stress she left behind. It becomes an absolute prerequisite to get a woman away from her home environment overnight once every three months, if you want to keep your marriage from burning out.

Here are some commonsense rules that ensure the stay will renew your marriage.

1. No talk about bills, children, in-laws, or other irritating topics allowed.

2. No briefcases, calls to the office, pagers, or cellular phones allowed.

3. No television, videos, or movies allowed (the attention is to be focused on each other, not on the actions of others).

4. Only recreational reading is permitted.

5. No dieting! (Ladies, it is no fun to take someone out for a fancy meal and hear them say, "Oh, I can't eat that!" This one time, eat it and enjoy it!)

6. Tell everyone you meet you are celebrating a romantic getaway, and watch them break their necks to help you celebrate in grand style.

7. Creatively show your partner through subtle romantic surprises how much you care!

Remember, relationships do not renew themselves. It is up to you to renew them constantly. Romance is only a part of married love, but it brings pleasure and delight. The challenge of being married is learning to keep a relationship romantic, interesting, and alive through all the changing years of marriage.

It isn't the time you put into being romantic today that will "fix" your marriage today. But it has a critical long-term effect on your marriage. How a couple spends their time alone together during the week becomes some of the most valuable hours of their lives and to a large extent determines their future happiness. Find romance wherever you can. Capture a moment here and a moment there. And hold on!

Maybe you've heard about the farmer and his wife who lived in the midwest. One day a tornado blew both of them out of the house into the barnyard. When the dust settled, the farmer saw his wife crying. "What are you crying for, woman?" he demanded. "You ain't hurt."

"I ain't cryin' cuz I'm hurt," she countered. "But do you realize this is the first time we've been out together in 14 years?"

May this never be said of you!

The Last Word

Have you ever thought of what your life might have been like had you not married your spouse? I have. Maybe I'd have been a near-recluse aging spinster (without nine grandchildren) who relied on the generosity of relatives to eke out an existence. I certainly would never have written 20-plus books on marriage and the family.

And I wonder what might have happened to Harry had I not shown up in his life. Harry certainly doesn't have the same fools-rush-in-where-angels-fear-to-tread zest for adventure and travel that I do. Together we make things possible for each other; we extend each other.

And there's more going on in our marriage than just what appears on the surface, something Spirit-filled. Perhaps we can reach higher and dig deeper than we could as two separate entities. Perhaps this is our contribution to God's work on earth.

When I slide into bed beside Harry at night and listen to his deep, rhythmic breathing, I feel a place of sanctuary. This is where I belong. Without his wisdom and strength, his hugs, his unfailing faith in things unseen, his dragging me out for occasional dinners at a favorite Italian haunt, maybe I'd implode.

Don't take yourself too seriously, and never fail to take your spouse seriously enough.

God has blessed me with a wonderful husband—one who loves the living daylights out of me. Our marriage is good, but not perfect. That doesn't lessen our love for each other or our commitment to the relationship. The wonder of it all is that God can use these two imperfect people, committed to each other in their imperfect marriage, to influence the world. Perhaps through our brutal honesty about ourselves and our marriage, He can reach others. God takes all our imperfections and makes something good from them.

• • •

As you have read the pages of this book, it is my hope you have found a few chuckles, a few inspirational thoughts, and a new determination to make your marriage the best it can be. Continual challenges lie just ahead, regardless of whether you are just starting out as husband and wife, are enmeshed in the turmoil of child-rearing years, or have just launched your children on their own.

Meet each changing stage as it comes—enthusiastically and confidently. Keep an open heart for the one you have married. Be willing to risk opening yourself honestly to that special person.

The reason we marry in the first place is to share our lives with someone we care about. Every couple goes through difficult stages. Sometimes what builds a stronger marriage is surviving a crisis and moving into the next stage.

Highly effective marriages arise out of the crises in which husband and wife work to resolve unsettling issues before they become major disasters. It takes teamwork to do this—two people who love, trust, and respect each other, who are totally committed to allowing God to rule in their lives. You will find that working through each crisis leads to a stronger, more fulfilling, and more successful marriage—one that will last through all the years to come.

---

[1] Jeanette C. Lauer and Robert H. Lauer, *Till Death Do Us Part* (New York: Harrington Press, 1986), p. 155.

[2] "The Funnybone Factor," *Virtue,* September/October 1992, p. 20.

[3] *Ibid.*

[4] Article in *Partnership,* November/December 1985, "Go Ahead and Laugh," by Sharon Alyne Stannigan, p. 45.

[5] Ruth Bell Graham, *It's My Turn* (Old Tappan, N.J.: Fleming H. Revell, 1982).

[6] *Till Death Do Us Part,* p. 155.

FOR CHRISTIAN COUNSELING:

New Life Clinic
(Christian Counseling Center)
820 West Spring Parkway, Suite 400
Plano, TX 75023
800-639-5433
Call to locate a New Life Clinic in your area.

Focus on the Family
Colorado Springs, CO 80995
719-531-3400
Ask for counseling referral.

Christian Association for Psychological Studies (CAPS)
Robert R. King, Jr., Ph.D., Exec. Secretary
P.O. Box 890279
Temecula, CA 92589-0279
909-965-2277
This is a referral service of counselors.

Fuller Psychological and Family Services
The Psychological Center
180 North Oakland Avenue
Pasadena, CA 91101
818-584-5555
Counselors are available by appointment.

Biola Counseling Center
13800 Biola Avenue
La Mirada, CA
310-903-4800
Counselors are available by appointment.

FOR HELP WITH SEXUAL PROBLEMS:

The American Association of Sex Educators, Counselors, and Therapists
435 North Michigan Avenue, Suite 1717
Chicago, IL 60611
For referrals to a sex therapist, send a note, stating your request, and a self-addressed, stamped envelope.
For a directory of certified sex therapists, send $15, plus a large, self-addressed, stamped envelope.

FOR HELP WITH PREMATURE EJACULATION:

Recovery of Male Potency (ROMP)
27211 Lasher Road, Suite 208
Southfield, MI 48034
810-357-1314
Offer brief telephone counseling and help in finding specialists who treat impotence. When writing for information, send a self-addressed, stamped envelope.

FOR INFORMATION REGARDING PROBLEM DRUGS:

The People's Pharmacy—LH
P.O. Box 52027
Durham, NC 27717
For a pamphlet listing problem drugs and alternative choices, request "Graedon's Guide to Drugs That Affect Sexuality" by sending $2 and a self-addressed, stamped envelope.

FOR HELP WITH SEXUAL ADDICTIONS:

Sex Addicts Anonymous (S.A.A.)
National Service Organization for S.A.A., Inc.
P.O. Box 70949
Houston, TX 77270
713-869-4902

Sexaholics Anonymous
Simi Valley, CA
805-581-3343

Sexual Compulsives Anonymous
Los Angeles, CA
213-859-5585

New York, NY
212-439-1123

Sex and Love Addicts Anonymous
Boston, MA
617-332-1845

Sex Offenders Anonymous (SOANON)
Van Nuys, CA 91409
818-244-6331

Blitchington, Peter and Evelyn. *Understanding the Male Ego.* Nashville: Thomas Nelson Publishers, 1984.

Burkett, Larry. *Debt-free Living.* Chicago: Moody Press, 1989.

Cowan, Carolyn Pope and Philip. *When Partners Become Parents: The Big Life Change for Couples.* New York: Basic Books, 1992.

DeAngelis, Barbara. *Are You the One for Me?* New York: Dell Books, 1992.

———. *Secrets About Men Every Woman Should Know.* New York: Delacorte Press, 1990.

Deutsch, Ronald M. *The Key to Feminine Response in Marriage.* New York: Ballantine Books, 1968.

Gottman, John. *Why Marriages Succeed or Fail.* New York: Simon & Schuster, 1994.

Gray, John. *Mars and Venus in the Bedroom.* New York: Harper Perennial, 1997.

———. *Men Are From Mars, Women Are From Venus.* New York: HarperCollins Publishers, 1993.

Harley, Willard F., Jr. *His Needs, Her Needs.* Grand Rapids: Fleming H. Revell, 1994.

———. *Love Busters.* Grand Rapids: Fleming H. Revell, 1992.

Hart, Archibald D. *The Sexual Man.* Dallas: Word Books, 1994.

Hite, Shere. *The Hite Report—A Nationwide Study of Female Sexuality.* New York: Dell Books, 1976.

Janus, Samuel S. and Cynthia L. *The Janus Report on Sexual Behavior.* New York: Wiley and Sons, Inc., 1993.

Joy, Donald M. *Men Under Construction.* Wheaton, Ill.: Victor Books, 1993.

Kaplan, Helen Singer. *How to Overcome Premature Ejaculation.* New York: Brunner/Mazel Publishers, 1989.

Kayser, Karen. *When Love Dies: The Process of Marital Disaffection.* New York: Guilford Press, 1993.

Kinder, Melvyn, and Connell Cowan. *Husbands and Wives: Exploding Marital Myths/Deepening Love and Desire.* New York: C. N. Potter, Inc., 1989.

Kreidman, Ellen. *Light Her Fire.* New York: Villard Books, 1991.

———. *Light His Fire.* New York: Dell Books, 1989.

LaHaye, Tim and Beverly LaHaye. *The Act of Marriage.* Grand Rapids: Zondervan Pub. House, 1976.

Lauer, Jeanette C. and Robert H. *Till Death Do Us Part: A Study and Guide to Long-Term Marriage.* Binghamton, N.Y.: Haworth Press, 1986.

Masters, William H. and Virginia E. Johnson. *Human Sexual Response.* Boston: Little, Brown & Co., 1966.

McManus, Michael J. *Marriage Savers: Helping Your Friends and Family Stay Married.* Grand Rapids: Zondervan Pub. House, 1993.

Notarius, Clifford, and Howard Markham. *We Can Work It Out: Making Sense of Marital Conflict.* New York: G. P. Putnam's Sons, 1993.

Penner, Clifford and Joyce. *The Gift of Sex: A Christian Guide to Sexual Fulfillment.*

Waco, Tex.: Word Books, 1981.

———. *Men and Sex.* Nashville: Thomas Nelson Publishers, 1997.

Penney, Alexandra. *How to Keep Your Man Monogamous.* New York: Bantam Books, 1989.

Ruben, Harvey L. *Supermarriage: Overcoming the Predictable Crises of Married Life.* New York: Bantam Books, 1986.

Tannen, Deborah. *That's Not What I Meant: How Conversational Style Makes or Breaks Relationships.* New York: William Morrow and Co., Inc., 1986.

Van Pelt, Nancy L. *Get Organized—Seven Secrets to Sanity for Stressed Women.* Hagerstown, Md.: Review and Herald Pub. Assn., 1998.

———. *How to Talk So Your Mate Will Listen and Listen So Your Mate Will Talk.* Grand Rapids: Fleming H. Revell, 1989.

———. *Smart Love—A Field Guide for Single Adults.* Grand Rapids: Fleming H. Revell, 1997.

Warren, Neil Clark. *Finding the Love of Your Life.* Colorado Springs, Colo.: Focus on the Family Publishing, 1992.

Wheat, Ed and Gaye. *Intended for Pleasure.* Old Tappan, N.J.: Fleming H. Revell Co., 1977.

Wright, H. Norman. *Holding On to Romance.* Ventura, Calif.: Regal Books, 1992.

———. *The Secrets of a Lasting Marriage.* Ventura, Calif.: Regal Books, 1995.

———. *Understanding the Man in Your Life.* Dallas: Word Publishing, 1987.